Odoo 11 Development Cookbook
Cookbook
Second Edition

Over 120 unique recipes to build effective enterprise and business applications

Alexandre Fayolle
Holger Brunn

BIRMINGHAM - MUMBAI

Odoo 11 Development Cookbook
Second Edition

Commissioning Editor: Aaron Lazar
Acquisition Editor: Akshay Ghadi
Content Development Editor: Francis Carneiro
Technical Editor: Akhil Nair
Copy Editor: Shaila Kusanale
Project Coordinator: Devanshi Doshi
Proofreader: Safis Editing
Indexer: Tejal Daruwale Soni
Graphics: Jason Monteiro
Production Coordinator: Deepika Naik

First published: April 2016
Second edition: January 2018

Production reference: 1180118

Published by Packt Publishing Ltd.
Livery Place
35 Livery Street
Birmingham
B3 2PB, UK.

ISBN 978-1-78847-181-7

>www.packtpub.com

`mapt.io`

Mapt is an online digital library that gives you full access to over 5,000 books and videos, as well as industry leading tools to help you plan your personal development and advance your career. For more information, please visit our website.

Why subscribe?

- Spend less time learning and more time coding with practical eBooks and Videos from over 4,000 industry professionals

- Improve your learning with Skill Plans built especially for you

- Get a free eBook or video every month

- Mapt is fully searchable

- Copy and paste, print, and bookmark content

PacktPub.com

Did you know that Packt offers eBook versions of every book published, with PDF and ePub files available? You can upgrade to the eBook version at `www.PacktPub.com` and as a print book customer, you are entitled to a discount on the eBook copy. Get in touch with us at `service@packtpub.com` for more details.

At `www.PacktPub.com`, you can also read a collection of free technical articles, sign up for a range of free newsletters, and receive exclusive discounts and offers on Packt books and eBooks.

Contributors

About the authors

Alexandre Fayolle started working with Linux and free software in the mid 1990s and quickly became interested in the Python programming language. In 2012, he joined Camptocamp to share his expertise on Python, PostgreSQL, and Linux with the team implementing Odoo. He currently manages projects for Camptocamp and is strongly involved in the Odoo Community Association. In his spare time, he likes to play jazz on the vibraphone.

> *I'd like to thank Daniel Reis for his work on the first edition of this book, and Nadège Gauffre for her patience and understanding while I was working on the Cookbook.*

Holger Brunn has been a fervent open source advocate since he came into contact with the open source market sometime in the nineties.

He has programmed for ERP and similar systems in different positions since 2001. For the last 10 years, he has dedicated his time to TinyERP, which became OpenERP and evolved into Odoo. Currently, he works at Therp BV in the Netherlands as a developer and is an active member of the Odoo Community Association (OCA).

About the reviewer

Yannick Vaucher is a strong believer in FOSS. Starting in 2011, he is employed by Camptocamp as an Odoo developer. Besides developing, he also teaches time-to-time technical Odoo formation to developers.

He joined the Odoo Community Association (OCA) as a core contributor and manages the Switzerland localization and Geospatial OCA projects. You may find multiple contributions to the Odoo module ecosystem have been made by him.

Packt is searching for authors like you

If you're interested in becoming an author for Packt, please visit `authors.packtpub.com` and apply today. We have worked with thousands of developers and tech professionals, just like you, to help them share their insight with the global tech community. You can make a general application, apply for a specific hot topic that we are recruiting an author for, or submit your own idea.

Table of Contents

Preface

Odoo, formerly known as OpenERP, is a great platform for developers. The framework, at its core, is very rich and allows building client-server applications from scratch, as well as adapting existing applications to your needs through a clever extension mechanism and a very modular design. The latest versions have brought a wealth of new possibilities with the addition of a full-featured website development stack. The scope is huge, and it is easy for newcomers to feel lost.

For years, Odoo developers have been learning their craft by reading the code of addon modules, which are built on top of the framework to provide enterprise management features.

While effective, this process is long and error-prone, since it is difficult to know whether the source code you are learning from uses the latest possibilities offered by the framework, or if you are looking at an older module that has not been updated to use these features. To make things worse, some code flows are intrinsically hard to follow because they're partly in the business logic layer, partly in the database layer, partly in the request handling layer, and partly in the client-side code.

This book is meant to save you time by tapping into the years of experience accumulated by long-time Odoo contributors to learn the current best practices in Odoo development by focusing on the new features of version 11, and also giving a solid base in the existing mature functionality of the framework. Since Odoo has a long tradition of guaranteeing backward compatibility, most of the presented material should still work with upcoming versions.

Who this book is for

If you are a Python developer who wants to develop highly efficient business applications with the latest Odoo framework and want a hands-on problem/solution book for all of your Odoo development-related issues, this book is for you! Some experience with the JavaScript programming language and web development is assumed to make the most of this book.

What this book covers

Chapter 1, *Installing the Odoo Development Environment*, begins with how to create a development environment for Odoo, start Odoo, create a configuration file, and activate the developer tools of Odoo.

Chapter 2, *Managing Odoo Server Instances*, is about addon installation and upgrading. It provides useful tips for working with addons installed from GitHub and organizing the source code of your instance.

Chapter 3, *Server Deployment*, provides advice on how to install and configure Odoo for production, including setting up a reverse proxy to encrypt network communications over HTTPS and ensuring that Odoo starts when the server boots.

Chapter 4, *Creating Odoo addon Modules*, explains the structure of an Odoo addon module and provides a step-by-step guide for creating a simple module from scratch.

Chapter 5, *Application Models*, focuses on Odoo model descriptions, and explains the various field types and the different inheritance models available in Odoo.

Chapter 6, *Basic Server-Side Development*, introduces the API of Odoo, presents the commonly used methods of the Model class, and explains how to write business logic methods. More advanced topics are covered in Chapter 9, *Advanced Server-Side Development*.

Chapter 7, *Module Data*, shows how to ship data along with the code of your module. It also explains how to write a migration script when a data model provided by an addon is modified in a new release.

Chapter 8, *Debugging and Automated Testing*, proposes some strategies for server-side debugging and provides an introduction to the Python debugger. It also explains how to write and run automated tests using YAML or Python for your addon modules. Client-side testing is covered in Chapter 15, *Web Client Development*.

Chapter 9, *Advanced Server-Side Development Techniques*, outlines more advanced topics useful when writing business methods, such as writing wizards to walk the user through a process, writing onchange methods, manipulating the execution context or bypassing the ORM to use raw SQL.

Chapter 10, *Backend Views*, teaches you how to write business views for your data models and how to call server-side methods from these views. It covers the usual views (list view, form view, and search view) as well as the views introduced in recent versions of Odoo (kanban, graph, calendar, pivot, and so on).

Chapter 11, *Access Security*, discusses how to control who has access to what in your Odoo instance by creating security groups, writing access control lists to define what operations are available to each group on a given model, and if necessary by writing record-level rules.

Chapter 12, *Internationalization*, takes you through the translation of the user interfaces of your addons and provides useful tricks about using GNU Gettext command line tools to manipulate translation files.

Chapter 13, *Automation, Workflows, Emails, and Printouts*, illustrates the different tools available in Odoo to implement business processes for your records. It also shows how server actions and automated rules can be used to support business rules, and how to generate emails and PDF documents with Odoo.

Chapter 14, *Web Server Development*, deals with the core of the web server in Odoo. It explains how to map URLs to methods and how to control who can access these URLs.

Chapter 15, *Web Client Development*, dives into the JavaScript part of Odoo and explains how you can provide new widgets and make RPC calls to the server. It also gives tips about debugging and testing this part of your code.

Chapter 16, *CMS Website Development*, shows how to customize websites built with Odoo, by writing your own templates and providing new snippets for use in the website builder.

To get the most out of this book

This books is meant for developers, and it is not a development tutorial. It expects you to be familiar with the Python programming language (especially in the backend development chapters), the JavaScript programming language (especially in the front end development chapters). Since the data files in the modules are often formatted as XML files, some knowledge of the XML syntactic rule is definitely welcome.

Odoo will run without problem on any recent GNU/Linux distribution. In order to simplify the code in the recipes, we chose to Debian GNU/Linux 9 (code name Stretch), so it will also help if you had some previous acquaintance with the apt-get command used to install software packages, and some notions about GNU/Linux system administration.

Download the example code files

You can download the example code files for this book from your account at `www.packtpub.com`. If you purchased this book elsewhere, you can visit `www.packtpub.com/support` and register to have the files emailed directly to you.

You can download the code files by following these steps:

1. Log in or register at `www.packtpub.com`.
2. Select the **SUPPORT** tab.
3. Click on **Code Downloads & Errata**.
4. Enter the name of the book in the **Search** box and follow the onscreen instructions.

Once the file is downloaded, please make sure that you unzip or extract the folder using the latest version of:

- WinRAR/7-Zip for Windows
- Zipeg/iZip/UnRarX for Mac
- 7-Zip/PeaZip for Linux

The code bundle for the book is also hosted on GitHub at `https://github.com/PacktPublishing/Odoo-11-Development-Coobook-Second-Edition`. We also have other code bundles from our rich catalog of books and videos available at `https://github.com/PacktPublishing/`. Check them out!

Conventions used

There are a number of text conventions used throughout this book.

`CodeInText`: Indicates code words in text, database table names, folder names, filenames, file extensions, pathnames, dummy URLs, user input, and Twitter handles. Here is an example: "Create a `virtualenv` and install the dependencies"

A block of code is set as follows:

```
from odoo import models, fields, api
class LibraryBook(models.Model):
    # [...]
    state = fields.Selection([('draft', 'Unavailable'),
                              ('available', 'Available'),
                              ('borrowed', 'Borrowed'),
                              ('lost', 'Lost')],
                             'State')
```

When we wish to draw your attention to a particular part of a code block, the relevant lines or items are set in bold:

```
def export_stock_level(self, stock_location):
    import pdb; pdb.set_trace()
    products = self.with_context(location=stock_location.id).search([])
    fname = join(EXPORTS_DIR, 'stock_level.txt')
    try:
        with open(fname, 'w') as fobj:
            for prod in products.filtered('qty_available'):
                fobj.write('%s\t%f\n' % (
                    prod.name, prod.qty_available))
    except IOError:
        raise exceptions.UserError('unable to save file')
```

Any command-line input or output is written as follows:

```
$ ../odoo/odoo-bin --save --config myodoo.cfg --stop-after-init
```

In the example above $ is the command line prompt, and it should not be typed. When the command line prompt is a hash sign (#), this means that the command must be run as the root user. Some command lines had to be wrapped on multiple lines due to the width of the pages. In these cases, there is a backslash (\) at the end of the line. When typing the command you may want to ignore these backslashes completely and not input them, entering the whole command on a single line. If you choose to type them, **you must not add any spaces after the backslash** and hit the Return key immediately to insert a new line character just after the backslash.

Bold: Indicates a new term, an important word, or words that you see onscreen. For example, words in menus or dialog boxes appear in the text like this. Here is an example: "Go to the **Settings** menu."

Warnings or important notes appear like this.

Tips and tricks appear like this.

Sections

In this book, you will find several headings that appear frequently (*Getting ready*, *How to do it...*, *How it works...*, *There's more...*, and *See also*).

To give clear instructions on how to complete a recipe, use these sections as follows:

Getting ready

This section tells you what to expect in the recipe and describes how to set up any software or any preliminary settings required for the recipe.

How to do it...

This section contains the steps required to follow the recipe.

How it works...

This section usually consists of a detailed explanation of what happened in the previous section.

There's more...

This section consists of additional information about the recipe in order to make you more knowledgeable about the recipe.

See also

This section provides helpful links to other useful information for the recipe.

Get in touch

Feedback from our readers is always welcome.

General feedback: Email `feedback@packtpub.com` and mention the book title in the subject of your message. If you have questions about any aspect of this book, please email us at `questions@packtpub.com`.

Errata: Although we have taken every care to ensure the accuracy of our content, mistakes do happen. If you have found a mistake in this book, we would be grateful if you would report this to us. Please visit `www.packtpub.com/submit-errata`, selecting your book, clicking on the Errata Submission Form link, and entering the details.

Piracy: If you come across any illegal copies of our works in any form on the internet, we would be grateful if you would provide us with the location address or website name. Please contact us at `copyright@packtpub.com` with a link to the material.

If you are interested in becoming an author: If there is a topic that you have expertise in and you are interested in either writing or contributing to a book, please visit `authors.packtpub.com`.

Reviews

Please leave a review. Once you have read and used this book, why not leave a review on the site that you purchased it from? Potential readers can then see and use your unbiased opinion to make purchase decisions, we at Packt can understand what you think about our products, and our authors can see your feedback on their book. Thank you!

For more information about Packt, please visit `packtpub.com`.

1
Installing the Odoo Development Environment

In this chapter, we will cover the following topics:

- Easy installation of Odoo from source
- Managing Odoo environments using the start command
- Managing Odoo server databases
- Storing the instance configuration in a file
- Activating the Odoo developer tools
- Updating Odoo from source

Introduction

There are lots of ways to set up an Odoo development environment. This chapter proposes one of these, although you will certainly find a number of other tutorials on the web explaining other approaches. Keep in mind that this chapter is about a development environment that has requirements different from a production environment, which will be covered in Chapter 3, *Server Deployment*.

Easy installation of Odoo from source

For Odoo deployment, it is recommended to use a **GNU/Linux** environment. You may be more at ease using **Microsoft Windows** or **Mac OS X**, but the fact is that most of the Odoo developers are using GNU/Linux, and you are much more likely to get support from the community for OS-level issues occurring on GNU/Linux than on Windows.

It is also recommended to develop using the same environment (the same distribution and the same version) as the one that will be used in production. This will avoid nasty surprises such as discovering, on the day of deployment, that some library has a different version than is expected, with slightly different and incompatible behavior. If your workstation is using a different OS, a good approach is to set up a virtual machine on your workstation and install a GNU/Linux distribution in the VM.

 To avoid copying files between your workstation where you are running your development environment and the virtual machine that runs Odoo, you can configure a SAMBA share inside the virtual machine and store the source code there. You can then mount the share on your workstation in order to edit the files easily.

This book assumes that you are running **Debian GNU/Linux** as its stable version (this is version 9, code name *Stretch* at the time of writing). **Ubuntu** is another popular choice, and since it is built on top of Debian, most of the examples in this book should work unchanged. Whatever Linux distribution you choose, you should have some notion of how to use it from the command line, and having a few ideas about system administration will certainly not cause any harm.

Getting ready

We assume that Linux is up and running and that you have an account with root access, either because you know the root password, or because `sudo` has been configured. In the following pages, we will use `$(whoami)` whenever the login of your work user is required in a command line. This is a shell command that will substitute your login in the command you are typing.

Some operations will definitely be easier if you have a **GitHub** account. Go to `https://github.com` and create one if you don't have one already.

How to do it...

To install Odoo from source, you need to follow these steps:

1. Run the following commands to install the main dependencies:

```
$ sudo apt-get update
$ sudo apt-get install -y git python3.5 postgresql nano virtualenv
\ xz-utils wget fontconfig libfreetype6 libx11-6 libxext6
libxrender1 \ node-less node-clean-css xfonts-75dpi
```

2. Download and install wkhtmltopdf:

```
$ wget -O wkhtmltox.tar.xz \
https://github.com/wkhtmltopdf/wkhtmltopdf/releases/download/0.12.4
/wkhtmltox-0.12.4_linux-generic-amd64.tar.xz
$ tar xvf wkhtmltox.tar.xz
$ sudo mv wkhtmltox/lib/* /usr/local/lib/
$ sudo mv wkhtmltox/bin/* /usr/local/bin/
$ sudo mv wkhtmltox/share/man/man1 /usr/local/share/man/
```

3. Now, use this to install the build dependencies:

```
$ sudo apt-get install -y gcc python3.5-dev libxml2-dev \
libxslt1-dev libevent-dev libsasl2-dev libssl1.0-dev libldap2-dev \
libpq-dev libpng-dev libjpeg-dev
```

4. Configure **PostgreSQL**:

```
$ sudo -u postgres createuser --createdb $(whoami)
$ createdb $(whoami)
```

5. Configure **git**:

```
$ git config --global user.name "Your Name"
$ git config --global user.email youremail@example.com
```

6. Clone the Odoo code base:

```
$ mkdir ~/odoo-dev
$ cd ~/odoo-dev
$ git clone -b 11.0 --single-branch\
https://github.com/odoo/odoo.git
$ cd odoo
```

7. Create an `odoo-11.0` **virtual environment** and activate it:

```
$ virtualenv -p python3 ~/odoo-11.0
$ source ~/odoo-11.0/bin/activate
```

8. Install the Python dependencies of Odoo in `virtualenv`:

```
$ pip3 install -r requirements.txt
```

9. Create and start your first Odoo instances:

```
$ createdb odoo-test
$ python3 odoo-bin -d odoo-test --addons-path=addons \
--db-filter=odoo-test$
```

10. Point your browser to `http://localhost:8069` and authenticate it using the **admin** account and `admin` as password.

> You can download the example code files for this book from your account at: `http://www.packtpub.com`. If you purchased this book elsewhere, you can visit `http://www.packtpub.com/support` and register to have the files emailed to you directly.
>
> You can download the code files by following these steps:
>
> - Log in or register to our website using your email address and password
> - Hover the mouse pointer on the **SUPPORT** tab at the top
> - Click on Code **Downloads & Errata**
> - Enter the name of the book in the **Search** box
> - Select the book for which you're looking to download the code files
> - Choose where you purchased this book from in the drop-down menu
> - Click on **Code Download**
>
> You can also download the Code Files by clicking on the **Code Files** button on the book's webpage at the Packt Publishing website. This page can be accessed by entering the book's name in the **Search** box. Note that you need to be logged in to your Packt account.

Once the file is downloaded, ensure that you unzip or extract the folder using the latest version of the following:

- WinRAR / 7-Zip for Windows
- Zipeg / iZip / UnRarX for Mac
- 7-Zip / PeaZip for Linux

How it works...

Dependencies come from various sources. First, you have the core dependencies of Odoo, the Python interpreter that is used to run the source code, and the PostgreSQL database server used to store the instance data. Git is used for source code versioning and getting the source code of Odoo itself.

Versions of Odoo prior to 11.0 ran with Python 2.7. Starting with Odoo 11.0, the minimum supported version of Python is 3.5. These two versions of Python are not compatible, so a module running on Python 2.7 (with Odoo 9.0 or 10.0, for instance) will require both porting to the specifics of Odoo 11.0 and porting to Python 3.

Since we will need to edit some files as `root` or as `postgres` (the PostgreSQL administrative user) on our server, we need to install a console-based text editor. We suggest `nano` as it is very simple to use, but feel free to choose any editor with which you feel at ease as long as it works on the console, such as `vim`, `e3`, or `emacs-nox`.

`Wkhtmltopdf` is a runtime dependency of Odoo used to produce PDF reports. The version required by Odoo 11.0 is 0.12.4, which is not included in the current GNU/Linux distributions. Fortunately for us, the maintainers of `wkhtmltopdf` provide pre-built packages for various distributions on `http://wkhtmltopdf.org/downloads.html`.

There are lots of other runtime dependencies that are Python modules, which we can install using `pip3` in a virtual environment. However, some of these Python modules can feature some dependencies on native C libraries, for which the Python bindings need to be compiled. Therefore, we install the development packages for these C libraries as well as the Python development package and a C compiler. Once these build dependencies are installed, we can use `pip3 install -r requirements.txt` (a file that comes from the Odoo source code distribution) to download, compile, and install the Python modules.

Virtual environments

Python **virtual environments**, or `virtualenv` for short, are isolated Python workspaces. They are very useful to Python developers because they allow different workspaces with different versions of various Python libraries to be installed, possibly on different Python interpreter versions.

You can create as many environments as you wish using the `virtualenv -p python3 path/to/newenv` command. This will create a `newenv` directory in the specified location, containing a `bin/` sub-directory and a `lib/python3.5` subdirectory. Don't forget `-p python3`, or you are likely to get a python 2.7 virtual environment that will not be able to run Odoo 11.0.

In `bin/`, you will find several scripts:

- `activate`: The script is not executed; it is sourced using the shell built-in `source` command. This will activate the environment by adjusting the `PATH` environment variable to include the `bin/` directory of the `virtualenv`. It also installs a shell function called deactivate, which you can run to exit the `virtualenv`, and changes the shell prompt to let you know which `virtualenv` is currently activated.
- `pip3`: This is a special version of the `pip3` command that acts inside the `virtualenv` only.
- `python3`: This is a wrapper around your system Python interpreter that uses the packages installed in the `virtualenv`.

 The shell built-in `source` command is also available as `.` (a single dot, followed by a space, and the path to the file to source). The shortcut form is perfectly fine, but we will stick to source in this book for readability.

There are two main ways of using a `virtualenv`. You may `activate` it as we show in the recipe (and call `deactivate` when you're done), or you may use the scripts in the `bin/` directory of the environment explicitly by calling them with their full path, in which case you don't need to `activate` the `virtualenv`. This is mainly a matter of taste, so you should experiment and find out which style suits you better for which case.

You may have executable Python scripts with the first line looking like the following:

```
#! /usr/bin/env python3
```

These will be easier to use with an activated `virtualenv`.

This is the case with the `odoo-bin` script, which you can call in the following way:

```
$ ./odoo-bin -d odoo-test --addons-path=addons --db-filter=odoo-test
```

PostgreSQL configuration

On a GNU/Linux system, Odoo works very well with the default values of `psycopg2` that the Python module used to access a PostgreSQL database:

- Passwordless authentication if the database user has the same name as the current user on local connections
- Local connection uses Unix domain sockets
- The database server listens on port `5432`

In that case, there is nothing special to do; we use the `postgres` administrative user to create a database user who shares our login name and gives it the right to create new databases. We then create a new database with the same name as the new user, which will be used as a default database when using the `psql` command.

When on a development server, it is okay to give the PostgreSQL user more rights and to use the `--superuser` command-line option rather than just `--createdb`. The net effect is that this user can then also create other users and globally manage the database instance. If you feel that `--superuser` is too much, you may still want to use `--createrole` in addition to `--createdb` when creating your database user. Avoid doing this on production servers as it will give additional leverage to an attacker exploiting a vulnerability in some part of the deployed code (refer to `Chapter 3`, *Server Deployment*).

If you want to use a database user with a different login, you will need to provide a password for the user. This is done by passing the `--pwprompt` flag on the command line when creating the user, in which case the command will prompt you for the password.

If the user has already been created and you want to set a password (or modify a forgotten password), you can use the following command:

```
$ psql -c "alter role $(whoami) with password 'newpassword'"
```

If this command fails with an error message saying that the database does not exist, it is because you did not create a database named after your login name in step 3. That's fine; just add the `--dbname` option with an existing database name, such as `--dbname template1`.

Git configuration

At some point in the book, you will need to use `git commit`. This will fail unless some basic configuration is performed; you need to provide Git with your name and email address. Git will remind you to do this with a nice error message, but you may as well do it now.

 This is also something to keep in mind if you are using a service such as *Travis* for continuous integration, and your test scripts need to perform some git merges; you have to provide a dummy name and email for the merging to succeed.

Downloading the Odoo source code

Downloading the Odoo code base is done by performing a git clone operation; be patient as this will take some time. The `--branch 11.0 --single-branch` options avoid downloading other branches and save a little time. The `--depth` option can also be used to avoid downloading the whole repository history, but the downside of that option is that you will not be able to explore that history when looking for issues.

Odoo developers also propose nightly builds, which are available as tarballs and distribution packages. The main advantage of using a `git clone` is that you will be able to update your repository when new bug fixes are committed in the source tree. You will also be able to easily test any proposed fixes and track regressions, so you can make your bug reports more precise and helpful for the developers.

Starting the instance

Now comes the moment you've been waiting for. To start our first instance, we first create a new empty database and then use the `odoo-bin` script with the following command-line arguments:

- `-d database_name`: Use that database by default.
- `--db-filter=database_name$`: Only try to connect to databases matching the supplied regular expression. One Odoo installation can serve multiple instances living in separate databases, and this argument limits the available databases. The trailing `$` is important as the regular expression is used in match mode; this avoids selecting names starting with the specified string.

- --addons-path=directory1,directory2,...: This is a comma separated list of directories in which Odoo will look for addons. This list is scanned at the instance creation time to populate the list of available addon modules in the instance.

If you are using a database user with a database login different from your Linux login, you need to pass the following additional arguments:

- --db_host=localhost: Use a TCP connection to the database server
- --db_user=database_username: Use the specified database login
- --db_password=database_password: The password to use to authenticate against the PostgreSQL server

To get an overview of all of the available options, use the --help argument. We will see much more about the odoo-bin script in this chapter as well as in Chapter 2, *Managing Odoo Server Instances*.

When Odoo is started on an empty database, it will first create the database structure needed to support its operations. It will also scan the addons path to find the available addon modules, and insert some into the initial records in the database. This includes the **admin** user with the default password admin, which you will use to authenticate with.

Odoo includes an HTTP server. By default, it listens on all local network interfaces on TCP port 8069, so pointing your web browser to http://localhost:8069/ leads you to your newly created instance.

There's more...

In the recipe, we downloaded the latest stable version of Odoo using the following command:

```
$ git clone -b 11.0 --single-branch https://github.com/odoo/odoo.git
```

This uses the official branch maintained by Odoo. One issue with this branch is that bug fixes contributed by the community are not always merged in a timely fashion. The **Odoo Community Association** (**OCA**) maintains a parallel branch in which fixes and improvements are peer-reviewed by the community and tend to be merged faster than on the official branch. It is not a fork of Odoo, and the latest version of Odoo is merged back into that branch daily. You may want to use it for your developments and deployments, in which case you need to clone Odoo like this:

```
$ git clone -b 11.0 --single-branch https://github.com/OCA/OCB.git odoo
```

Managing Odoo environments using the start command

We will often want to use custom or community modules with our Odoo instance. Keeping them in a separate directory makes it easier to install upgrades to Odoo or troubleshoot issues from our custom modules. We just have to add that directory to the addons path, and they will be available in our instance, just like the core modules are.

It is possible to think about this module directory as an Odoo environment. The Odoo start command makes it easy to organize Odoo instances as directories, each with its own modules.

Getting ready

For this recipe, we need to have already installed Odoo. We assume that it will be at ~/odoo-dev/odoo, and that the virtualenv is activated.

This means that the following command should successfully start an Odoo server:

```
$ ~/odoo-dev/odoo/odoo-bin
```

How to do it...

To create a work environment for your instance, you need to follow these steps:

1. Change to the directory where Odoo is:

```
$ cd ~/odoo-dev
```

2. Choose a name for the environment and create a directory for it:

```
$ mkdir my-odoo
```

3. Change to that directory and start an Odoo server instance for that environment:

```
$ cd my-odoo/
$ ../odoo/odoo-bin start
```

How it works...

The Odoo `start` command is a shortcut to start a server instance using the current directory. The directory name is automatically used as the database name (for the `-d` option), and the current directory is automatically added to the addons path (the `--addons-path` option), as long as it contains an Odoo addon module. In the preceding recipe, you won't see the current directory in the addons path because it doesn't contain any modules yet.

There's more...

By default, the current directory is used, but the `--path` option allows you to set a specific path to use instead. For example, this will work from any directory:

```
$ ~/odoo-dev/odoo/odoo-bin start --path=~/odoo-dev/my-odoo
```

The database to use can also be overridden using the usual `-d` option. In fact, all of the other usual `odoo-bin` command-line arguments, except `--addons-path`, will work. For example, to set the server listening port, use the following command:

```
$ ../odoo/odoo-bin start -p 8080
```

As we can see, the Odoo `start` command can be a convenient way to quickstart Odoo instances with their own module directory.

Managing Odoo server databases

When working with Odoo, all of the data of your instance is stored in a PostgreSQL database. All of the standard database management tools you are used to are available, but Odoo also proposes a web interface for some common operations.

Getting ready

We assume that your work environment is set up, and you have an instance running. Do not start it using the `odoo-bin start` command shown in the previous recipe, as it configures the server with some options that interfere with multi database management.

How to do it...

The Odoo database management interface provides tools to create, duplicate, remove, back up, and restore a database. There is also a way to change the master password that is used to protect access to the database management interface.

Accessing the database management interface

To access the database, the following steps need to be performed:

1. Go to the login screen of your instance (if you are authenticated, log out).
2. Click on the **Manage Databases** link. This will navigate to `http://localhost:8069/web/database/manager` (you can also point your browser directly to that URL).

Setting or changing the master password

If you've set up your instance with default values, and not yet modified it as explained in the following section, the database management screen will display a warning, telling you that the **master password** is not set and advising you to set one with a direct link:

To set the master password, you need to perform the following:

1. Click on the **Set Master Password** button. You will get a dialog box asking you to provide the **New Master Password**:

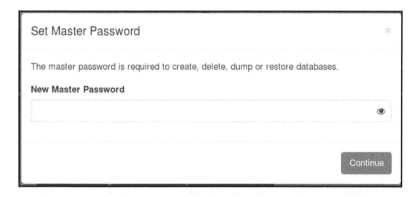

2. Type in a non-trivial new password and click on **Continue**

If the master password is already set, click on the **Set Master Password** button at the bottom of the screen to change it. In the displayed dialog box, type the previous master password and the new one, and then click on **Continue**.

The master password is in the server configuration file under the `admin_password` key. If the server was started without specifying a configuration file, a new one will be generated in `~/.odoorc`. See the next recipe for more information about the configuration file.

Creating a new database

This dialog box can be used to create a new database instance that will be handled by the current Odoo server:

1. In the database management screen, click on the **Create Database** button at the bottom of the screen:

2. Fill in the form, as follows:
   - **Master Password**: The master password for this instance.
   - **Database Name**: Input the name of the database you wish to create.
   - **Password:** Type the password you want to set for the admin user of the new instance.
   - **Language**: Select the language you wish to be installed by default in the new database in the drop-down list.
   - **Country**: Select the country of the main company in the drop-down list.
   - **Load demonstration data**: Check this box to have demonstration data. This is useful to run interactive tests or set up a demonstration for a customer, but it should not be checked for a database meant to contain production data.

If you wish to use the database to run the automated tests of the modules (refer to `Chapter 8`, *Debugging and Automated Testing*), you need to have the demonstration data, as the vast majority of the automated tests in Odoo depend on these records to run successfully.

3. Click on the **Continue** button, and wait a little until the new database is initialized. You will then be redirected to the instance, connected as the administrator.

Troubleshooting: If you are redirected to a login screen, this is probably because the `--db-filter` option was passed to Odoo and the new database name did not match the new database name. Note that the `odoo-bin start` command does this silently, making only the current database available. To work around this, simply restart Odoo without the `start` command, as shown in the first recipe of this chapter. If you have a configuration file (refer to the *Storing the instance configuration in a file* recipe later in this chapter), then check that the `db_filter` option is unset or set to a value matching the new database name.

Duplicating a database

Very often, you will have an existing database and you want to experiment with it to try a procedure or run a test, but without modifying the existing data. The answer is simple—duplicate the database and run the tests on the copy. Repeat this as many times as required:

1. In the database management screen, click on the **Duplicate Database** link next to the name of the database you wish to clone:

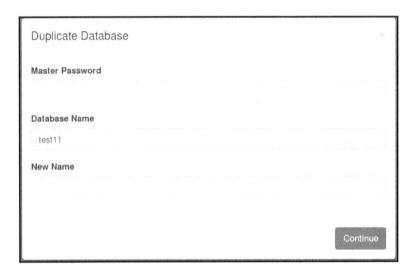

2. Fill in the form as follows:
   - **Master Password**: The master password of the Odoo server
   - **New Name**: The name you want to give to the copy

3. Click on the **Continue** button
4. You can then click on the name of the newly created database in the database management screen to access the login screen for that database

Removing a database

When you have finished your tests, you will want to clean up the duplicated databases. To do this, perform the following steps:

1. In the database management screen, click on the **Delete Database** link next to the name of the database you want to remove:

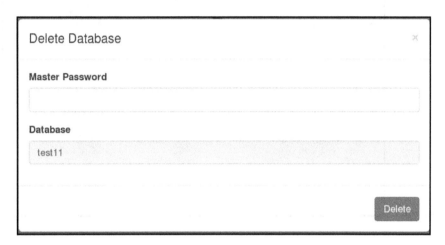

2. Fill in the form; enter the **Master Password**, which is the master password of the Odoo server
3. Click on the **Delete** button

Caution! Potential data loss!

If you selected the wrong database, and have no backup, there is no way to recover the lost data.

Backing up a database

For creating a backup, the following steps need to be performed:

In the database management screen, click on the **Backup Database** link next to the database you want to

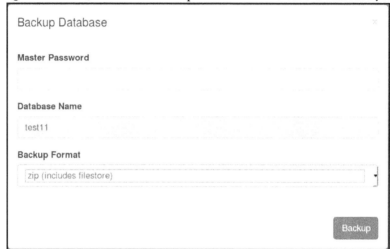

back up:

1. Fill in the form:
   - **Master Password**: The master password of the Odoo server.
   - **Backup Format**: Always use **zip** for a production database, as it is the only real full backup format. Only use the **pg_dump** format for a development database where you don't really care about the file store.

3. Click on the **Backupbutton.** The backup file will be downloaded to your browser.

Restoring a database backup

If you need to restore a backup, this is what you need to do:

1. In the database management screen, click on the **Restore Database** button at the bottom of the screen:

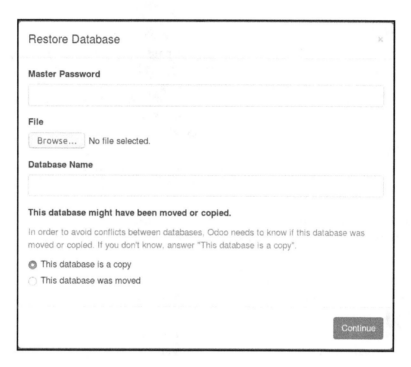

2. Fill in the form:
    - **Master Password**: The master password of the Odoo server.
    - **File**: A previously downloaded Odoo backup.
    - **Database Name**: Provide the name of the database in which the backup will be restored. The database must not exist on the server.
    - **This database might have been moved or copied**: Choose "**This database was moved**" if the original database was on another server, or if it has been deleted from the current server. Otherwise, choose "**This database is a copy**", which is a safe default.

3. Click on the **Continue** button.

It is not possible to restore a database on top of itself. If you try to do this, you will get an error message (**Database restore error: Database already exists**). You need to remove the database first.

How it works...

These features, apart from the **Change master password** screen, run PostgreSQL administration commands on the server and report back through the web interface.

The master password is a very important piece of information that only lives in the Odoo server configuration file and is never stored in the database. There used to be a default value of admin, but using this value is a security liability as it is well known. In Odoo v9 and later, this is identified as an "unset" master password, and you are urged to change it when accessing the database administration interface. Even if it is stored in the configuration file under the admin_passwd entry, this is not the same as the password of the admin user; these are two independent passwords; the master password is set for an Odoo server process, which itself can handle multiple database instances, each of which has an independent admin user with his own password.

 Security considerations: Remember that we are considering a development environment in this chapter. The Odoo database management interface is something that needs to be secured when you are working on a production server, as it gives access to a lot of sensitive information, especially if the server hosts Odoo instances for several different clients. This will be covered in Chapter 3, *Server Deployment*.

To create a new database, Odoo uses the PostgreSQL createdb utility and calls the internal Odoo function to initialize the new database in the same way as when you start Odoo on an empty database.

To duplicate a database, Odoo uses the --template option of createdb, passing the original database as an argument. This essentially duplicates the structure of the template database in the new database using internal and optimized PostgreSQL routines, which is much faster than creating a backup and restoring it (especially when using the web interface that requires downloading the backup file and uploading it again).

Backup and restore operations use the `pg_dump` and `pg_restore` utilities, respectively. When using the `zip` format, the backup will also include a copy of the file store that contains a copy of the documents when you configure Odoo to not keep these in the database, which is the default in 11.0. Unless you configure it otherwise, these files live in `~/.local/share/Odoo/filestore`.

If the backup gets large, downloading it may fail, either because the Odoo server itself is not able to handle the large file in memory or the server runs behind a reverse proxy (refer to `Chapter 3`, *Server Deployment*) because there is a limit to the size of HTTP responses set in the proxy. Conversely, for the same reasons, you will likely experience issues with the database restore operation. When you start running into these issues, it is time to invest in a more robust external backup solution.

There's more...

Experienced Odoo developers generally don't use the database management interface, and perform the operations from the command line. To initialize a new database with demo data, for instance, the following one-liner can be used:

```
$ createdb testdb && odoo-bin -d testdb
```

The additional bonus of this command line is that you can request the installation of addons while you are at it using, for instance, `-i sale,purchase,stock` (more on this in `Chapter 2`, *Managing Odoo Server Instances*).

To duplicate a database, stop the server and run the following commands:

```
$ createdb -T dbname newdbname
$ cd ~/.local/share/Odoo/filestore # adapt if you have changed the data_dir
$ cp -r dbname newdbname
$ cd -
```

Note that in the context of development, the file store is often omitted.

The use of `createdb -T` only works if there are no active sessions on the database, which means you have to shut down your Odoo server before duplicating the database from the command line.

To remove an instance, run the following command:

```
$ dropdb dbname
$ rm -rf ~/.local/share/Odoo/filestore/dbname
```

To create a backup (assuming that the PostgreSQL server is running locally), use the following command:

```
$ pg_dump -Fc -f dbname.dump dbname
$ tar cjf dbname.tgz dbname.dump ~/.local/share/Odoo/filestore/dbname
```

To restore the backup, run the following command:

```
$ tar xf dbname.tgz
$ pg_restore -C -d dbname dbname.dump
```

Caution!

If your Odoo instance uses a different user to connect to the database, you need to pass `-U username` so that the correct user is the owner of the restored database.

Storing the instance configuration in a file

The `odoo-bin` script has dozens of options, and it is tedious to remember them all and to remember to set them properly when starting the server. Fortunately, it is possible to store them all in a configuration file and to only specify by hand the ones you want to alter, for example, for development.

How to do it...

To generate a configuration file for your Odoo instance, run the following command:

```
$ odoo-bin --save --config myodoo.cfg --stop-after-init
```

You can add additional options, and their values will be saved in the generated file. All the unset options will be saved with their default value set. To get a list of possible options, use this:

```
$ odoo-bin --help | less
```

This will provide you with some help about what the various options perform. To convert from the command line form to the configuration form, use the long option name, remove the leading dashes, and convert the dashes in the middle to underscores:
`--without-demo` becomes `without_demo`. This works for most options, but there are a few exceptions listed in the next section.

Edit the `myodoo.cfg` file (use the table in the following section for some parameters you may want to change). Then, to start the server with the saved options, run the following command:

```
$ odoo-bin -c myodoo.cfg
```

The `--config` option is commonly abbreviated as `-c`.

How it works...

At start up, Odoo loads its configuration in three passes. First, a set of default values for all options is initialized from the source code, then the configuration is parsed, and any value defined in the file overrides the defaults. Finally, the command-line options are analyzed and their values override the configuration obtained from the previous pass.

As mentioned earlier, the names of the configuration variables can be found from the names of the command-line options by removing the leading dashes and converting the middle dashes to underscores. There are a few exceptions, notably the following:

Command line	Configuration file
`--db-filter`	`dbfilter`
`--no-http`	`http_enable = True/False`
`--database`	`db_name`
`--dev`	`dev_mode`
`--i18n-import` / `--i18n-export`	Unavailable

Here's a list of options commonly set through the configuration file:

Option	Format	Usage
`without_demo`	Comma separated list of module names, or `all` (to disable demo data for all modules) or `False` (to enable demo data for all modules)	Prevents module demo data from being loaded.
`addons_path`	Comma separated list of paths	A list of directory names in which the server will look for addons (refer to `Chapter 2`, *Managing Odoo Server instances*).
`admin_passwd`	Text	The master password (take a look at the preceding recipe).
`data_dir`	Path to a directory	A directory in which the server will store session information, addons downloaded from the internet, and documents if you enable the file store.
`db_host`	Host name	The name of the server running the PostgreSQL server. Use `False` to use local Unix Domain sockets, and `localhost` to use TCP sockets locally.
`db_user`	Database user login	
`db_password`	Database user password	This is generally empty if `db_host` is `False` and `db_user` has the same name as the user running the server. Read the man page of `pg_hba.conf` for more information on this.
`database`	Database name	Used to set the database name on which some commands operate by default. This does not limit the databases on which the server will act. Refer to the following `dbfilter` option for this.

`dbfilter`	A regular expression	The expression should match the name of the databases considered by the server. If you run the website, it should match a single database, so it will look like `^databasename$`. More information on this is in `Chapter 3`, *Server Deployment*.
`http_interface`	IP address of a network interface	Defaults to `0.0.0.0`, which means that the server listens on all interfaces.
`http_port` `longpolling_port`	Port number	The ports on which the Odoo server will listen. You will need to specify both to run multiple Odoo servers on the same host; `longpolling_port` is only used if `workers` is not `0`. `http_port` defaults to `8069` and `longpolling_port` to `8072`.
`logfile`	Path to a file	The file in which Odoo will write its logs.
`log_level`	Log verbosity level	Specify the level of logging. Accepted values (in increasing verbosity order): `critical`, `error`, `warn`, `info`, `debug`, `debug_rpc`, `debug_rpc_answer`, `debug_sql`.
`workers`	Integer	The number of worker processes. Refer to `Chapter 3`, *Server Deployment*, for more information.
`no_database_list`	True / False	Set to True to disable listing of databases. See `Chapter 3`, *Server Deployment*, for more information.

 The parsing of the configuration file by Odoo is now using the Python `ConfigParser` module. However, the implementation in Odoo 11.0 has changed, and it is no longer possible to use variable interpolation. So, if you are used to defining values for variables from the values of other variables using the `%(section.variable)s` notation, you will need to change your habits and revert to explicit values.

Activating the Odoo developer tools

When using Odoo as a developer, you need to know how to activate **Developer Mode** in the web interface to access the advanced settings menu and developer information.

How to do it...

To activate Developer Mode in the web interface, do as follows:

1. Connect to your instance and authenticate as `admin`
2. Go to the **Settings** menu
3. Locate the **Share the love** card, which should be on the right of the screen:

4. Click on the **Activate the developer mode** link

5. Wait for the UI to reload

It is also possible to activate the developer mode by editing the URL; before the # sign, insert `?debug`. For instance, if you are starting from `http://localhost:8069/web#menu_id=102&action=94`, then you need to change this to `http://localhost:8069/web?debug=#menu_id=102&action=94`. To exit the developer mode, you can do either of these:

- Edit the URL and remove that string
- Close your browser tab and open a new one
- Use the **Deactivate the developer mode** link displayed in the **Share the love card** when the Developer mode is active

How it works...

When in developer mode, two things happen:

1. You get tooltips when hovering over a field in a form view or over a column in list view, providing technical information about the field (internal name, type, and so on)
2. A drop-down menu with a **Bug** icon is displayed next to the user's menu in the top-right corner, giving access to technical information about the model being displayed, the various related view definitions, the workflow, custom filter management, and so on

There is a variant of the developer mode—the **Developer mode (with assets)**. This mode behaves as the normal developer mode, but additionally, the JavaScript and CSS code sent to the browser is not minified, which means that the web development tools of your browser are easy to use for debugging the JavaScript code (more on this in Chapter 15, *Web Client Development*).

Caution!

Test your addons both with and without developer mode, as the unminified versions of the JavaScript libraries can hide bugs that only bite you in the minified version.

Updating Odoo from source

In the first recipe, we saw how to install Odoo from source using the `git` repository. The main benefit of this setting is being able to update the source code of Odoo using `git` to get the latest bug fixes.

Getting ready

Stop any instance currently running with the Odoo source you are about to update.

Make a backup of all the databases you care about in case something goes bad. This is obviously something you need to do for production databases. Refer to the *Managing Odoo server databases* recipe for instructions.

Then, make a note of the current version of the source you are running. The best way is to create a lightweight tag using the following command:

```
$ cd ~/odoo-dev/odoo
$ git checkout 11.0
$ git tag 11.0-before-update-$(date --iso)
```

How to do it...

To update the source code of Odoo, use the following command:

```
$ git pull --ff-only origin 11.0
```

This will fetch the latest version of the source code committed to the current branch.

To update an instance running on this code, run the following command:

```
$ ./odoo-bin -c myodoo.cfg --stop-after-init -u base
```

 -u is the shortcut notation for the --update option of odoo-bin.

If you don't have a database set in the configuration file, you will have to add the -d database_name option. This command is to be repeated for all of the instances running with this version of the source code.

If the update fails, don't panic, because you have backups:

1. Read the error message carefully and save it to a file, as it will be useful to make a bug report later
2. If you cannot figure out what the problem is, restore the service; restore the Odoo source code to the previous version, which is known to work using the tag you set before updating the source version:

```
$ git reset --hard 11.0-before-update-$(date --iso)
```

3. Drop the broken databases and restore them from the backups you made (refer to the *Managing Odoo server databases* recipe for instructions)
4. Restart your instances and tell your users that the upgrade has been postponed

 Note that in real life, this should never happen on a production database, because you would have tested the upgrade beforehand on a copy of the database, fixed the issues, and only done the upgrade on the production server after ensuring that it runs flawlessly. However, sometimes you still get surprises, so even if you are really sure, make a backup.

How it works...

Updating the source code is done by ensuring that we are on the correct branch using git checkout, and then fetching the new revisions using git pull. The --ff-only option will cause a failure if you have local commits not present in the remote repository. If this happens and you want to keep your changes, you can use git pull (without --ff-only) to merge the remote changes with yours; otherwise, use git reset --hard origin/11.0 to force the update, discarding your local modifications.

The update command uses the following options:

- -c: Specifies the configuration file
- --stop-after-init: Stops the instance when the update is over
- -u base or --update base: Requests the update of the base module

When updating a module, Odoo does the following:

- It updates the database structure for the models defined in the module for which the structure changes. For updates on the stable branch of Odoo, there should be no such changes, but this can happen for your own addons or third party addons.
- It updates the database records stored in data files of the module, most notably the views. It then recursively updates the installed modules that have declared a dependency on the module.

Since the base module is an implicit dependency of all Odoo modules, updating it will trigger an update of all of the installed modules in your instance. To update all installed modules, the alias all can be used instead of base.

2
Managing Odoo Server Instances

In this chapter, we will learn the following recipes:

- Configuring the addons path
- Updating the addon modules list
- Standardizing your instance directory layout
- Installing and upgrading local addon modules
- Installing addon modules from GitHub
- Applying changes to addons
- Applying and trying proposed pull requests

Introduction

In Chapter 1, *Installing the Odoo Development Environment*, we saw how to set up an Odoo instance using only the standard core addons, which are shipped by the editor. This chapter focuses on adding noncore addons to an Odoo instance, be it your own addons, or third-party addons, such as the ones maintained by the **Odoo Community Association** (**OCA**).

About the terminology – addon versus module

In this book, we will use the term *addon* or *addon module* to refer to a Python package that respects the expected format to be installed in Odoo. The user interface often uses the words *app* or *module* for this, but we prefer keeping the term *module* for Python modules or packages that are not necessarily Odoo addons, and *app* for addon modules that are properly defined as applications, that is, have an entry in the main menu of Odoo.

Configuring the addons path

The addons path is a configuration parameter that lists the directories, which will be searched for addon modules by Odoo when it initializes a new database.

Directories listed in the addons path are expected to contain subdirectories, each of which is an addon module.

Getting ready

This recipe assumes that you have an instance ready, with a configuration file generated as described in Chapter 1, *Installing the Odoo Development Environment*. The source code of Odoo is available in ~/odoo-dev/odoo, and the configuration file is in ~/odoo-dev/my-instance.cfg.

How to do it...

To add the ~/odoo-dev/local-addons directory to the addons path of the instance, follow these steps:

1. Edit the configuration file for your instance ~/odoo-dev/my-instance.cfg
2. Locate the line starting with addons_path =. By default, it should look like the following:

   ```
   addons_path = ~/odoo-dev/odoo/odoo/addons,~/odoo-dev/odoo/addons
   ```

3. Modify the line by appending a comma followed by the name of the directory you want to add to the addons path:

```
addons_path = ~/odoo-dev/odoo/odoo/addons,
~/odoo-dev/odoo/addons,~/odoo-dev/local-addons
```

4. Restart your instance:

```
$ ~/odoo-dev/odoo/odoo-bin -c my-instance.cfg
```

How it works...

When Odoo is restarted, the configuration file is read. The value of the addons_path variable is expected to be a comma-separated list of directories. Relative paths are accepted, but they are relative to the current working directory and therefore should be avoided in the configuration file.

At this point, the new addons present in ~/odoo-dev/local-addons are not available in the list of available addon modules of the instance. For this, you need to perform an extra operation explained in the next recipe, *Updating the addon modules list*.

There's more...

When you call the odoo-bin script for the first time to initialize a new database, you can pass the --addons-path command-line argument with a comma-separated list of directories. This will initialize the list of available addon modules with all of the addons found in the supplied addons path. When you do this, you have to explicitly include the base addons directory (odoo/odoo/addons) as well as the core addons directory (odoo/addons). Be careful if you put a space after the commas, as you will need to quote the list of directories.

A small difference with the preceding recipe is that the local addons must not be empty; they must contain at least one subdirectory, which has the minimal structure of an addon module. We will see in detail in Chapter 4, *Creating Odoo addon modules*, how to write your own modules. In the meantime, here's a quick hack produce, something that will make Odoo happy:

```
$ mkdir -p ~/odoo-dev/local-addons/dummy
$ touch ~/odoo-dev/local-addons/dummy/__init__.py
$ echo '{"name": "dummy", "installable": False}' > \
~/odoo-dev/local-addons/dummy/__manifest__.py
```

You can use the `--save` option to also save the path to the configuration file:

```
$ odoo/odoo-bin -d mydatabase \
--addons-path="odoo/odoo/addons,odoo/addons,~/odoo-dev/local-addons" \
--save -c ~/odoo-dev/my-instance.cfg --stop-after-init
```

In this case, using relative paths is okay, since they will be converted to absolute paths in the configuration file.

 Since Odoo only checks directories in the addons path for the presence of addons when the path is set from the command line, not when the path is loaded from a configuration file, the dummy module is no longer necessary. You may, therefore, remove it (or keep it for some time until you're sure that you won't need to create a new configuration file).

Updating the addon modules list

As we said in the preceding recipe, when you add a directory to the addons path, just restarting the Odoo server is not enough to be able to install one of the new addon modules. A specific action is required for Odoo to scan the addons path and update the list of the available addon modules.

Getting ready

Start your instance and connect to the instance using the Administrator account and activate the developer mode (refer to `Chapter 1`, *Installing the Odoo Development Environment*).

How to do it...

To update the list of the available addon modules in your instance, you need to perform the following steps:

1. Open the **Apps** menu:

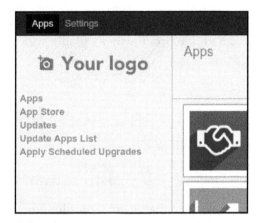

2. Click on **Update Apps List**:

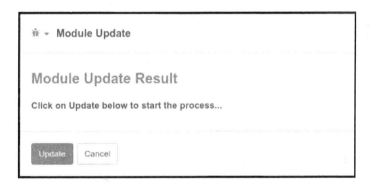

3. In the dialog, click on the **Update** button.
4. At the end of the update, you can click on the **Apps** entry to see the updated list of the available addon modules. You will need to remove the default filter on **Apps** in the search box to see all of them.

How it works...

When the Update button is clicked on, Odoo will read the addons path configuration variable, and for each directory in the list, it will look for immediate subdirectories containing an addon manifest file, which is a file named __manifest__.py, stored in the addon module directory. Odoo reads the manifest, expecting to find a Python dictionary. Unless the manifest contains a key installable set to False, the addon module metadata is recorded in the database. If the module was already present, the information is updated; otherwise, a new record is created. If a previously available addon module is not found, the record is not deleted from the list.

Standardizing your instance directory layout

We recommend that your development and production environments all use a similar directory layout. This standardization will prove helpful when you have to perform maintenance operations, and it will also ease your day-to-day work.

This recipe creates a directory structure that groups files having similar life cycles or similar purpose together in standardized subdirectories. Feel free to alter this structure to suit your needs, but ensure that you have this documented somewhere.

How to do it...

To create the proposed instance layout, you need to perform the following steps:

1. Create one directory per instance:

```
$ mkdir ~/odoo-dev/projectname
$ cd ~/odoo-dev/projectname
```

2. Create a Python virtualenv in a subdirectory called env/:

```
$ virtualenv -p python3 env
```

3. Create some subdirectories, as follows:

```
$ mkdir src local bin filestore logs
```

The functions of the subdirectories are as follows:

- `src/`: This contains the clone of Odoo itself and of the various third-party addon projects (refer to step 4 in this recipe)
- `local/`: This is used to save your instance-specific addons
- `bin/`: This includes various helper executable shell scripts
- `filestore/`: This is used as a file store
- `logs/` (optional): This is used to store the server log files

4. Clone Odoo and install the requirements (refer to `Chapter 1`, *Installing the Odoo Development Environment*, for details):

```
$ git clone https://github.com/odoo/odoo.git src/odoo
$ env/bin/pip3 install -r src/odoo/requirements.txt
```

5. Save the following shell script as `bin/odoo`:

```
#!/bin/sh
ROOT=$(dirname $0)/..
PYTHON=$ROOT/env/bin/python3
ODOO=$ROOT/src/odoo/odoo-bin
$PYTHON $ODOO -c $ROOT/projectname.cfg "$@"
exit $?
```

6. Make the script executable:

```
$ chmod +x bin/odoo
```

7. Create an empty dummy local module:

```
$ mkdir -p local/dummy
$ touch local/dummy/__init__.py
$ echo '{"name": "dummy", "installable": False}' >\
local/dummy/__manifest__.py
```

8. Generate a configuration file for your instance:

```
$ bin/odoo --stop-after-init --save \
  --addons-path src/odoo/odoo/addons,src/odoo/addons,local \
  --data-dir filestore
```

9. Add a `.gitignore` file, asking to exclude `filestore/`, `env/`, `logs/` and `src/`:

```
# dotfiles, with exceptions:
.*
!.gitignore
# python compiled files
*.py[co]
# emacs backup files
*~
# not tracked subdirectories
/env/
/src/
/filestore/
/logs/
```

10. Create a Git repository for this instance and add the files you've added to git:

```
$ git init
$ git add .
$ git commit -m "initial version of projectname"
```

How it works...

We generate a clean directory structure with clearly labeled directories and dedicated roles; especially, we separate the following:

- The code maintained by other people (in `src/`)
- The `local` specific code
- The `filestore` of the instance

By having one `virtualenv` per project, we are sure that the project's dependencies will not interfere with the dependencies of other projects that can be running a different version of Odoo or use different third-party addon modules, which need different versions of Python dependencies. This comes at the cost of a little disk space.

In a similar way, using separate clones of Odoo and third-party addon modules for our different projects, we are able to let each of these evolve independently and only install updates on the instances that need them, hence reducing the risk of introducing regressions.

The `bin/odoo` script allows us to run the server without having to remember the various paths or activate the `virtualenv`. It also sets the configuration file for us. You can add additional scripts in there to help you in your day-to-day work, for instance, a script to check out the different third-party projects that you need to run your instance.

Regarding the configuration file, we only show the bare minimum options to set up here, but you obviously can set more, such as the database name, the database filter, or the port on which the project listens. Refer to Chapter 1, *Installing the Odoo Development Environment*, for more information on this topic.

Finally, by managing all of this in a Git repository, it becomes quite easy to replicate the setup on a different computer and share the development among a team.

Speedup tip

To ease project creation, you can create a template repository containing the empty structure, and fork that repository for each new project. This will save you from retyping the bin/odoo script and the .gitignore file, and any other template file you need (continuous integration configuration, README.md, ChangeLog, and so on).

See also

If you like this approach, we suggest trying out the build-out recipe in Chapter 3, *Server Deployment*, which goes one step further in this way using build-out to create the instance environment. The same concepts are applied in the docker recipe, also in Chapter 3, *Server Deployment*.

Installing and upgrading local addon modules

The core of the functionality of Odoo comes from the addon modules. You have a wealth of addons available as part of Odoo itself as well as addon modules that you can download from the internet or write yourself.

In this recipe, we will show how to install and upgrade addon modules through the web interface and from the command line.

The main benefits of using the command line for these operations are being able to act on more than one addon at a time and having a clear view of the server logs as the installation or update progresses, which is very useful when in the development mode or when scripting the installation of an instance.

Getting ready

You have an Odoo instance with its database initialized, the addons path properly set, and the addons list up to date.

How to do it...

There are two possible methods to install or update addons: you can use the web interface or the command line.

From the web interface

To install a new addon module in your database using the web interface, use the following steps:

1. Connect to the instance using the **Administrator** account. Open the **Apps** menu:

2. Click on **Apps**

3. Use the search box to locate the addon you want to install. Here are few tips to help you in this task:
    - Activate the **Not Installed** filter
    - If looking for a specific functionality addon rather than a broad functionality addon, remove the **Apps** filter
    - Type a part of the module name in the search box, and use this as a **Module** filter
    - You may find that using the list view gives something more readable

4. Click on the **Install** button under the module name (in the icons view or in the form view)

To update an already installed module in your database, use the following steps:

1. Connect to the instance using the **Administrator** account.

2. Open the **Apps** menu.

3. Click on **Apps**:

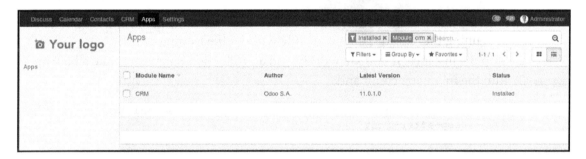

4. Use the search box to locate the addon you want to install. Here are a few tips:
    - Activate the **Installed** filter
    - If looking for a specific functionality addon rather than a broad functionality addon, remove the **Apps** filter
    - Type a part of the addon module name in the search box, and use this a **Module** filter
    - You may find that using the list view gives something more readable

5. Display the module in the form view, and click on the **Upgrade** button under the module name

From the command line

To install some new addons in your database, follow the following steps:

1. Find the names of the addons. This is the name of the directory containing the `__manifest__.py` file without the leading path.
2. Stop the instance. If you are working on a production database, make a backup.
3. Run the following command:

```
$ odoo/odoo-bin -c instance.cfg -d dbname -i addon1,addon2 \
--stop-after-init
```

 You may omit `-d dbname` if this is set in your configuration file.

4. Restart the instance.

To update an already installed addon module in your database, follow the steps given here:

1. Find the name of the addon module to update; this is the name of the directory containing the `__manifest__.py` file without the leading path.
2. Stop the instance. If you are working on a production database, make a backup.
3. Run the following command:

```
$ odoo/odoo-bin -c instance.cfg -d dbname -u addon1 \
--stop-after-init
```

 You may omit `-d dbname` if this is set in your configuration file.

4. Restart the instance.

How it works...

The addon module installation and update are two closely-related processes, but there are some important differences, as highlighted in the next two sections.

Addon installation

When you install an addon, Odoo checks its list of available addons for an uninstalled addon with the supplied name. It also checks for the dependencies of that addon and, if any, it will recursively install them before installing the addon.

The installation process of a single module consists of the following steps:

1. If any, run the addon `preinit` hook
2. Load the model definitions from the Python source code and update the database structure if necessary (refer to `Chapter 5`, *Application Models*, for details)
3. Load the data files of the addon and update the database contents if necessary (refer to `Chapter 7`, *Module Data*, for details)
4. Install the addon demo data if demo data is enabled in the instance
5. If any, run the addon `postinit` hook
6. Run a validation of the view definitions of the addon
7. If demo data is enabled and test is enabled, run the tests of the addon (refer to `Chapter 8`, *Debugging and Automated Testing*, for details)
8. Update the module state in the database
9. Update the translations in the database from the addon's translations (refer to `Chapter 12`, *Internationalization*, for details)

> The `preinit` and `postinit` hooks are defined in the __manifest__.py file using the `pre_init_hook` and `post_init_hook` keys, respectively. The value of the key is the name of a Python function, which must be defined in the __init__.py file of the addon module. The preinit (respectively postinit) hook is called with a database cursor (respectively a database cursor and a registry object) and may perform modification in the database to prepare (respectively finalize) the module installation. Note that these are not run when the module is updated (you can use migration steps for this; see the following).

Addon update

When you update an addon, Odoo checks in its list of available addon modules for an installed addon with the given name. It also checks for the reverse dependencies of that addon (these are the addons that depend on the updated addon), and, if any, it will recursively update them.

The update process of a single addon module consists of the following steps:

1. Run the addon module's premigration steps, if any (refer to `Chapter 7`, *Module Data*, for details).
2. Load the model definitions from the Python source code and update the database structure if necessary (refer to `Chapter 5`, *Application Models*, for details).
3. Load the data files of the addon and update the database contents if necessary (refer to `Chapter 7`, *Module Data*, for details).
4. Update the addon's demo data if demo data is enabled in the instance.
5. If any, run the addon post migration steps (refer to `Chapter 7`, *Module Data*, for details).
6. Run a validation of the view definitions of the addon.
7. If demo data is enabled and test is enabled, run the tests of the addon (refer to `Chapter 8`, *Debugging and Automated Testing*, for details).
8. Update the module state in the database.
9. Update the translations in the database from the addon's translations (refer to `Chapter 12`, *Internationalization*, for details).

 Note that updating an addon module that is not installed does nothing at all. However, installing an addon module that is already installed reinstalls the addon, which can have some unintended effects with some data files containing data that is supposed to be updated by the user and not updated during the normal module update process (refer to *Using the noupdate and forcecreate flags* in `Chapter 7`, *Module Data*). There is no risk of error from the user interface, but this can happen from the command line.

There's more...

Be careful about the dependency handling. Consider an instance where you want to have the `sale`, `sale_stock`, and `sale_specific` addons installed, with `sale_specific` depending on `sale_stock`, and `sale_stock` depending on `sale`. To install all three, you only need to install `sale_specific`, as it will recursively install the `sale_stock` and `sale` dependencies. To update all three, you need to update `sale`, as this will recursively update the reverse dependencies `sale_stock` and `sale_specific`.

Another tricky part is when you add a dependency to an addon that already has a version installed. To continue with the previous example, imagine that you add a dependency on `stock_dropshipping` in `sale_specific`. Updating the addon `sale_specific` will not automatically install the new dependency, neither will requesting the installation of `sale_specific`. In this situation, you can get very nasty error messages because the Python code of the addon is not successfully loaded, but the data of the addon and the models tables in the database are present. To solve this, you need to stop the instance and manually install the new dependency.

Installing addon modules from GitHub

GitHub is a great source of third-party addons. A lot of Odoo partners use GitHub to share the addons they maintain internally, and the **Odoo Community Association (OCA)** collectively maintains several hundreds of addons on GitHub. Before starting to write your own addon, ensure that you check that nothing already exists that you can use as is or as a starting point.

This recipe will show you how to clone the *partner-contact* project of the OCA from GitHub and make the addon modules it contains available in your instance.

Getting ready

Suppose you want to change the way addresses are handled in your instance; your customer needs a third field in addition to Odoo's two fields (`street` and `street2`) to store addresses. You can certainly write your own addon to add a field on `res.partner`, but the issue is a bit trickier than it seems if you want the address to be properly formatted on invoices. Fortunately, someone on a mailing list tells you about the `partner_address_street3` addon that is maintained by the OCA as part of the *partner-contact* project.

The paths used in this recipe reflect the layout proposed in the *Standardizing your instance directory layout* recipe.

How to do it...

To install `partner_address_street3`, follow these steps:

1. Go to your project's directory:

   ```
   $ cd ~/odoo-dev/my-odoo/src
   ```

2. Clone the 11.0 branch of the partner-contact project in the `src/` directory:

   ```
   $ git clone --branch 11.0 \
   https://github.com/OCA/partner-contact.git src/partner-contact
   ```

3. Change the addons path to include that directory and update the addons list of your instance (refer to the *Configure the addons path* and *Update the addon modules list* recipes of this chapter). The `addons_path` line of `instance.cfg` should look like this:

   ```
   addons_path = ~/odoo-dev/my-odoo/src/odoo/odoo/addons, \
   ~/odoo-dev/my-odoo/src/odoo/addons, \
   ~/odoo-dev/my-odoo/src/, \
   ~/odoo-dev/local-addons
   ```

4. Install the `partner_address_street3` addon (take a look at the previous recipe, *Installing and upgrading local addon modules*).

How it works...

All of the Odoo Community Association code repositories have their addons contained in separate subdirectories, which is coherent with what is expected by Odoo regarding the directories in the addons path; therefore, just cloning the repository somewhere and adding that location in the addons path is enough.

There's more...

Some maintainers follow a different approach and have one addon module per repository, living at the root of the repository. In that case, you need to create a new directory, which you will add to the addons path and clone all of the addons from that maintainer you need in this directory. Remember to update the addon modules list each time you add a new repository clone.

Applying changes to addons

Most addons available on GitHub are subject to change and do not follow the rules that Odoo enforces for its stable release. They may receive bug fixes or enhancements, including issues or feature requests that you submitted, and these changes may introduce database schema changes or updates in the data files and views. This recipe explains how to install the updated versions.

Getting ready

Suppose you reported an issue with `partner_address_street3` and received a notification that the issue was solved in the last revision of the 11.0 branch of the *partner-contact* project; you will want to update your instance with this latest version.

How to do it...

To apply a source modification to your addon from GitHub, you need to perform the following steps:

1. Stop the instance using that addon
2. Make a backup if it is a production instance (refer to the *Manage Odoo server databases* recipe in `Chapter 1`, *Installing the Odoo Development Environment*)
3. Go to the directory where *partner-contact* was cloned:

   ```
   $ cd ~/odoo-dev/my-odoo/src
   ```

4. Create a local tag for the project so that you can revert to that version in case things break:

   ```
   $ git checkout 11.0
   $ git tag 11.0-before-update-$(date --iso)
   ```

5. Get the latest version of the source code:

   ```
   $ git pull --ff-only
   ```

6. Update the `partner_address_street3` addon in your databases (refer to the *Install and upgrade local addon modules* recipe)
7. Restart the instance

How it works...

This is just a simple application of all the previous recipes we've seen; we get a new version of the addon and update it in our instances.

If `git pull --ff-only` fails, you can revert to the previous version using this command:

```
$ git reset --hard 11.0-before-update-$(date --iso)
```

Then, you can try `git pull` (without `--ff-only`), which will cause a merge, but this means you have local changes on the addon.

See also

If the update step breaks, refer to the *Updating Odoo from Source* recipe in `Chapter 1`, *Installing the Odoo Development Environment*, for the recovery instructions. Remember to always test an update on a copy of a database production first.

Applying and trying proposed pull requests

In the **GitHub** world, a **Pull Request** (**PR**) is a request made by a developer for the maintainers of a project to include some new developments. Such a PR may contain a bug fix or a new feature. These requests are reviewed and tested before being pulled in the main branch.

This recipe explains how to apply a PR to your Odoo project in order to test an improvement or a bug fix.

Getting ready

As in the previous recipe, suppose you reported an issue with `partner_address_street3` and received a notification that the issue was solved in a pull request, which is not yet merged in the 11.0 branch of the project. The developer asks you to validate the fix in PR #123. You need to update a test instance with this branch.

You should not try out such branches directly on a production database, so first create a test environment with a copy of the production database (refer to `Chapter 1`, *Installing the Odoo Development Environment*, and `Chapter 3`, *Server Deployment*).

How to do it...

To apply and try out a GitHub pull request for an addon, you need to perform the following steps:

1. Stop the instance.
2. Go to the directory where partner-contact was cloned:

   ```
   $ cd ~/odoo-dev/my-odoo/src
   ```

3. Create a local tag for the project so that you can revert to that version in case things break:

   ```
   $ git checkout 11.0
   $ git tag 11.0-before-update-$(date --iso)
   ```

4. Pull the branch of the `pull` request. The easiest way is to use the number of the PR, which should have been communicated to you by the developer. In our example, this is the pull request number `123`:

   ```
   $ git pull origin pull/123/head
   ```

5. Update the `partner_address_street3` addon module in your database and restart the instance (refer to the *Installing and upgrading local addon modules* recipe).
6. Test the update—try to reproduce your issue, or try out the feature you wanted.

If it does not work, comment on the PR page of GitHub, explaining what you did and what did not work so that the developer can update the PR.

If it works, say so on the PR page too; this is an essential part of the PR validation process, and it will speed up the merging in the main branch.

How it works...

We are using a GitHub feature that enables pull requests to be pulled by number using the `pull/`*nnnn*`/head` branch name, where *nnnn* is the number of the PR. The git pull command will merge the remote branch in ours, applying the changes in our code base. After this, we update the addon module, test, and report back to the author of the change about any failure or success.

There's more...

You can repeat step four for different pull requests in the same repository if you want to test them simultaneously. If you are really happy with the result, you can create a branch to keep a reference to the result of the applied changes:

```
$ git checkout -b 11.0-custom
```

Using a different branch will help you remember that you are not using the version from GitHub, but a custom one.

> The `git branch` command can be used to list all the local branches you have in your repository.

From then on, if you need to apply the latest revision of the 11.0 branch from GitHub, you will need to pull them without using `--ff-only`:

```
$ git pull origin 11.0
```

3
Server Deployment

In this chapter, we will cover these recipes:

- Installing Odoo for production use
- Adapting the configuration file for production
- Setting up Odoo as a system service
- Configuring a reverse proxy and SSL with nginx and Let's Encrypt
- Using buildout for repeatable builds
- Using Docker to run Odoo

Introduction

We have seen in Chapter 1, *Installing the Odoo Development Environment*, in the recipe Easy installation from source, and in Chapter 2, *Managing Odoo Server Instances*, in the recipe Standardizing your instance directory layout, how to set up a development environment. The requirements for a production environment are slightly different. This chapter covers the specificity of the deployment of Odoo.

Installing Odoo for production use

Installing Odoo in the production phase is not very different from installing Odoo for development. While there are several possible approaches, this recipe proposes a setup that is close to the development installation explained in Chapter 1, *Installing the Odoo Development Environment*, in the recipe *Easy installation from source*, and in Chapter 2, *Managing Odoo Server Instances*, in the recipe *Standardize your instance directory layout*.

Getting ready

We expect that you have a development instance ready. In this recipe, we assume the following:

- The project of your instance is managed in the same way as suggested in `Chapter 2`, *Managing Odoo Server Instances*, in the *Standardize your instance directory layout* recipe. We will use `https://github.com/yourlogin/project.git`. This repository should contain the configuration file of the instance used during development, the specific addons of the instance, and any helper script that you may have created in the context of the project.

Caution:

If the configuration files of your project include security information such as passwords, you should not push the project on a public service such as GitHub. Use an internal Git repository or a private GitHub project.

- The deployment server is running Debian Stretch (but it should work with little change on derived distributions such as Ubuntu; see `Chapter 1`, *Installing the Odoo Development Environment*, for more on this).
- You have `root` access to the final server using `ssh` or `sudo`. If you don't, you will have to find a system administrator to assist you in the configuration.
- You know the final fully qualified domain name under which the server will be accessed.

How to do it...

To install Odoo for production, you need to carry out the following steps:

1. As root, install the dependencies and build dependencies:

```
# apt-get update
# apt-get install git python3.5 postgresql nano virtualenv \
      gcc python3.5-dev libxml2-dev libxslt1-dev \
      libevent-dev libsasl2-dev libldap2-dev libpq-dev \
      libpng-dev libjpeg-dev node-less node-clean-css \
      xfonts-75dpi xfonts-base wget xz-utils
# wget -O wkhtmltox.tar.xz \
https://github.com/wkhtmltopdf/wkhtmltopdf/releases/download/0.12.4/wkh
tmltox-0.12.4_linux-generic-amd64.tar.xz
# tar xvf wkhtmltox.tar.xz
```

```
# mv wkhtmltox/lib/* /usr/local/lib/
# mv wkhtmltox/bin/* /usr/local/bin/
# mv wkhtmltox/share/man/man1 /usr/local/share/man/
```

2. As root, create a user called odoo:

```
# adduser odoo
```

3. Configure the PostgreSQL database:

```
# sudo -u postgres createuser odoo
# sudo -u postgres createdb -O odoo odoo_project
```

4. As odoo, clone the project repository:

```
# su odoo
$ mkdir ~/odoo-prod
$ cd ~/odoo-prod
$ git clone https://github.com/yourlogin/project.git project
$ mkdir -p project/src
```

5. As the odoo user, clone the Odoo source code:

```
$ cd project/src
$ git clone -b 11.0 --single-branch
https://github.com/odoo/odoo.git odoo
```

6. Create virtualenv and install the dependencies:

```
$ virtualenv -p python3 ~/env-odoo-11.0
$ source ~/env-odoo-11.0/bin/activate
$ pip3 install -r odoo/requirements.txt
```

7. Clone all third-party addon repositories in the project/src subdirectory:

```
$ git clone -b 11.0 https://github.com/OCA/partner-contact.git
```

8. Create the ~/odoo-prod/project/bin directory:

```
$ mkdir ~/odoo-prod/project/bin
```

9. Create a script to easily start Odoo in the production environment in ~/odoo-prod/project/bin/start-odoo:

```
#! /bin/sh
PYTHON=~odoo/env-odoo-11.0/bin/python3
```

```
ODOO=~odoo/odoo-prod/project/src/odoo/odoo-bin
CONF=~odoo/odoo-prod/project/production.conf
${PYTHON} ${ODOO} -c ${CONF} "$@"
```

10. Make the script executable:

```
$ chmod +x ~/odoo-prod/project/bin/start-odoo
```

11. As `root`, uninstall `gcc`:

```
# apt-get remove gcc
```

How it works...

Most of the recipe is identical to what is described in `Chapter 1`, *Installing the Odoo Development Environment*, but there are a few key differences.

We are using a dedicated system user with login `odoo`. This enables us to control who has access to the account, for example, by configuring the `sudo` or `ssh` authorized keys. It also allows us to give this user as few permissions as possible, in case the instance is compromised.

The database user linked to this account does not have any privilege, not even database creation. We create the database externally, just once. In case the instance is compromised, an attacker won't be able to create additional databases on the server.

The Odoo script we are creating will be used in the recipe *Set up Odoo as a system service* later in this chapter. It uses the `production.conf` configuration file, which is explained in the next recipe, *Adapting the configuration file for production*.

We uninstall `gcc` at the end of the process so that if an attacker gains access, he will not be able to use this to recompile executables locally.

At the end of this recipe, your server is not ready yet. You will need to refer to the recipes *Adapting the configuration file for production, Set up Odoo as a system service*, and *Configure a reverse proxy and SSL*, which are described in this chapter.

There's more...

Here are a few more important points to consider when preparing the deployment of your instance.

Server dimensioning

What should you use for a server? Pretty much any physical server these days is more than enough to handle an average sized Odoo instance with about 20 simultaneous users. Since virtual machines typically have fewer resources provisioned, you will need to pay a little more attention to this if you are planning to run on a VM. Here are a few key figures to get you started. Obviously, they will need fine tuning to match your use of Odoo.

A small Odoo instance needs at least 1 GB of RAM. Don't be shy on this; the last thing you want to happen is your server swapping. 2 to 4 GB is a good starting point. Give your server, at the very least, two CPU/cores. If you are running the PostgreSQL server on the same host, provision at least four CPU/cores, and add 1 GB of RAM for the database. The additional CPU/cores will be used by the Odoo workers that are covered in the next recipe, *Adapting the configuration file for production*.

The source code of your instance will eat up 1 to 2 GB of hard disk if you are keeping the Git history, which we recommend in this recipe. The file store (`data_dir` in the configuration file) will grow as the instance is used, and the growth heavily depends on what you are doing in the instance. Start with 5 GB, which should give you plenty of time before getting full, and monitor the disk usage. If you are running the database on the same host, give plenty of disk space to the partition that will contain the database working files, starting at 50 GB.

You will also need space for the on-site backups, both of the database and the file store. A lot can depend on your backup plan; 200 GB is a good starting point.

PostgreSQL tuning

Discussing **PostgreSQL tuning** is beyond the scope of this book. You may want to check out the books *PostgreSQL 9 Admin Cookbook* or *PostgreSQL 9.0 High Performance*, both from Packt Publishing, for an in-depth coverage of these topics.

The default configuration of PostgreSQL is generally very conservative and is meant to prevent the database server from hogging all the system resources. On production servers, you can safely increase some parameters in the `postgresql.conf` file to get better performance. Here are some settings for PostgreSQL 9.6 you can use to get started:

```
max_connections = 80
shared_buffers = 256MB
effective_cache_size = 768MB
work_mem = 3276kB
maintenance_work_mem = 64MB
min_wal_size = 2GB
```

```
max_wal_size = 4GB
checkpoint_completion_target = 0.9
wal_buffers = 7864kB
default_statistics_target = 100
```

You will need to restart PostgreSQL after modifying these settings.

The `pgtune` utility can help in finding more suitable configuration. An online version is available at `http://pgtune.leopard.in.ua/`:

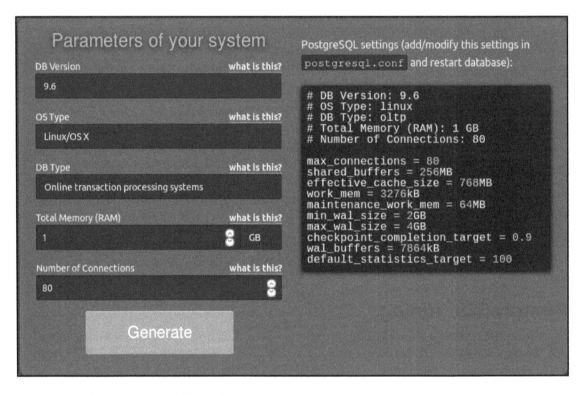

Connect to the website and fill in the form:

- **DB Version**: Use the database version you have installed (by default 9.6 in Debian Stretch)
- **OS Type**: **Linux**
- **DB Type**: Choose **Online transaction processing system**, as Odoo instances are heavy users of transactions

- **Total Memory (RAM)**: Put the amount of RAM you want to allocate to PostgreSQL; this will be almost all of it if you are using a dedicated server (see later)
- **Number of Connections**: The max number of simultaneous queries your database server will accept

If your instance is heavily loaded, you will benefit from separating the database server and the Odoo server onto two different hosts. Don't use two virtual machines running on the same physical server if you are getting down to this; use two physical servers with a high speed network connection between both. In that case, you will need to ensure that the `pg_hba.conf` file on the database server host allows password authenticated connections on the database from the Odoo server, and that the `postgresql.conf` file lets the PostgreSQL server listen in on the network interface connecting both servers.

Source code version

When cloning Odoo and the third-party dependencies, you may want to ensure that you are using the exact same revision as the one you had in developments. There are several ways to do this:

- You can manually mark down the version SHA1 of the local revision in a file, record this in the project repository, and ensure that you are using the same revision on the production server
- You can use tags or branches on forks of these repositories in your GitHub account
- You can use `git submodule` to tie these revisions to the repository of your project (visit `https://git-scm.com/book/en/v2/Git-Tools-Submodules` for some documentation on this handy tool)
- You can use buildout to manage the various dependencies and freeze the revisions (refer to the *Use buildout for repeatable builds* recipe for more information on this)

Why not use the Linux distribution packages provided by Odoo?
You can do that and you will get started much faster because a lot of things are handled for you by the packages. However, there are a few issues with using the packaged source; most importantly, you cannot easily patch the source code of Odoo, which is easier if you run from the source. Granted, this is not something you have to do every day, but being able to use the standard development tools to achieve this, rather than manually applying and tracking patches on production servers, is a precious help and a gain of time. You may also be using the Odoo Community Association branch of Odoo (`https://github.com/OCA/OCB`), for which no packages are provided.

Backups

The recipe does not cover **backups**. At the very least, you should have the cron task on the server running a daily backup. A simple and basic solution is to edit the `crontab` file as root by running `crontab -e` and to add the following lines:

```
@daily su postgres -c pg_dumpall | gzip >\
  /backups/postgresql-$(date +%u).dump.gz
@daily tar czf /backups/odoo-filestore-$(date +%u).tgz \
/home/odoo/odoo-prod/project/filestore
```

Don't forget to create the `/backups` directory. The backup files should not be stored on the same hard disk, and ideally, they would be mirrored on a server in a different physical location. Check these backups on a regular basis; having backups that you can't restore when you need them is useless.

The proposed solution is to keep daily backups of the last 7 days, which means you will lose one day of work in case of a problem. There are more advanced solutions available for PostgreSQL that allow point-in-time recovery. You will find more information about this in the book *PostgreSQL 9 Admin Cookbook*, Packt Publishing. Similarly, there are many Linux tools, such as duplicity (`http://duplicity.nongnu.org/`), which you can use for file backups allowing easy management.

See also

For more information on the Odoo Community Association branch of Odoo, see the recipe *Easy installation from source* in `Chapter 1`, *Installing the Odoo Development Environment*.

Adapting the configuration file for production

In Chapter 1, *Installing the Odoo Development Environment*, we have seen how to save the configuration of the instance in a file. We used the default values for lots of parameters, and if you've followed the *Standardize your instance directory layout* recipe in Chapter 2, *Managing Odoo Server Instances*, as well as the previous recipe for the production installation, you should now have that same configuration file in the production environment. This recipe shows how to derive a configuration file that is suitable for use in production.

Getting ready

We assume that you have installed Odoo on the production server with the previous recipe, *Install Odoo for production*. We assume that you will be running PostgreSQL on the same server as Odoo.

You may want to install the pwgen utility to generate random passwords.

We are describing the steps here as if you were running them on the production server, but they can also be executed on your development server, since the new configuration file is added to the Git repository of the project that we use to deploy on the production server.

How to do it...

To adapt the configuration file for production, you need to follow these steps:

1. Create a new configuration file for production based on the development file:

   ```
   $ cd ~/odoo-prod/project
   $ cp development.conf production.conf
   ```

2. Edit the production configuration file production.conf.
3. Change the addons path to match the production base directory:

   ```
   addons_path = /home/odoo/odoo-prod/project/src/odoo/addons,
   /home/odoo/odoo-prod/project/src/odoo/odoo/addons,
   /home/odoo/odoo-prod/project/src/partner-contact
   ```

4. Change the data directory:

```
data_dir = /home/odoo/odoo-prod/project/filestore
```

5. Change the server log path to match the production base directory:

```
logfile = /home/odoo/odoo-prod/project/logs/odoo.log
```

6. Configure log rotation:

```
logrotate = True
```

7. Configure the logging handlers:

```
log_level = warn
log_handler = :WARNING,werkzeug:CRITICAL,odoo.service.server:INFO
```

8. Adapt the database connection parameters:

```
db_host = False
db_maxconn = 64
db_name = odoo-project
db_password = False
db_port = False
db_template = template1
db_user = False
```

9. Configure the database filter, and disable database listing:

```
dbfilter = odoo-project$
list_db = False
```

10. Change the master password using a random password generated with pwgen :

```
admin_password = use a random password
```

11. Configure Odoo to run with workers:

```
workers = 4
# limit_memory_hard: 4GB
limit_memory_hard = 4294967296
# limit_memory_soft: 640MB
limit_memory_soft = 671088640
limit_request = 8192
limit_time_cpu = 120
limit_time_real = 300
```

12. Only listen on the local network interface:

    ```
    http_interface = 127.0.0.1
    ```

13. Save the file, and add it to the Git repository:

    ```
    $ git add production.conf
    $ git commit -m "add production configuration file"
    ```

How it works...

Most of the parameters shown in this recipe are explained in the *Manage Odoo server instances* recipe in `Chapter 1`, *Installing the Odoo Development Environment*.

In steps 3, 4, and 5, we change the addons path and the log file. In case you are developing in an environment with the same layout as the production environment, this is required because Odoo expects absolute paths in the configuration file.

Step 6 enables log rotation. This will cause Odoo to configure the logging module to archive the server logs on a daily basis, and to keep the old logs for 30 days. This is useful on production servers to avoid logs eventually consuming all the available disk space.

Step 7 configures the logging level. The proposed setting is very conservative and will only log messages with at least the `WARNING` level, except for `werkzeug` (`CRITICAL`) and `odoo.service.server` (`INFO`). For more information on the log filtering, refer to `Chapter 8`, *Debugging and Automated Testing*, where you will find the recipe, *Producing server logs to help debug methods*. Feel free to tune this to your taste.

Step 8 configures the database settings. This will work if you are running the PostgreSQL database server locally and have set it up as explained in the previous recipe. If you're running PostgreSQL on a different server, you will need to replace the `False` values with the appropriate connection settings for your database instance.

Step 9 restricts the database available to the instance by configuring a database filter. We also disable the database listing, which is not strictly necessary given that the regular expression we set in `dbfilter` can only match one single database. It is still a good thing to do though, in order to avoid displaying the list of databases to anyone, and to avoid users connecting to the wrong database.

Step 10 sets a nontrivial master password for the instance. The master password is used for database management through the user interface, and a few community addons also use it for extra security before performing actions that can lead to data loss. You really need to set this to a nontrivial value. We propose using the `pwgen` utility to generate a random password, but any other method is also valid.

Step 11 configures Odoo to work with **workers**. In this mode, Odoo will create a number of worker processes (in this example, 4) to handle HTTP requests. This has several advantages over the default configuration in which the request handling is performed in separate threads, which are given as follows:

- Requests can be handled in parallel, making better use of multiple cores or CPUs on the server (Python threads are penalized by the existence of the **Global Interpreter Locks** (**GIL**) in the Python interpreter).
- It is possible to terminate one of the workers depending on resource consumption. The following table gives the various resource limits that can be configured:

Parameter	Suggested value	Description
`limit_memory_hard`	4294967296	This is the maximum amount of RAM a worker will be able to allocate. We recommend using 4 GB as some processes launched by Odoo can allocate some large amounts of RAM.
`limit_memory_soft`	671088640	If a worker ends up consuming more than this limit (640 MB in our setting), it will be terminated after it finishes processing the current request.
`limit_request`	8192	A worker will be terminated after having processed this many requests.
`limit_time_cpu`	120	This is the maximum amount of CPU time allowed to process a request.
`limit_time_real`	300	This is the maximum amount of wall clock time allowed to process a request.

Step 12 configures the internal Odoo web server to only listen on the local interface. This means the instance will not be reachable from other servers. This enables us to configure a **reverse proxy** on the same server to access the server and to force encrypted connections. Take a look at the *Configure a reverse proxy and SSL* recipe later in this chapter.

There's more...

When running with workers, you may encounter some issues specific to this mode:

- If you get strange errors when running with workers, with `lessc` or `wkhtmltopdf` not working as intended (for example, prematurely exiting with a -11 or -6 status), then you likely have `limit_memory_hard` set to a value that is too low. Try raising it a bit, as the default value is notoriously too low.
- If you get timeout errors when performing long operations (this includes CSV imports and exports and addon module installations), try increasing the `limit_time_cpu` and `limit_time_real` parameters, as there too the default value is quite low. If you have a reverse proxy, you may want to check its timeout limit too (too low a limit in the reverse proxy will not prevent the transactions from completing, but will display an error message in the user's browser, which can cause them to retry the import and unnecessarily put some load on the server).
- If your instance gets completely stuck when printing reports, try raising the number of workers. This can be a deadlock caused by `wkhtmltopdf` blocking up all the available workers while printing.

> In any case, always validate the setup before going to production, and remember to test printing reports when enabling workers.

Setting up Odoo as a system service

For a production instance, it is very important that the Odoo server gets started when the computer reboots. On current Linux systems, this is achieved through a `systemd` configuration. If your OS is not using `systemd`, you will have to check the documentation to obtain this result.

Getting ready

We assume that you followed the first two recipes to install and configure your Odoo instance. Especially the deployed source of Odoo, which is at `/home/odoo/odoo-prod/project/src/odoo/`, and the configuration file of the instance, which is at `/home/odoo/odoo-prod/project/production.conf`. The scripts also makes use of the `start-odoo` script created in step 9 of the *Install Odoo for production* recipe.

How to do it...

To configure `systemd` to start Odoo, you need to perform the following steps:

1. As root, create a file called `/lib/systemd/system/odoo.service`, with the following contents:

```
[Unit]
Description=Odoo 11.0
After=postgresql.service
[Service]
Type=simple
User=odoo
Group=odoo
WorkingDirectory=/home/odoo/odoo-prod/project
ExecStart=/home/odoo/odoo-prod/project/bin/start-odoo
[Install]
WantedBy=multi-user.target
```

2. As root, register the service:

```
# systemctl enable odoo.service
```

3. As root, start the service:

```
# service odoo start
```

4. To stop the service, you can run the following:

```
# service odoo stop
```

How it works...

Systemd uses some configuration files or scripts to know which programs must run when the server boots. The configurations provided in the recipe will need small adaptations to match the paths of your instance.

 Don't forget to reboot your server and check that Odoo is properly started!

There's more...

If you are using the buildout method described in the *Use buildout for repeatable builds* recipe, you will need to adapt the paths to use the start_odoo script created by the recipe.

Configuring a reverse proxy and SSL with nginx and Let's Encrypt

In order to avoid all the information between the user's browsers and the Odoo server that is to be sent in clear over the network, it is necessary to use the HTTPS protocol that encrypts the exchanges. Odoo cannot do this natively, and it is necessary to configure a **reverse proxy** that will handle the encryption and decryption on behalf of the Odoo server. This recipe shows how to use nginx (http://nginx.net) for this. We will also show how to use **Let's Encrypt** (https://letsencrypt.org) to manage the certificate and renewal if your organisation does not have its own way of getting a signed **SSL certificate**.

Getting ready

You should know the public name of the server and configure your DNS accordingly. In this recipe, we will use odoo.example.com as the name of your server.

Make sure that port 80 and 443 of the server are reachable from outside using the DNS name you will be using if you are getting the SSL certificate from Let's Encrypt.

How to do it...

In order to access your instance using HTTPS via nginx, you need to follow these steps:

1. As root, install the Let's Encrypt client, certbot:

```
# apt-get install certbot
```

2. As root, request a certificate from Let's Encrypt (don't forget to change the email and the address of the server):

```
# certbot certonly --standalone -n --agree-tos\
 -m youremail@example.com -d odoo.example.com
```

3. As root, install nginx:

```
# apt-get install nginx
```

4. As root, create a configuration file in /etc/nginx/sites-available/odoo-80:

```
server {
  listen [::]:80 ipv6only=off;
  server_name odoo.example.com;
  access_log /var/log/nginx/odoo80.access.log combined;
  error_log /var/log/nginx/odoo80.error.log;
  location / {
    rewrite ^/(.*) https://odoo.example.com:443/$1 permanent;
  }
}
```

5. Create a configuration file in /etc/nginx/sites-available/odoo-443:

```
server {
  listen [::]:443 ipv6only=off;
  server_name odoo.example.com;
  ssl on;
  ssl_certificate
  /etc/letsencrypt/live/odoo.example.com/fullchain.pem;
  ssl_certificate_key
  /etc/letsencrypt/live/odoo.example.com/privkey.pem;
  access_log /var/log/nginx/odoo443.access.log combined;
  error_log /var/log/nginx/odoo443.error.log;
  client_max_body_size 128M;
  gzip on;
  proxy_read_timeout 600s;
  index index.html index.htm index.php;
```

```
   add_header Strict-Transport-Security "max-age=31536000";
   proxy_set_header Host $http_host;
   proxy_set_header X-Real-IP $remote_addr;
   proxy_set_header X-Forward-For $proxy_add_x_forwarded_for;
   proxy_set_header X-Forwarded-Proto https;
   proxy_set_header X-Forwarded-Host $http_host;
   location / {
     proxy_pass http://localhost:8069;
     proxy_read_timeout 6h;
     proxy_connect_timeout 5s;
     proxy_redirect http://$http_host/ https://$host:$server_port/;
     add_header X-Static no;
     proxy_buffer_size 64k;
     proxy_buffering off;
     proxy_buffers 4 64k;
     proxy_busy_buffers_size 64k;
     proxy_intercept_errors on;
   }
   location /longpolling/ {
     proxy_pass http://localhost:8072;
   }
   location ~ /[a-zA-Z0-9_-]*/static/ {
     proxy_pass http://localhost:8069;
     proxy_cache_valid 200 60m;
     proxy_buffering on;
     expires 864000;
   }
 }
```

6. As root, link the configuration file in /etc/nginx/sites-enabled/:

```
# ln -s /etc/nginx/sites-available/odoo80\
  /etc/nginx/sites-enabled/odoo80
# ln -s /etc/nginx/sites-available/odoo443\
  /etc/nginx/sites-enabled/odoo443
```

7. As root, remove /etc/nginx/sites-enabled/default:

```
# rm /etc/nginx/sites-enabled/default
```

8. As Odoo, edit the production configuration file of the instance to enable
   proxy_mode:

```
proxy_mode = True
```

9. As root, restart your `odoo` instance and `nginx`:

```
# service odoo restart
# service nginx restart
```

10. As root, create a cron file `/etc/cron.d/letsencrypt` to ensure that the certificate will get renewed with the following content:

```
11 5 * * * certbot renew
```

How it works...

We are using nginx as a reverse HTTP proxy. Incoming HTTP and HTTPS connections are handled by nginx, which delegates the processing of the requests to the Odoo server. The Odoo server is configured to only listen on the local loop back interface (`127.0.0.1`) on port `8069` for normal requests (`http_port`) and port `8072` for the long polling requests (`longpolling_port`). You may need to adapt the port numbers to your configuration:

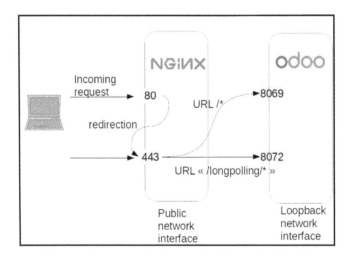

The recipe sets up two files. The first one is the configuration for incoming connections on port 80 using the HTTP protocol. We don't want these because they are in clear text, meaning that the passwords can be sniffed. Therefore, we set up nginx to redirect the URLs permanently to port 443 using the encrypted HTTPS protocol.

The second file is a bit more complex and configures the way nginx should handle connections using the HTTPS protocol:

- The first configuration block configures the SSL protocol, the encryption key, and certificate, as well as the log file's location.
- The second block sets some headers on the requests to handle the proper reverse proxying over HTTPS.
- The `location /` block defines the default processing of incoming requests; they will be proxied to the Odoo server listening on port `8069`.
- The `location /longpolling` block handles queries made on URLs starting with
  `/longpolling`, which are then forwarded to Odoo on port `8072`. These connections are used by the bus addon module to send notifications to the web client.
- The `location ~ /[a-zA-Z0-9_-]*/static/` block uses a regular expression to match the URLs of the static files of Odoo modules. These files are rarely updated, and so we ask nginx to cache them in order to lighten the load on the Odoo server.

The `certbot` program is a command-line utility that eases interacting with letsencrypt.org. The complete documentation is available at `https://certbot.eff.org/docs/`. In this recipe, we use two subcommands:

- `certbot certonly <options>` will request a signed certificate from letsencrypt for the domains passed to the `-d` option. Use the `-m` option to specify your email address. The `--standalone` option requests certbot to set up a local temporary web server which Let's Encrypt will attempt to contact to check that you do control the domain for which you are requesting a certificate. It is therefore important that the command is run on the server which will be hosting Odoo, that the DNS is pointing to that server and that no firewall is blocking port 80 and 443 on the server.

This check is done by connecting to `http://<yourdomain>:80/.well-known/acme`. The `--standalone` mode of certbot creates a temporary web server listening on this port and able to answer the request, but for this only works if no other process is listening on port 80 and if the external firewall is letting external connections on that port pass.

- `certbot renew` checks for certificates pending renewal, and automatically renews them. By default, Let's Encrypt certificates have a validity of 90 days, which is quite short. Thanks to this utility, which we run on a daily basis, certificates which are about to expire are automatically renewed.

The Odoo Community Association has a module available in the `OCA server-tools project` called `letsencrypt`. At the time of writing this, the module is `available for Odoo 10` but not for Odoo 11, although it will most certainly be ported rapidly (and when it is, it will be available at `https://github.com/OCA/server-tools/tree/11.0/letsencrypt`). The aim of this module is to help you set up Let's Encrypt for your Odoo server.

There's more...

This recipe focuses on the nginx configuration. You may be more familiar with other tools such as the Apache web server and `mod_proxy`. In this case, you can of course use these to achieve a similar setup.

If you would rather not rely on Let's Encrypt and prefer using another Certification Authority (CA), you can use the following process:

1. Install `openssl`:

```
$ sudo apt-get install openssl
```

2. Generate the key for your server:

```
$ mkdir ~/sslkey
$ openssl genrsa -out ~/sslkey/server.key 2048
```

3. Generate a signing request:

```
$ openssl req -new -key ~/sslkey/server.key\
-out ~/sslkey/server.csr
```

4. The preceding command will ask you a series of questions about your company and your Odoo server's URL. Don't get these wrong or your certificate will be unusable.

5. You will be able to send the file, `~/sslkey/server.csr`, to a **Certification Authority** (**CA**) of your choice. The CA will send you back a file called `server.crt`.

6. You will need to store the file in the directory `/etc/nginx/ssl/` together with the file `server.key` generated in step 2:

```
# mkdir -p /etc/nginx/ssl
# chown www-data /etc/nginx/ssl
# mv server.key server.crt /etc/nginx/ssl
# chmod 710 /etc/nginx/ssl
# chown root:www-data /etc/nginx/ssl/*
# chmod 640 /etc/nginx/ssl/*
```

7. Then, in the nginx configuration file `/etc/nginx/sites-available/odoo-443` provided in the recipe, rewrite the `ssl_certificate` and `ssl_certificate_key` lines, as follows:

```
ssl_certificate /etc/nginx/ssl/server.crt;
ssl_certificate_key /etc/nginx/ssl/server.key;
```

8. Finally, restart nginx

See also

- For more information about the various nginx configuration options, see `http://nginx.org/en/docs/`
- For a tutorial on the configuration of Apache2 as a reverse proxy and the use of a personal certification authority, take a look at `http://antiun.github.io/odoo-reverse-proxy-howto/`

Using buildout for repeatable builds

So far, we have been manually setting up our instances. This cries for automation, and maybe you have already written a shell script to download the proper version of the addons your instance needs and streamlined the process. It turns out that there is a tool meant to help with doing this called **buildout**. Buildout is a Python-based build system for creating, assembling, and deploying applications from multiple parts, some of which may be non-Python-based. It lets you create a buildout configuration and reproduce the same software later.

This recipe shows how you can start using buildout to ensure you have the same setup in the development and production servers.

 At the time of writing this, the buildout recipe has not been adapted to work with Odoo 11.0 and Python3. This section is based on what is likely to be the correct way to use this tool, but you may encounter slight differences. Be sure to check the documentation.

Getting ready

We assume that your instance only has a dependency on the server-tools and partner-contact projects of the Odoo Community Association, and that your user-specific addon modules are living in the `local/addons` subdirectory of the project.

We also expect you to have installed the build dependencies of Odoo. Refer to steps 1 to 3 of the *Install Odoo for production* recipe in this chapter. This recipe is better used first on a development machine and later deployed on a production server.

How to do it...

In order to use buildout to build your project, you need to follow these steps:

1. On your development server, create a new work directory:

```
$ mkdir ~/odoo-dev/project-buildout
$ cd ~/odoo-dev/project-buildout
```

2. Create a file called `buildout.cfg`:

```
[buildout]
parts = odoo
```

```
[odoo]
recipe = anybox.recipe.odoo:server
OCA = https://github.com/OCA
version = git https://github.com/odoo/odoo.git odoo 11.0 depth=1
addons = git ${odoo:OCA}/server-tools.git parts/server-tools 11.0
    git ${odoo:OCA}/partner-contact.git parts/partner-contact 11.0
    local local/addons

options.limit_memory_hard = 4294967296
options.limit_memory_soft = 671088640
options.limit_request = 8192
options.limit_time_cpu = 120
options.limit_time_real = 300
options.http_port = 8069
options.longpolling_port = 8072
options.workers = 0

[versions]
zc.buildout = 2.9.5
# you will need to update the following line
# once the version supporting Odoo 11.0 is known.
# anybox.buildout.odoo = 1.9.1
setuptools = 19.7

setuptools = 19.7

Babel = 2.3.4
decorator = 4.0.10
docutils = 0.12
ebaysdk = 2.1.5
feedparser = 5.2.1
gevent = 1.1.2
greenlet = 0.4.10
jcconv = 0.2.3
html2text = 2016.9.19
Jinja2 = 2.8
lxml = 3.5.0
Mako = 1.0.4
MarkupSafe = 0.23
mock = 2.0.0
num2words = 0.5.4
ofxparse = 0.16
passlib = 1.6.5
Pillow = 3.4.1
psutil = 4.3.1
psycogreen = 1.0
psycopg2 = 2.7.1
pydot = 1.2.3
```

```
pyldap = 2.4.28
pyparsing = 2.1.10
PyPDF2 = 1.26.0
pyserial = 3.1.1
python-dateutil = 2.5.3
pytz = 2016.7
pyusb = 1.0.0
PyYAML = 3.12
qrcode = 5.3
reportlab = 3.3.0
requests = 2.11.1
six = 1.10.0
suds-jurko = 0.6
vatnumber = 1.2
vobject = 0.9.3
Werkzeug = 0.11.11
XlsxWriter = 0.9.3
xlwt = 1.3.0
xlrd = 1.0.0
```

3. Create a configuration file for the production environment in `prod.cfg`:

```
[buildout]
extends = buildout.cfg

[odoo]
options.limit_memory_hard = 4294967296
options.limit_memory_soft = 671088640
options.limit_request = 8192
options.limit_time_cpu = 120
options.limit_time_real = 300
options.workers = 4

options.data_dir = project/filestore

options.http_interface = 127.0.0.1
options.http_port = 8069
options.longpolling_port = 8072

options.log_level = warn
options.log_handler =
:WARNING,werkzeug:CRITICAL,odoo.service.server:INFO

options.admin_password = generate with pwgen -s 16 1

options.listdb = False
options.db_host = False
```

```
options.db_port = False
options.db_user = False
options.db_name = odoo_project
options.dbfilter = ^odoo_project$
options.proxy_mode = True
```

4. Create a configuration file for the development environment in `dev.cfg`:

```
[buildout]
extends = buildout.cfg

[odoo]
options.db_name = odoo_dev
options.dbfilter = ^odoo_dev$
options.log_level = info
```

5. Create a `virtualenv` without `setuptools`:

```
$ virtualenv -p python3 sandbox --no-setuptools
```

6. Download the current version of the `bootstrap.py` file:

```
$ wget
https://raw.github.com/buildout/buildout/master/bootstrap/bootstrap.py
```

7. Run the `bootstrap.py` script:

```
$ sandbox/bin/python3 bootstrap.py
```

8. On your development machine, you can create a development environment by running the following:

```
$ bin/buildout -c dev.cfg
```

9. On the production server, you can create a production environment by running the following:

```
$ bin/buildout -c prod.cfg
```

10. To start the instance, run the following:

```
$ bin/start_odoo
```

11. Commit the files to Git (you may also want to add a `.gitignore` file):

```
$ git init
```

```
$ git add buildout.cfg prod.cfg dev.cfg bootstrap.py local/addons
$ git commit -m "initialize project with buildout"
```

How it works...

Buildout works by processing a configuration file, which is called `buildout.cfg` by default. This file uses a syntax close to `ConfigParser` (with a few extensions) to describe the desired target environment. There is one mandatory section, `[buildout]`, which contains a `parts` entry listing the sections to process. Most sections have a `recipe` entry that gives the name of a buildout recipe to use to build the section. There are lots of recipes available (take a look at `http://www.buildout.org/en/latest/docs/recipelist.html` for a partial listing), and different recipes can be combined in a single configuration file. Each recipe supports its own configuration settings. Recipes are Python modules, usually made available from PyPI.

Buildout configuration files are extensible and support parameterization:

- A configuration file can extend another one; configuration settings are added or overwritten by the extending file.
- Configuration settings can refer to the value of other settings using the `${section:name}` syntax.
- In step 1, we prepare our base `buildout.cfg` configuration file. We define a section called `[odoo]` and set the `anybox.recipe.odoo` parameter as the buildout recipe in charge for this section. Here are the settings we use:
  - `version`: This defines the Odoo version we want. Here, we are using the latest version from the 9.0 branch on GitHub. The depth options limit the Git clone depth to speed up the installation.
  - `OCA`: This is a custom setting used to simplify the URLs of the OCA addons we are listing in the following settings, using the `${odoo:OCA}` variable.
  - `addons`: This lists the addons directories to install, one by one. The syntax is `protocol URL destination revision options`. The Git protocol will use Git to clone a repository. The local protocol will use a local directory (and revision must not be provided in this case). Other available protocols are `hg` (for mercurial repositories), `svn` (subversion), `bzr` (bazaar). The revision can be a tag, a branch, or a commit identifier.

The [versions] section is a standardized buildout section used to specify the versions of the Python dependencies that will be installed in the environment. It is important to fix the version of zc.buildout, anybox.buildout.odoo, and setuptools in this section to ensure the repeatability of the build, which is what we do in the first two lines of the section. The anybox.buildout.odoo recipe is able to find the names of the dependencies from the Odoo server version, but not the versions. To generate this list, we copied the requirements.txt file for the Odoo codebase and replaced the == operator with =.

 As we write this chapter, the adaptation of anybox.recipe.odoo to work with Python3 and Odoo 11.0 are not finalized. We are therefore unable to suggest a version number which will be compatible; you will need to check the documentation.

The prod.cfg and dev.cfg files extend the base configuration defined in buildout.cfg. In the [odoo] section, they both define settings with names starting with options. (Mind the dot): buildout will use these when generating a configuration file for the instance with the options set as specified in the configuration file. If you've read the recipe *Adapting the configuration file for production* in this chapter, the prod.cfg file should be familiar.

In order to ensure that the buildout environment is insulated from the system Python, we use a virtualenv (called sandbox in this recipe) configured to not have setuptools available. We use this virtualenv to run the bootstrap.py script that we downloaded from the buildout source code repository. The role of bootstrap.py is to prepare things for buildout to work, including installing buildout itself. A script, bin/buildout, is created in the directory of the build to run buildout.

You can then manage your buildout configuration in a version management system such as Git. It is recommended that you store the bootstrap.py file together with the buildout configuration file; this file evolves with buildout, and since we are freezing the version of buildout in the configuration file, we need to keep the bootstrap.py file that we know will work with this version.

To run buildout, just execute the bin/buildout script with the -c option to specify a configuration file. This will do several things:

- Odoo gets installed in the parts/ subdirectory
- The specified addons are installed in the specified subdirectory (we recommend that you use parts/ for this too)

- The dependencies of Odoo and any additional dependencies are installed in the `eggs/` subdirectory
- A configuration file is created in `etc/odoo.cfg` with the appropriate value for `addons_path` and all the options specified in the buildout configurations
- A helper script `bin/start_odoo` is created; it uses the generated configuration file and the installed Python dependencies

There's more...

If one addon module that you need requires an external Python dependency, you can add it to the `[odoo]` section using the `eggs` setting. For instance, to add `unicodecsv` to the buildout, use the following:

```
[odoo]
eggs += unicodecsv

[versions]
unicodecsv = 0.14.1
```

Temporary merges

During development, it can be useful to merge pending pull requests in the various projects used by the project. The buildout recipe supports this through the merges option. Suppose your project uses OCA/partner-contact and OCA/product-attribute, and you need to merge the PR 237 and 249 on partner-contact and the PR 132 on product attribute, then you can write the following in your buildout configuration file:

```
[odoo]
OCA = https://github.com/OCA
version = git https://github.com/odoo/odoo.git odoo 11.0 depth=1
addons = git ${odoo:OCA}/partner-contact.git parts/partner-contact 11.0
    git ${odoo:OCA}/product-attribute.git parts/product-attribute  11.0
    merges = git origin parts/partner-contact pull/237/head
    git origin parts/partner-contact pull/249/head
    git origin parts/product-attribute pull/132/head
```

The syntax for the merge option using the git protocol is `<remote> <local repository> <refspec>`. We use here the reference for pull requests provided by GitHub.

A word of caution

This feature is very useful during development but should be avoided for deployment in production. The merged branches can evolve and be rebased or overwritten without notice. It is better that your deployment depends on non-merged PR so as to use a personal fork of the project on which you will do the merges yourself to ensure that you get repeatable builds. Also, note that the buildout freeze-to option, which is explained next, does not work with merges.

Freezing a buildout

To ease deployment, it is possible to use some advanced commands. The freeze-to option can be used to generate a buildout configuration file that freezes the revisions of Odoo and all the addons:

```
$ bin/buildout -c prod.cfg -o odoo:freeze-to=frozen-prod.cfg
```

You can then run buildout with the frozen-prod.cfg file to get the exact same versions of the files.

You can also extract the source code to a separate directory, with the extract-downloads-to option:

```
$ bin/buildout -c frozen-prod.cfg \ -o odoo:extract-downloads-to=../production
```

The directory production now contains a release.cfg file, and a parts/ directory with the source code (but not the git history). If the target server is running the same version of Linux as the server you are working on, you can deploy the production environment without compiling any dependency by performing the following steps:

1. Copy the required file to the production/ directory:

```
$ cp -r develop-eggs eggs buildout.cfg prod.cfg bootstrap.py \
../production
```

2. Make an archive of that:

```
$ cd ..
$ tar cjf production-1.0.tar.bz2
```

3. Copy that archive on the production server using a suitable procedure (USB key or `rsync`, for instance).

4. On the production server, unpack the archive and install the version with the following:

```
$ tar xf production-1.0.tar.bz2
$ cd production
$ virtualenv sandbox --no-setuptools
$ sandbox/bin/python bootstrap.py
$ bin/buildout -c release.cfg
```

See also

- The full documentation for the buildout recipe is available at `http://docs.anybox.fr/anybox.recipe.odoo/current/index.html`

Using Docker to run Odoo

Docker is a project meant to make **Linux Containers** (**LXC**) easy to manage by providing high level tools. These containers can be used to ease the distribution of applications and their dependencies. There is a whole ecosystem built around Docker, meant to ease the deployment and management of dockerized applications. Discussing the details is far beyond the scope of this recipe and the interested reader may want to check the book *Learning Docker* from Packt Publishing, for more in-depth explanations.

In this recipe, we will see how to build a Docker image on your development workstation and run it on a production server.

Getting ready

We assume that Docker is installed both on your development station and on the production server. The instructions to install Docker Community Edition for Debian GNU/Linux are on `https://docs.docker.com/engine/installation/linux/docker-ce/debian/` (and the instructions for installing Docker for other platforms are close by).

You will also need `docker-compose`, which is packaged for Debian stretch:

```
# apt-get install docker-compose
```

This recipe uses the layout suggested in the *Standardizing your instance directory layout* recipe from `Chapter 2`, *Managing Odoo server instances*. It assumes that you have a clone of the Odoo repository in `src/odoo`.

How to do it...

If you want to work with Docker, there are two steps:

- Building the image
- Running a container based on that image

Building a Docker image

To build a Docker image from your development environment, follow the following steps:

1. Go to the project directory, and a file called `.dockerignore` with the following content:

```
env
**/*~
**/*.pyc
**/.git
filestore
```

2. Create a file `bin/docker-entrypoint.sh` with the following content:

```
#!/bin/bash
ODOO=/srv/odoo/src/odoo/odoo-bin

$ODOO --addons-path="$ODOO_ADDONS_PATH" \
       -d "$ODOO_DB_NAME" \
       --db_host="$ODOO_DB_HOST" \
       --db_user="$ODOO_DB_USER" \
       --db_password="$ODOO_DB_PASSWORD" \
       --no-database-list \
       --db-filter="$ODOO_DB_FILTER" \
       --db_port="$ODOO_DB_PORT" \
       --data-dir=/filestore "$@"
```

3. Make the file executable:

```
$ chmod +x bin/docker-entrypoint.sh
```

4. Create a file called `Dockerfile` with the following content:

```
FROM debian:stretch
LABEL version="1.1" \
      maintainer="Alexandre Fayolle
      <alexandre.fayolle@camptocamp.com>" \
      description="Example docker image for the bookshelf project"

CMD ["/srv/odoo/bin/odoo"]
ENV ODOO_ADDONS_PATH="src/odoo/odoo/addons,src/odoo/addons,local/" \
    ODOO_DB_HOST=odoo \
    ODOO_DB_NAME=odoodb \
    ODOO_DB_filter=odoodb$ \
    ODOO_LIST_DB=False \
    ODOO_DB_USER=odoo \
    ODOO_DB_PASSWORD=odoo \
    ODOO_DB_PORT=5432 \
    LANG=C.UTF-8 \
    LC_ALL=C.UTF-8

VOLUME ["/filestore"]

WORKDIR /srv/odoo


COPY src/odoo/requirements.txt /srv/odoo/src/odoo/

RUN mkdir local bin \
    && \
    apt-get update \
    && \
    apt-get install -y \
        fontconfig \
        libfreetype6 \
        libx11-6 \
        libxext6 \
        libxrender1 \
        node-clean-css \
        node-less \
        python3-pip \
        virtualenv \
        python3.5 \
```

```
        wget \
        xfonts-75dpi \
        xfonts-base \
        xz-utils \
        zlib1g \
    && \
    apt-get install -y \
        gcc \
        libevent-dev \
        libjpeg-dev \
        libldap2-dev \
        libpng-dev \
        libpq-dev \
        libsasl2-dev \
        libxml2-dev \
        libxslt1-dev \
        python3.5-dev \
    && \
    pip3 install --no-cache-dir -r src/odoo/requirements.txt \
    && \
    apt-get remove --purge --autoremove -y \
        gcc \
        g++ \
    && \
    wget -qO wkhtmltox.tar.xz \
https://github.com/wkhtmltopdf/wkhtmltopdf/releases/download/0.12.4
/wkhtmltox-0.12.4_linux-generic-amd64.tar.xz \
    && \
    tar -xf wkhtmltox.tar.xz \
    && \
    install wkhtmltox/lib/* /usr/lib \
    && \
    install wkhtmltox/bin/* /usr/bin \
    && \
    rm -rf wkhtmltox wkhtmltox.tar.xz \
    && \
    apt-get remove --purge -y \
        libevent-dev \
        libjpeg-dev \
        libldap2-dev \
        libpng-dev \
        libpq-dev \
        libsasl2-dev \
        libxml2-dev \
        libxslt1-dev \
        python3.5-dev \
        wget \
        xz-utils\
```

```
                 && \
                 apt-get clean \
                 ;

         COPY . /srv/odoo
         RUN mv bin/docker-entrypoint.sh bin/odoo
```

5. Build the docker image with this command:

   $ docker build -t yourcompany/yourproject .

6. Create a file called `docker-compose.yml` with the following content:

```yaml
version: '2'
services:
  odoo:
    build: .
    image: yourcompany/yourproject
    depends_on:
      - db
    volumes:
      - "data-odoo:/filestore"
    environment:
      - ODOO_DB_USER=odoo
      - ODOO_DB_PASSWORD=odoo
      - ODOO_DB_NAME=odoodb
      - ODOO_DB_HOST=db
      - ODOO_ADMIN_PASSWORD=randompass
    ports:
      - 8069
      - 8072
    restart: always

  db:
    image: postgres:9.6
    environment:
      - POSTGRES_USER=odoo
      - POSTGRES_PASSWORD=odoo
      - POSTGRES_DB=odoodb
      - PG_SYSTEM_SHARED_BUFFERS=256MD
      - PG_SYSTEM_MAINTENANCE_WORK_MEM=256MB
      - PG_SYSTEM_WAL_BUFFERS=8MB
      - PG_SYSTEM_EFFECTIVE_CACHE_SIZE=1024MB
    volumes:
      - "data-db:/var/lib/postgresql/data"

volumes:
```

```
data-odoo:
data-db:
```

7. Save your Docker image:

```
$ docker save yourcompany/yourproject | gzip >
yourproject.image.tar.gz
```

Running Odoo in a container

To deploy the Docker image on the production server, things are much easier :

1. Copy the Docker image to the production server, using `scp` or a USB key
2. Load the image on the server like this:

```
$ gunzip -c yourproject.image.tar.gz | docker load
```

3. Copy the `docker-compose.yml` file to the production server, and place it for instance in `/srv/odoo/yourproject/`:

```
$mkdir -p /srv/odoo/yourproject
$ mv docker-compose.yml /srv/odoo/yourproject
```

4. Start the Docker composition:

```
$ docker-compose up -d
```

How it works...

Docker allows you to create system images and then ship them around to run them on other servers. Docker images are created by writing a `Dockerfile`, which describes how to add layers generally to a pre-existing Dockerfile. In our case, we start with a Debian stable image (in the `FROM` line from the file). After adding some descriptive `LABEL`, we configure the `ENTRYPOINT` and command (`CMD`) of the image, which will be run when we start the container. The `ENV` section provides some configuration settings which will be used by the entry point script to run Odoo the way we want. The `VOLUME` line is used to provision a place where persistent data will be stored. This is important because Docker containers are essentially transient, and all the data inside a container will be lost when the container is stopped, unless it is placed in a Docker volume.

Then, the Dockerfile has a number of RUN commands that are the instructions for actually building the environment: we install buildtime and runtime dependencies, and uninstall the buildtime dependencies. Finally, we COPY the contents of the current directory to the container. The .dockerignore file is used to avoid copying unnecessary files.

With the Dockerfile ready, we can now build the image. The docker build command takes two parameters : the name of the image and a path to the directory. The name of the images are normally formed as companyname/projectname, but you may use just projectname for testing.

We use the docker save command to produce a tarball dump of the image in order to ship it later to the production server, where the docker load command can be used to load it back into the Docker environment.

At this point, we could run our instance using a local PostgreSQL installation, by configuring PostgreSQL to listen on all network interfaces, and running:

```
docker run -e ODOO_DB_HOST=db_server_name \
    yourcompany/yourproject
```

However, to get a feel of the benefits of Docker, we build a docker composition by writing a docker-compose.yml file. A Docker composition describes several Docker containers which are going to work together in a private virtual network. In our case, we will add a second container to run the PostgreSQL. Inside the docker-compose.yml file, we list the containers we will use, and specify their configuration: the environment variables values we are setting (overriding the ones from the images), the dependencies between the containers... Then, from a directory that contains the composition file, we can use the docker-compose command to control the stack:

```
$ docker-compose up -d   # start the stack as a daemon
$ docker compose logs -f odoo  # monitor the output
                               # odoo container
$ docker compose down  # stop the stack
```

There's more...

The way we set up the Docker image in this recipe is merely a starting point. You will probably want to tune a lot of parameters, add options to the entry point to ease the management of the instance, modify the composition file to allow running Odoo from mounts of your local checkouts of the sources rather than requiring a rebuild each time you edit a module... all of which is far beyond the scope of this book.

Odoo proposes Docker images on Docker Hub (`https://hub.docker.com/_/odoo/`). In the same way, we do not advise using the Debian packages of Odoo or the nightly builds provided by Odoo, and we do not advise using the Docker images for production, as they make it impractical to test patches sent by Odoo. However, to set up test instances or demo instances, the approach can certainly be considered.

Docker is a huge universe, and offers a wealth of options. You may want to publish your images on a Docker image repository, and use Docker push and Docker pull to publish and retrieve the Docker images of your projects. You may want to run a container management platform such as `Rancher` to run your images on a cluster of servers with load balancing. Alternatively, you can integrate the image building step with your continuous integration environment to publish snapshots of your developments for testing.

4

Creating Odoo Addon Modules

In this chapter, we will cover the following topics:

- Creating and installing a new addon module
- Completing the addon module manifest
- Organizing the addon module file structure
- Adding Models
- Adding Menu Items and Views
- Adding Access Security
- Using scaffold to create a module

Introduction

Now that we have a development environment and know how to manage Odoo server instances and databases, you can learn how to create Odoo addon modules.

Our main goal here is to understand how an addon module is structured and the typical incremental workflow to add components to it. The various components mentioned in the recipe names of this chapter will be covered extensively in subsequent chapters.

For this chapter, you are expected to have Odoo installed and also expected to follow the recipes in Chapter 1, *Installing the Odoo Development Environment*. You are also expected to be comfortable in discovering and installing extra addon modules, as described in Chapter 2, *Managing Odoo Server Instances*.

Creating and installing a new addon module

In this recipe, we will create a new module, make it available in our Odoo instance, and install it.

Getting ready

We will need an Odoo instance ready to use.

If the first recipe in Chapter 1, *Installing the Odoo Development Environment*, was followed, Odoo should be available at ~/odoo-dev/odoo. For explanation purposes, we will assume this location for Odoo, although any other location of your preference can be used.

We will also need a location for our Odoo modules. For the purpose of this recipe, we will use a local-addons directory alongside the odoo directory, at ~/odoo-dev/local-addons.

How to do it...

The following steps will create and install a new addon module:

1. Change the working directory in which we will work and create the addons directory where our custom module will be placed:

    ```
    $ cd ~/odoo-dev
    $ mkdir local-addons
    ```

2. Choose a technical name for the new module and create a directory with that name for the module. For our example, we will use my_module:

    ```
    $ mkdir local-addons/my_module
    ```

 A module's **technical name** must be a valid Python identifier; it must begin with a letter, and only contain letters (preferably lowercase), numbers, and underscore characters.

3. Make the Python module importable by adding an __init__.py file:

    ```
    $ touch local-addons/my_module/__init__.py
    ```

4. Add a minimal module manifest for Odoo to detect it. Create a __manifest__.py file with this line:

```
{'name': 'My module'}
```

5. Start your Odoo instance including our module directory in the addons path:

```
$ odoo/odoo-bin --addons-path=odoo/addon/,local-addons/
```

 If the --save option is added to the Odoo command, the addons path will be saved in the configuration file. Next time you start the server, if no addons path option is provided, this will be used.

6. Make the new module available in your Odoo instance; log in to Odoo using admin, enable the **Developer Mode** in the **About** box, and in the Apps top menu, select **Update Apps List**. Now, Odoo should know about our Odoo module.

7. Select the **Apps** menu at the top and, in the search bar in the top-right, delete the default **Apps filter** and search for my_module. Click on its **Install** button, and the installation will be concluded.

How it works...

An Odoo module is a directory containing code files and other assets. The directory name used is the module's technical name. The name key in the module manifest is its title.

The __manifest__.py file is the module manifest. It contains a Python dictionary with information about the module, the modules it depends on, and the data files that it will load.

In the example, a minimal manifest file was used, but in real modules, we will want to add a few other important keys. These are discussed in the *Completing the module manifest* recipe, which we will see next.

The module directory must be Python-importable, so it also needs to have an __init__.py file, even if it's empty. To load a module, the Odoo server will import it. This will cause the code in the __init__.py file to be executed, so it works as an entry point to run the module Python code. Due to this, it will usually contain import statements to load the module Python files and submodules.

Known modules can be installed directly from the command line using the --init or -i option. This list is initially set when you create a new database, from the modules found on the addons path provided at that time. It can be updated in an existing database with the **Update Module List** menu.

Completing the addon module manifest

The manifest is an important piece for Odoo modules. It contains important information about the module and declares the data files that should be loaded.

Getting ready

We should have a module to work with, already containing a __manifest__.py manifest file. You may want to follow the previous recipe to provide such a module to work with.

How to do it...

We will add a manifest file and an icon to our addon module:

1. To create a manifest file with the most relevant keys, edit the module __manifest__.py file to look like this:

```
{
    'name': "Title",
    'summary': "Short subtitle phrase",
    'description': """Long description""",
    'author': "Your name",
    'license': "AGPL-3",
    'website': "http://www.example.com",
    'category': 'Uncategorized',
    'version': '11.0.1.0.0',
    'depends': ['base'],
    'data': ['views.xml'],
    'demo': ['demo.xml'],
}
```

2. To add an icon for the module, choose a PNG image to use and copy it to static/description/icon.png.

How it works...

The remaining content is a regular Python dictionary, with keys and values. The example manifest we used contains the most relevant keys:

- `name`: This is the title for the module.
- `summary`: This is the subtitle with a one-line description.
- `description`: This is a long description written in plain text or the **ReStructuredText** (**RST**) format. It is usually surrounded by triple quotes, and is used in Python to delimit multiline texts. For an RST quickstart reference, visit `http://docutils.sourceforge.net/docs/user/rst/quickstart.html`.
- `author`: This is a string with the name of the authors. When there is more than one, it is common practice to use a comma to separate their names, but note that it still should be a string, not a Python list.
- `license`: This is the identifier for the license under which the module is made available. It is limited to a predefined list, and the most frequent option is `AGPL-3`. Other possibilities include `LGPL-3`, `Other OSI approved license`, and `Other proprietary`.
- `website`: This is a URL people should visit to know more about the module or the authors.
- `category`: This is used to organize modules in areas of interest. The list of the standard category names available can be seen at `https://github.com/odoo/odoo/blob/11.0/odoo/addons/base/module/module_data.xml`. However, it's also possible to define other new category names here.
- `version`: This is the modules' version numbers. It can be used by the Odoo app store to detect newer versions for installed modules. If the version number does not begin with the Odoo target version (for example, `11.0`), it will be automatically added. Nevertheless, it will be more informative if you explicitly state the Odoo target version, for example, using `11.0.1.0.0` or `11.0.1.0` instead of `1.0.0` or `1.0`.
- `depends`: This is a list with the technical names of the modules it directly depends on. If none, we should at least depend on the `base` module. Don't forget to include any module defining XML IDs, Views, or Models referenced by this module. That will ensure that they all load in the correct order, avoiding hard-to-debug errors.

- `data`: This is a list of relative paths to the data files to load with module installation or upgrade. The paths are relative to the module root directory. Usually, these are XML and CSV files, but it's also possible to have YAML data files. These are discussed in depth in Chapter 7, *Module Data*.
- `demo`: This is the list of relative paths to the files with demonstration data to load. These will only be loaded if the database was created with the **Demo Data** flag enabled.

The image that is used as the module icon is the PNG file at `static/description/icon.png`.

> Odoo is expected to have significant changes between major versions, so modules built for one major version are likely to not be compatible with the next version without conversion and migration work. Due to this, it's important to be sure about a module's Odoo target version before installing it.

There's more...

Instead of having the long description in the module manifest, it's possible to have it in its own file. Since version 8.0, it can be replaced by a README file, with either a `.txt`, `.rst`, or an `.md` (Markdown) extension. Otherwise, include a `description/index.html` file in the module.

This HTML description will override a description defined in the manifest file.

There are a few more keys that are frequently used:

- `application`: If this is `True`, the module is listed as an application. Usually, this is used for the central module of a functional area
- `auto_install`: If this is `True`, it indicates that this is a "glue" module, which is automatically installed when all of its dependencies are installed
- `installable`: If this is `True` (the default value), it indicates that the module is available for installation

Organizing the addon module file structure

An addon module contains code files and other assets such as XML files and images. For most of these files, we are free to choose where to place them inside the module directory.

However, Odoo uses some conventions on the module structure, so it is advisable to follow them.

Getting ready

We are expected to have an addon module directory with only the __init__.py and __manifest__.py files. In this recipe, we suppose this is local-addons/my_module.

How to do it...

To create the basic skeleton for the addon module, perform the given steps:

1. Create the directories for code files:

```
$ cd local-addons/my_module
$ mkdir models
$ touch models/__init__.py
$ mkdir controllers
$ touch controllers/__init__.py
$ mkdir views
$ mkdir security
$ mkdir data
$ mkdir demo
$ mkdir i18n
$ mkdir -p static/description
```

2. Edit the module's top __init__.py file so that the code in subdirectories is loaded:

```
from . import models
from . import controllers
```

This should get us started with a structure containing the most used directories, similar to this one:

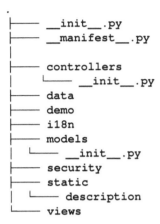

```
├──── __init__.py
├──── __manifest__.py
│
├──── controllers
│     └──── __init__.py
├──── data
├──── demo
├──── i18n
├──── models
│     └──── __init__.py
├──── security
├──── static
│     └──── description
└──── views
```

How it works...

To provide some context, an Odoo addon module can have three types of files:

- The **Python code** is loaded by the __init__.py files, where the .py files and code subdirectories are imported. Subdirectories containing code Python, in turn, need their own __init__.py.
- **Data files** that are to be declared in the data and demo keys of the __manifest__.py module manifest in order to be loaded are usually XML and CSV files for the user interface, fixture data, and demonstration data. There can also be YAML files, which can include some procedural instructions that are run when the module is loaded, for instance, to generate or update records programmatically rather than statically in an XML file.
- **Web assets** such as JavaScript code and libraries, CSS, and QWeb/HTML templates also play an important part. There are declared through an XML file extending the master templates to add these assets to the web client or website pages.

The addon files are to be organized in these directories:

- `models/` contains the backend code files, creating the Models and their business logic. A file per Model is recommended, with the same name as the model, for example, `library_book.py` for the `library.book` model. These are addressed in depth in Chapter 5, *Application Models*.
- `views/` contains the XML files for the user interface, with the actions, forms, lists, and so on. As with models, it is advised to have one file per model. Filenames for website templates are expected to end with the `_template` suffix. Backend views are explained in Chapter 10, *Backend Views*, and website views are addressed in Chapter 16, *CMS Website Development*.
- `data/` contains other data files with module initial data. Data files are explained in Chapter 7, *Module Data*.
- `demo/` contains data files with demonstration data, useful for tests, training, or module evaluation.
- `i18n/` is where Odoo will look for the translation `.pot` and `.po` files. Refer to Chapter 12, *Internationalization*, for more detail. These files don't need to be mentioned in the manifest file.
- `security/` contains the data files defining access control lists, usually a `ir.model.access.csv` file, and possibly an XML file to define access Groups and Record Rules for row level security. Take a look at Chapter 11, *Access Security*, for more details on this.
- `controllers/` contains the code files for the website controllers, and for modules providing that kind of feature. Web controllers are covered in Chapter 14, *Web Server Development*.
- `static/` is where all web assets are expected to be placed. Unlike other directories, this directory name is not just a convention, and only files inside it can be made available for the Odoo web pages. They don't need to be mentioned in the module manifest, but will have to be referred to in the web template. This is discussed in detail in Chapter 16, *CMS Website Development*.

When adding new files to a module, don't forget to declare them either in the `__manifest__.py` (for data files) or `__init__.py` (for code files); otherwise, those files will be ignored and won't be loaded.

Adding models

Models define the data structures to be used by our business applications. This recipe shows how to add a basic model to a module.

We will use a simple book library example to explain this; we want a model to represent books. Each book has a name and a list of authors.

Getting ready

We should have a module to work with. If we follow the first recipe in this chapter, we will have an empty my_module. We will use that for our explanation.

How to do it...

To add a new Model, we add a Python file describing it and then upgrade the addon module (or install it, if it was not already done). The paths used are relative to our addon module location (for example, ~/odoo-dev/local-addons/my_module/):

1. Add a Python file to the models/library_book.py module with the following code:

```
from odoo import models, fields
class LibraryBook(models.Model):
    _name = 'library.book'
    name = fields.Char('Title', required=True)
    date_release = fields.Date('Release Date')
    author_ids = fields.Many2many(
        'res.partner',
        string='Authors'
    )
```

2. Add a Python initialization file with code files to be loaded by the models/__init__.py module with the following code:

```
from . import library_book
```

3. Edit the module Python initialization file to have the models/ directory loaded by the module:

```
from . import models
```

4. Upgrade the Odoo module, either from the command line or from the apps menu in the user interface. If you look closely at the server log while upgrading the module, you should see this line:

```
odoo.modules.registry: module my_module: creating or updating
database table
```

After this, the new `library.book` model should be available in our Odoo instance. If we have the technical tools activated, we can confirm that by looking it up at **Settings** | **Technical** | **Database Structure** | **Models**.

How it works...

Our first step was to create a Python file where our new module was created.

Odoo models are objects derived from the Odoo `Model` Python class.

When a new model is defined, it is also added to a central model registry. This makes it easier for other modules to make modifications to it later.

Models have a few generic attributes prefixed with an underscore. The most important one is _name, providing a unique internal identifier to be used throughout the Odoo instance.

The model fields are defined as class attributes. We began defining the `name` field of the `Char` type. It is convenient for models to have this field, because by default, it is used as the record description when referenced from other models.

We also used an example of a relational field, `author_ids`. It defines a many-to-many relation between `Library Books` and the partners. A book can have many authors and each author can have written many books.

There's much more to say about models, and they will be covered in depth in `Chapter 5`, *Application Models*.

Next, we must make our module aware of this new Python file. This is done by the __init__.py files. Since we placed the code inside the `models/` subdirectory, we need the previous __init__ file to import that directory, which should in turn contain another __init__ file importing each of the code files there (just one, in our case).

Changes to Odoo models are activated by upgrading the module. The Odoo server will handle the translation of the model class into database structure changes.

Although no example is provided here, business logic can also be added to these Python files, either by adding new methods to the Model's class, or by extending the existing methods, such as `create()` or `write()`. This is addressed in `Chapter 6`, *Basic Server-Side Development*.

Adding Menu Items and Views

Once we have Models for our data structure needs, we want a user interface for our users to interact with them. This recipe builds on the `Library Book` Model from the previous recipe and adds a menu item to display a user interface featuring list and form Views.

Getting ready

The addon module implementing the `library.book` Model, provided in the previous recipe, is needed. The paths used are relative to our addon module location (for example, `~/odoo-dev/local-addons/my_module/`).

How to do it...

To add a view, we will add an XML file with its definition to the module. Since it is a new Model, we must also add a menu option for the user to be able to access it.

Be aware that the sequence of the following steps is relevant, since some of them use references to IDs defined in the preceding steps:

1. Create the XML file to add the data records describing the user interface `views/library_book.xml`:

    ```
    <?xml version="1.0" encoding="utf-8"?>
    <odoo>
      <!-- Data records go here -->
    </odoo>
    ```

2. Add the new data file to the addon module manifest, `__manifest__.py` by adding it to `views/library_book.xml`:

    ```
    {
        'name': "Library Books",
        'summary': "Manage your books",
    ```

```
'depends': ['base'],
'data': ['views/library_book.xml'],
}
```

3. Add the action that opens the Views in the `library_book.xml` file:

```
<act_window
    id="library_book_action"
    name="Library Books"
    res_model="library.book" />
```

4. Add the menu item to the `library_book.xml` file, making it visible to the users:

```
<menuitem
    id="library_book_menu"
    name="Library"
    action="library_book_action"
    parent=""
    sequence="5" />
```

If you try and upgrade the module now, you should be able to see a new top menu option (you might need to refresh your web browser). Clicking on it should work and will open Views for `Library Books` that are automatically generated by the server:

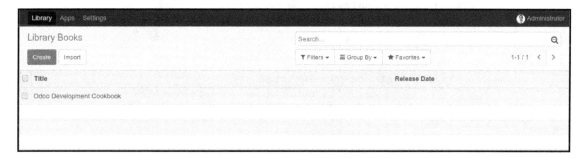

5. Add a custom form view to the `library_book.xml` file:

```
<record id="library_book_view_form" model="ir.ui.view">
  <field name="name">Library Book Form</field>
  <field name="model">library.book</field>
  <field name="arch" type="xml">
    <form>
      <group>
        <field name="name"/>
        <field name="author_ids" widget="many2many_tags"/>
      </group>
```

```
        <group>
          <field name="date_release"/>
        </group>
      </form>
    </field>
  </record>
```

6. Add a custom Tree (List) view to the `library_book.xml` file:

```
<record id="library_book_view_tree" model="ir.ui.view">
  <field name="name">Library Book List</field>
  <field name="model">library.book</field>
  <field name="arch" type="xml">
    <tree>
      <field name="name"/>
      <field name="date_release"/>
    </tree>
  </field>
</record>
```

7. Add custom `Search` options to the `library_book.xml` file:

```
<record id="library_book_view_search" model="ir.ui.view">
  <field name="name">Library Book Search</field>
  <field name="model">library.book</field>
  <field name="arch" type="xml">
    <search>
      <field name="name"/>
      <field name="author_ids"/>
      <filter string="No Authors"
              domain="[('author_ids','=',False)]"/>
    </search>
  </field>
</record>
```

How it works...

At the low level, the user interface is defined by records stored in special Models. The first two steps create an empty XML file to define the records to be loaded and then add them to the module's list of data files to be installed.

Data files can be anywhere inside the module directory, but the convention is for the user interface to be defined inside a `views/` subdirectory using file names after the Model the interface is for. In our case, the `library.book` interface is in the `views/library_book.xml` file.

The next step is to define a Window Action to display the user interface in the main area of the web client. The Action has a target Model defined by `res_model` and sets the title to display to the user using `name`. These are just the basic attributes. It supports additional attributes, giving much more control on how the Views are rendered, such as what Views are to be displayed, adding filters on the records available, or setting default values. These are discussed in detail in `Chapter 10`, *Backend Views*.

In general, data records are defined using a `<record>` tag, but in our example, the Window Action was defined using the `<act_window>` tag. This is a shortcut to create records for the `ir.actions.act_window` Model, where Window Actions are stored.

Similarly, menu items are stored in the `ir.ui.menu` Model, but a convenience `<menuitem>` shortcut tag is available and was used.

These are the menu item's main attributes used here:

- `name`: This is the menu item text to be displayed.
- `action`: This is the identifier of the action to be executed. We use the ID of the Window Action created in the previous step.
- `sequence`: This is used to set the order at which the menu items of the same level are presented.
- `parent`: This is the identifier for the parent menu item. Our example menu item had no parent, meaning that it is to be displayed at the top of the menu.

At this point, our module can display a menu item, and clicking on it opens Views for the `Library Books` model. Since nothing specific is set on the Window Action, the default is to display a List (or Tree) view and a form view.

We haven't defined any of these views, so Odoo will automatically create them on the fly. However, we will surely want to control how our views look, so in the next two steps, a form and a tree view are created.

Both views are defined with a record on the `ir.ui.view` model. The attributes we used are as follows:

- `name`: This is a title identifying this view. It is frequent to see the XML ID repeated here, but it can perfectly be a more human readable title.

If the `name` field is omitted, Odoo will generate one using the model name and the type of view. This is perfectly fine for the standard view of a new model. It is recommended to have a more explicit name when you are extending a view, as this will make your life easier when you are looking for a specific view in the user interface of Odoo.

- `model`: This is the internal identifier of the target model, as defined in its `_name` attribute.
- `arch`: This is the view architecture, where its structure is actually defined. This is where different types of views differ from each other.

Form views are defined with a top `<form>` element, and its canvas is a two-column grid. Inside the form, `<group>` elements are used to vertically compose fields. Two groups result in two columns with fields, which are added using the `<field>` element. Fields use a default widget according to their data type, but a specific widget can be used with the help of the `widget` attribute.

Tree views are simpler; they are defined with a top `<tree>` element containing `<field>` elements for the columns to be displayed.

Finally, we added a Search view to expand the search option in the box at the top-right. Inside the `<search>` top-level tag, we can have the ;`<field>` and `<filter>` elements. Field elements are additional fields that can be searched from the box. Filter elements are predefined filter conditions that can be activated with a click.

Adding Access Security

When adding a new data model, you need to define who can create, read, update, and delete records. When creating a totally new application, this can involve defining new user groups.

This recipe builds on the `Library Book` Model from the previous recipes and defines a new group of users to control who can work book records.

Getting ready

The addon module implementing the `library.book` model, provided in the previous recipe, is needed. The paths used are relative to our addon module location (for example, `~/odoo-dev/local-addons/my_module/`).

How to do it...

The security rules we want to add in this recipe are as follows:

- Everyone will be able to read library book records
- A new group of users called "Librarians" will have the right to create, read, update, and delete book records

To implement this, you need to perform the following steps:

1. Create a file called `security/groups.xml` with the following content:

```xml
<?xml version="1.0" encoding="utf-8"?>
<odoo>
  <record id="group_librarian" model="res.groups">
    <field name="name">Librarians</field>
  </record>
</odoo>
```

2. Add a file called `security/ir.model.access.csv` with the following content:

```
id,name,model_id:id,group_id:id,perm_read,perm_write,perm_create,perm_unlink
acl_book,library.book default,model_library_book,,1,0,0,0
acl_book_librarian,library.book_librarian,model_library_book,group_librarian,1,1,1,1
```

3. Add both files in the data entry of `__manifest__.py`:

```python
# ...
'data': [
    'security/groups.xml',
    'views/library_book.xml',
    'security/ir.model.access.csv',
],
# ...
```

The newly defined security rules will be in place once you update the addon in your instance.

How it works...

We are providing two new data files that we add to the addon module's manifest so that the installation or update of the module will load them in the database:

- The `security/groups.xml` file defines a new security group by creating a `res.groups` record.
- The `ir.model.access.csv` file associates permissions on models with groups. The first line has an empty `group_id:id` column, which means that the rule applies to everyone. The last line gives all privileges to members of the group we just created.

> The order of the files in the data section of the manifest is important; the file creating the security groups must be loaded before the file listing the access rights, as the access right's definition depends on the existence of the groups. Since the views can be specific to a security group, we recommend putting the group's definition file in the list to be on the safer side.

More information on security is available in the recipes from `Chapter 11`, *Access Security*.

Using scaffold to create a module

When creating a new Odoo module, there is some boilerplate that needs to be set up. To help quick start new modules, Odoo provides the `scaffold` command.

The recipe shows how to create a new module using the `scaffold` command, which will put in place a skeleton of the file directories to use.

Getting ready

We need Odoo installed and a directory for our custom modules.

We will assume that Odoo is installed at `~/odoo-dev/odoo` and our custom modules will be at `~/odoo-dev/local-addons`.

How to do it...

The scaffold command is used from the command line:

1. Change the working directory to where we will want our module to be. This can be whatever directory you choose, but within an addons path to be useful. Following the directory choices used in the previous recipe, it should be as follows:

   ```
   $ cd ~/odoo-dev/local-addons
   ```

2. Choose a technical name for the new module, and use the scaffold command to create it. For our example, we will choose my_scaffolded:

   ```
   $ ~/odoo-dev/odoo/odoo-bin scaffold my_scaffolded
   ```

3. Edit the __manifest__.py default module manifest provided and change the relevant values. You will surely want to at least change the module title in the name key.

This is how the generated addon module should look like:

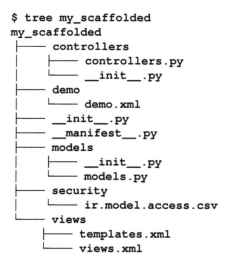

```
$ tree my_scaffolded
my_scaffolded
├──── controllers
│     ├──── controllers.py
│     └──── __init__.py
├──── demo
│     └──── demo.xml
├──── __init__.py
├──── __manifest__.py
├──── models
│     ├──── __init__.py
│     └──── models.py
├──── security
│     └──── ir.model.access.csv
└──── views
      ├──── templates.xml
      └──── views.xml
```

You should now edit the various generated files and adapt them to the purpose of your new module.

How it works...

The `scaffold` command creates the skeleton for a new module based on a template.

By default, the new module is created in the current working directory, but we can provide a specific directory to create the module, passing it as an additional parameter. Consider this example:

```
$ ~/odoo-dev/odoo/odoo-bin scaffold my_module ~/odoo-dev/local-addons
```

A `default` template is used, but a `theme` template is also available for website theme authoring. To choose a specific template, the `-t` option can be used. We are also allowed to use a path for a directory with a template.

This means that we can use our own templates with the `scaffold` command. The built-in themes can be used as a guide, and they can be found in the `./odoo/cli/templates` Odoo subdirectory. To use our own template, we can use something like this:

```
$ ~/odoo-dev/odoo/odoo-bin scaffold -t path/to/template my_module
```

5
Application Models

In this chapter, we will cover the following topics:

- Defining the Model representation and order
- Adding data fields to a Model
- Using a float field with configurable precision
- Adding a monetary field to a Model
- Adding relational fields to a Model
- Adding a hierarchy to a Model
- Adding constraint validations to a Model
- Adding computed fields to a Model
- Exposing related fields stored in other models
- Adding dynamic relations using Reference fields
- Adding features to a Model using inheritance
- Using abstract Models for reusable Model features
- Using delegation inheritance to copy features to another Model

Introduction

In order to concisely get the point through, the recipes in this chapter make small additions to an existing addon module. We chose to use the module created by the recipes in Chapter 4, *Creating Odoo Addon Modules*. To better follow the examples here, you should have that module created and ready to use.

Defining the Model representation and order

Models have structural attributes defining their behavior. These are prefixed with an underscore and the most important is _name, which defines the internal global identifier for the model.

There are two other attributes we can use, one to set the field used as a representation or title for the records, and another one to set the order they are presented in.

Getting ready

This recipe assumes that you have an instance ready with my_module, as described in Chapter 4, *Creating Odoo Addon Modules*.

How to do it...

The my_module instance should already contain a Python file called models/library_book.py, which defines a basic model. We will edit it to add a new class-level attribute after _name:

1. To add a human-friendly title to the model, add the following:

   ```
   _description = 'Library Book'
   ```

2. To have records sorted, by default, first from newer to older and then by title, add the following:

   ```
   _order = 'date_release desc, name'
   ```

3. To use the short_name field as the record representation, add the following:

   ```
   _rec_name = 'short_name'
   short_name = fields.Char('Short Title', required=True)
   ```

When we're done, our `library_book.py` file should look like this:

```
from odoo import models, fields
class LibraryBook(models.Model):
    _name = 'library.book'
    _description = 'Library Book'
    _order = 'date_release desc, name'
    _rec_name = 'short_name'
    name = fields.Char('Title', required=True)
    short_name = fields.Char('Short Title', required=True)
    date_release = fields.Date('Release Date')
    author_ids = fields.Many2many('res.partner', string='Authors')
```

We should then upgrade the module to have these changes activated in Odoo.

How it works...

The first step adds a friendlier description title to the model's definition. This is not mandatory, but can be used by some addons. For instance, it is used by the tracking feature in the `mail` addon module for the notification text when a new record is created. For more details, refer to `Chapter 13`, *Automation and Workflows*.

By default, Odoo orders the records using the internal `id` value. However, this can be changed to use the fields of our choice by providing an `_order` attribute with a string containing a comma-separated list of field names. A field name can be followed by the `desc` keyword to have it sorted in reverse order.

Only fields stored in the database can be used. Non-stored computed fields can't be used to sort records.

> The syntax for the `_order` string is similar to SQL `ORDER BY` clauses, although it's stripped down. For instance, special clauses such as `NULLS FIRST` are not allowed.

Model records have a representation used when they are referenced from other records. For example, a `user_id` field with the value 1 represents the **Administrator** user. When displayed in a form view, Odoo will display the username rather than the database ID. By default, the `name` field is used. In fact, that is the default value for the `_rec_name` attribute, and that's why it's convenient to have a `name` field in our models.

If no `name` field exists in the model, a representation is generated with the model and record identifiers, similar to (library.book, 1).

There's more...

Record representation is available in a magic `display_name` computed field, and has been added automatically to all models since version 8.0. Its values are generated using the `name_get()` model method, which was already in existence in the previous Odoo versions.

The default implementation of `name_get()` uses the `_rec_name` attribute to find which field holds the data; that should use to generate the display name. For more sophisticated representations, we can override its logic. The method must return a list of tuples with two elements: the ID of the record and the Unicode string representation for the record.

For example, to have the title and its release date in the representation, such as Moby Dick (1851-10-18), we can define the following:

```
def name_get(self):
  result = []
    for record in self:
     result.append(
     (record.id,
     "%s (%s)" % (record.name, record.date_release)
      ))
return result
```

Adding data fields to a Model

Models are meant to store data, and this data is structured in fields. Here, we will learn about the several types of data that can be stored in fields, and how to add them to a model.

Getting ready

This recipe assumes that you have an instance ready with the `my_module` addon module available, as described in `Chapter 4`, *Creating Odoo Addon Modules*.

How to do it...

The my_module addon module should already have a models/library_book.py defining a basic Model. We will edit it to add new fields:

1. Use the minimal syntax to add fields to the Library Books model:

```
from odoo import models, fields
class LibraryBook(models.Model):
    # ...
    short_name = fields.Char('Short Title')
    notes = fields.Text('Internal Notes')
    state = fields.Selection(
        [('draft', 'Not Available'),
         ('available', 'Available'),
         ('lost', 'Lost')],
        'State')
    description = fields.Html('Description')
    cover = fields.Binary('Book Cover')
    out_of_print = fields.Boolean('Out of Print?')
    date_release = fields.Date('Release Date')
    date_updated = fields.Datetime('Last Updated')
    pages = fields.Integer('Number of Pages')
    reader_rating = fields.Float(
        'Reader Average Rating',
        digits=(14, 4),  # Optional precision (total, decimals),
    )
```

2. All these fields support a few common attributes. As an example, we can edit the preceding pages field to add them:

```
pages = fields.Integer(
    string='Number of Pages',
    default=0,
    help='Total book page count',
    groups='base.group_user',
    states={'lost': [('readonly', True)]},
    copy=True,
    index=False,
    readonly=False,
    required=False,
    company_dependent=False,
    )
```

3. The `Char` fields support a few specific attributes. As an example, we can edit the `short_name` field to add them:

```
short_name = fields.Char(
    string='Short Title',
    size=100,  # For Char only
    translate=False,  # also for Text fields
    )
```

4. The HTML fields also have specific attributes:

```
description = fields.Html(
    string='Description',
    # optional:
    sanitize=True,
    strip_style=False,
    translate=False,
    )
```

Upgrading the module will make these changes effective in the Odoo model.

How it works...

Fields are added to models by defining an attribute in its Python class. The non-relational field types available are as follows:

- `Char` for string values.
- `Text` for multi-line string values.
- `Selection` for selection lists. This has a list of values and description pairs. The value that is selected is what gets stored in the database, and it can be a string or an integer. The description is automatically translatable.

 While integer keys are nice, you must be aware that Odoo interprets `0` as "unset" internally and will not display the description if the stored value is zero, which can happen, so you will need to take this into account.

- `Html` is similar to the text field, but is expected to store rich text in the HTML format.
- `Binary` fields store binary files, such as images or documents.
- `Boolean` stores `True/False` values.

- `Date` stores date values. The ORM handles them in the string format, but they are stored in the database as dates. The format used is defined in `odoo.fields.DATE_FORMAT`.

- `Datetime` for date-time values. They are stored in the database in a naive date time, in UTC time. The ORM represents them as a string and also in UTC time. The format used is defined in `odoo.fields.DATETIME_FORMAT`.

- The `Integer` fields need no further explanation.

- The `Float` fields store numeric values. The precision can optionally be defined with a total number of digits and decimal digits pairs.

- `Monetary` can store an amount in a certain currency; it is also explained in another recipe.

The first step in the recipe shows the minimal syntax to add to each field type. The field definitions can be expanded to add other optional attributes, as shown in step 2.

Here's an explanation for the field attributes used:

- `string` is the field's title, used in UI view labels. It's actually optional; if not set, a label will be derived from the field name by adding title case and replacing underscores with spaces.

- `size` only applies to `Char` fields and is the maximum number of characters allowed. In general, it is advised not to use it.

- `translate`, when set to `True`, makes the field translatable; it can hold a different value depending on the user interface language.

- `default` is the default value. It can also be a function that is used to calculate the default value. For example, `default=_compute_default`, where `_compute_default` is a method defined on the model before the field definition.

- `help` is an explanation text displayed in the UI tooltips.

- `groups` makes the field available only to some security groups. It is a string containing a comma-separated list of XML IDs for security groups. This is addressed in more detail in `Chapter 11`, *Access Security*.

- `states` allows the user interface to dynamically set the value for the `readonly`, `required`, and `invisible` attributes, depending on the value of the `state` field. Therefore, it requires a `state` field to exist and be used in the form view (even if it is invisible). The name of the `state` attribute is hardcoded in Odoo and cannot be changed.

- `copy` flags whether the field value is copied when the record is duplicated. By default, it is `True` for non-relational and `Many2one` fields and `False` for `One2many` and computed fields.
- `index`, when set to `True`, makes for the creation of a database index for the field, sometimes allowing faster searches. It replaces the deprecated `select=1` attribute.
- The `readonly` flag makes the field read-only by default in the user interface.
- The `required` flag makes the field mandatory by default in the user interface.
- The `sanitize` flag is used by HTML fields and strips its content from potentially insecure tags. Using this performs a global clean up of the input. If you need finer control, there are a few more keywords you can use, which only work if `sanitize` is enabled:
    - `sanitize_tags=True` to remove tags that are not part of a white list (this is the default)
    - `sanitize_attributes=True` to additionally only remove attributes that are not part of a white list
    - `sanitize_style=True` to remove style properties that are not part of a white list
    - `strip_style=True` to remove all style elements
    - `strip_class=True` to remove the class attributes

> The various white list mentioned here are defined in `odoo/tools/mail.py`.

- The `company_dependent` flag makes the field store different values per company. It replaces the deprecated `Property` field type.

There's more...

The `Selection` field also accepts a function reference instead of a list as its "selection" attribute. This allows for dynamically generated lists of options. You can find an example relating to this in the *Adding dynamic relations using Reference fields* recipe in this chapter, where a selection attribute is also used.

The `Date` and `Datetime` field objects expose a few utility methods that can be convenient.

For `Date`, we have the following:

- `fields.Date.from_string(string_value)` parses the string into a date object.
- `fields.Date.to_string(date_value)` represents the `Date` object as a string.
- `fields.Date.today()` returns the current day in string format. This is appropriate to use for default values.
- `fields.Date.context_today(record, timestamp)` returns day of `timestamp` (or the current day, if `timestamp` is omitted) in string format according to the timezone of the record's (or record set) context.

For `Datetime`, we have the following:

- `fields.Datetime.from_string(string_value)` parses the string into a `datetime` object.
- `fields.Datetime.to_string(datetime_value)` represents the `datetime` object as a string.
- `fields.Datetime.now()` returns the current day and time in string format. This is appropriate to use for default values.
- `fields.Datetime.context_timestamp(record, timestamp)` converts a `timestamp` naive date-time into a timezone-aware date-time using the timezone in the context of `record`. This is not suitable for default values, but can be used for instances when sending data to an external system.

Other than the basic fields, we also have relational fields: `Many2one`, `One2many`, and `Many2many`. These are explained in the *Adding relational fields to a Model* recipe of this chapter.

It's also possible to have fields with automatically computed values, defining the computation function with the `compute` field attribute. This is explained in the *Adding computed fields to a Model* recipe.

A few fields are added by default in Odoo models, so we should not use these names for our fields. These are the `id` field, for the record's automatically generated identifier, and a few audit log fields, which are as follows:

- `create_date` is the record creation timestamp
- `create_uid` is the user who created the record
- `write_date` is the last recorded edit timestamp
- `write_uid` is the user who last edited the record

The automatic creation of these log fields can be disabled by setting the `_log_access=False` model attribute.

Another special column that can be added to a model is `active`. It must be a Boolean flag allowing for mark records as inactive. Its definition looks like this:

```
active = fields.Boolean('Active', default=True)
```

By default, only records with `active` set to `True` are visible. To have them retrieved, we need to use a domain filter with `[('active', '=', False)]`. Alternatively, if the `'active_test': False` value is added to the environment's context, the ORM will not filter out inactive records.

 In some cases, you may not be able to modify the context to get both active and inactive records. In this case, you can use the `['|', ('active', '=', True), ('active', '=', False)]` domain.
Caution: `[('active', 'in' (True, False))]` does not work as you might expect. Odoo is looking explicitly for an `('active', '=', False)` clause in the domain, and it will not find it and will default to restricting the search on active records only.

Using a float field with configurable precision

When using float fields, we may want to let the end user configure the precision that is to be used. The **Decimal Precision Configuration** module addon provides this ability.

We will add a **Cost Price** field to the Library Book model, with a user-configurable number of digits.

Getting ready

We will reuse the `my_module` addon module from Chapter 4, *Creating Odoo Addon Modules*.

How to do it...

We need to install the `decimal_precision` module, add a "Usage" entry for our configuration, and then use it in the model field:

1. Ensure that the Decimal Accuracy module is installed; select **Apps** from the top menu, remove the default filter, search for the **Decimal Precision Configuration** app, and install it if it's not already installed:

2. Activate **Developer Mode** from the link in the **Settings** menu (refer to the *Activating the Odoo developer tools* recipe in `Chapter 1`, *Installing the Odoo Development Environment*). This will enable the **Settings** | **Technical** menu.

3. Access the Decimal Precision configurations. To do this, open the **Settings** top menu and select **Technical** | **Database Structure** | **Decimal Accuracy**. We should see a list of the currently defined settings.

4. Add a new configuration, setting **Usage** to **Book Price** and choosing the **Digits** precision:

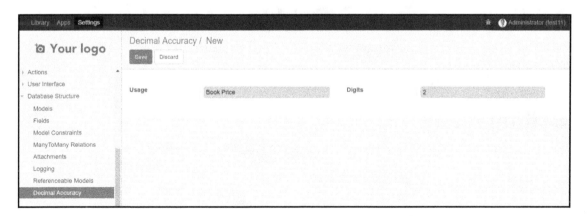

5. Add the new dependency to the __manifest__.py manifest file. It should be similar to this:

```
{    'name': 'Chapter 05 code',
     'depends': ['base', 'decimal_precision],
     'data': ['views/library_book.xml'] }
```

6. To add the model field using this decimal precision setting, edit the models/library_book.py file by adding the following:

```
from odoo.addons import decimal_precision as dp
# ...
class LibraryBook(models.Model):
    # ...
    cost_price = fields.Float(
        'Book Cost', dp.get_precision('Book Price))
```

How it works...

The get_precision() function looks up the name in the Decimal Accuracy's **Usage** field and returns a tuple representing 16-digit precision with the number of decimals defined in the configuration.

Using this function in the field definition, instead of having it hard-coded, allows the end user to configure it according to their needs.

Adding a monetary field to a Model

Odoo has special support for **monetary** values related to a **currency**. Let's see how to use it in a model.

Getting ready

We will reuse the my_module addon module from Chapter 4, *Creating Odoo Addon Modules*.

How to do it...

The monetary field needs a complementary currency field to store the currency for the amounts.

The `my_module` already has a `models/library_book.py` defining a basic model. We will edit this to add the required fields:

1. Add the field to store the currency that is to be used:

```
class LibraryBook(models.Model):
    # ...
    currency_id = fields.Many2one(
        'res.currency', string='Currency')
```

2. Add the monetary field to store our amount:

```
class LibraryBook(models.Model):
    # ...
    retail_price = fields.Monetary(
        'Retail Price',
        # optional: currency_field='currency_id',
        )
```

Now, upgrade the addon module, and the new fields should be available in the Model. They won't be visible in views until they are added to them, but we can confirm their addition by inspecting the Model fields in **Settings | Technical | Database Structure | Models**.

How it works...

Monetary fields are similar to Float fields, but Odoo is able to represent them correctly in the user interface since it knows what their currency is through a second field for that purpose.

This currency field is expected to be named `currency_id`, but we can use whatever field name we like as long as it is indicated using the `currency_field` optional parameter.

> This is very useful when you need to maintain amounts in different currencies in the same record, for example, in the currency of the sale order and in the currency of the company. You can configure two fields as `fields.Many2one(res.currency)` and use the first one for the first amount and the other one for the second amount.

You might like to know that the decimal precision for the amount is taken from the currency definition (the `decimal_precision` field of the `res.currency` model).

Adding relational fields to a Model

Relations between Odoo Models are represented by relational fields. We can have three different types of **relations**:

- **many-to-one**, commonly abbreviated as **m2o**
- **one-to-many**, commonly abbreviated as **o2m**
- **many-to-many**, commonly abbreviated as **m2m**

Looking at the Library Books example, we can see that each book can have one publisher, so we can have a many-to-one relation between books and publishers.

From the publisher's point of view, each publisher can have many books. So, the previous many-to-one relation implies a one-to-many reverse relation.

Finally, there are cases where we can have a many-to-many relation. In our example, each book can have several (many) authors. Also, inversely, each author can have written many books. Looking at it from either side, this is a many-to-many relation.

Getting ready

We will reuse the `my_module` addon module from Chapter 4, *Creating Odoo Addon Modules*.

How to do it...

Odoo uses the Partner model, `res.partner`, to represent persons, organizations, and addresses. So, we should use it for authors and publishers. We will edit the `models/library_book.py` file to add these fields:

1. Add to `Library Books` the many-to-one field for the book's publisher:

```
class LibraryBook(models.Model):
    # ...
    publisher_id = fields.Many2one(
        'res.partner', string='Publisher',
        # optional:
```

```
        ondelete='set null',
        context={},
        domain=[],
        )
```

2. To add the one-to-many field for a publisher's books, we need to extend the partner model. For simplicity, we will add that to the same Python file:

```
class ResPartner(models.Model):
    _inherit = 'res.partner'
    published_book_ids = fields.One2many(
        'library.book', 'publisher_id',
        string='Published Books')
```

 The _inherit attribute we use here will be explained in the *Adding features to a Model using inheritance* recipe later in this chapter.

3. The many-to-many relation between books and authors was already created, but let's revisit it:

```
class LibraryBook(models.Model):
    # ...
    author_ids = fields.Many2many(
        'res.partner', string='Authors')
```

4. The same relation, but from authors to books, should be added to the partner model:

```
class ResPartner(models.Model):
    # ...
    authored_book_ids = fields.Many2many(
        'library.book',
        string='Authored Books',
        # relation='library_book_res_partner_rel'  # optional
        )
```

Now, upgrade the addon module, and the new fields should be available in the Model. They won't be visible in views until they are added to them, but we can confirm their addition by inspecting the Model fields in **Settings** | **Technical** | **Database Structure** | **Models**.

How it works...

Many-to-one fields add a column to the database table of the model, storing the database ID of the related record. At the database level, a foreign key constraint will also be created for it, ensuring that the stored IDs are a valid reference to a record in the related table. No database index is created for these relation fields, but this should often be considered; it can be done by adding the `index=True` attribute.

We can see that there are four more attributes we can use for many-to-one fields. The `ondelete` attribute determines what happens when the related record is deleted. For example, what happens to Books when their publisher record is deleted? The default is `'set null'`, setting an empty value on the field. It can also be `'restrict'`, which prevents the related record from being deleted, or `'cascade'`, which causes the linked record to also be deleted.

The last two (`context` and `domain`) are also valid for the other relational fields. They are mostly meaningful on the client side, and at the model level, act just as default values to be used in the client-side views:

- `context` adds variables to the client context when clicking through the field to the related record's view. We can, for example, use it to set default values for new records created through that view.
- `domain` is a search filter used to limit the list of related records available.

Both context and domain are explained in more detail in `Chapter 10`, *Backend Views*.

One-to-many fields are the reverse of many-to-one relations, and although they are added to models just like other fields, they have no actual representation in the database. Instead, they are programmatic shortcuts and enable views to represent these lists of related records.

Many-to-many relations also don't add columns in the tables for the models. This type of relation is represented in the database using an intermediate relation table, with two columns to store the two related IDs. Adding a new relation between a Book and an Author creates a new record in the relation table with the ID for the Book and the ID for the Author.

Odoo automatically handles the creation of this relation table. The relation table name is, by default, built using the name of the two related models, alphabetically sorted, plus a `_rel` suffix. However, we can override it using the `relation` attribute.

A case to keep in mind is when the two table names are large enough for the automatically generated database identifiers to exceed the PostgreSQL limit of 63 characters. As a rule of thumb, if the names of the two related tables exceed 23 characters, you should use the `relation` attribute to set a shorter name. In the next section, we will go into more detail on this.

There's more...

The `Many2one` fields support an additional `auto_join` attribute. It is a flag that allows the ORM to use SQL joins on this field. Due to this, it bypasses the usual ORM control such as user access control and record access rules. On a specific case, it can solve a performance issue, but it is advised to avoid using it.

We have seen the shortest way to define the relational fields. For completeness, these are the attributes specific to this type of field:

The `One2many` field attributes are as follows:

- `comodel_name`: This is the target model identifier and is mandatory for all relational fields, but it can be defined position-wise without the keyword
- `inverse_name`: This applies only to `One2many` and is the field name in the target model for the inverse `Many2one` relation
- `limit`: This applies to `One2many` and `Many2many` and sets an optional limit on the number of records to read that are used at the user interface level

The `Many2many` field attributes are as follows:

- `comodel_name`: (as defined earlier)
- `relation`: This is the name to use for the table supporting the relation, overriding the automatically defined name
- `column1`: This is the name for the `Many2one` field in the relational table linking to this model
- `column2`: This is the name for the `Many2one` field in the relational table linking to `comodel`

For `Many2many` relations, in most cases, the ORM will take perfect care of the default values for these attributes. It is even capable of detecting inverse `Many2many` relations, detecting the already existing `relation` table, and appropriately inverting the `column1` and `column2` values.

However, there are two cases where we need to step in and provide our own values for these attributes. One is the case where we need more than one `Many2many` relation between the same two models. For this to be possible, we must provide ourselves the `relation` table name for the second relation, which must be different from the first relation. The other case is when the database names of the related tables are long enough for the automatically generated relation name to exceed the 63 character PostgreSQL limit for database object names.

The relation table's automatic name is `<model1>_<model2>_rel`. However, this relation table also creates an index for its primary key with the following identifier:

    <model1>_<model2>_rel_<model1>_id_<model2>_id_key

This primary key also needs to meet the 63 characters limit. So, if the two table names combined exceed a total of 63 characters, you will probably have trouble meeting the limits and will need to manually set the `relation` attribute.

Adding a hierarchy to a Model

Hierarchies are represented using model relations with itself; each record has a parent record in the same model and also has many child records. This can be achieved by simply using many-to-one relations between the model and itself.

However, Odoo also provides improved support for this type of field using the **Nested set model** (https://en.wikipedia.org/wiki/Nested_set_model). When activated, queries using the `child_of` operator in their domain filters will run significantly faster.

Staying with the Library Books example, we will build a hierarchical category tree that can be used to categorize books.

Getting ready

We will reuse the `my_module` addon module from `Chapter 4`, *Creating Odoo Addon Modules*.

How to do it...

We will add a new Python file, `models/library_book_categ.py`, for the category tree, shown as follows:

1. To have the new Python code file loaded, add this line to `models/__init__.py`:

```
from . import library_book_categ
```

2. To create the Book Category model with the parent and child relations, create the `models/library_book_categ.py` file with the following:

```
from odoo import models, fields, api
class BookCategory(models.Model):
    _name = 'library.book.category'
    name = fields.Char('Category')
    parent_id = fields.Many2one(
        'library.book.category',
        string='Parent Category',
        ondelete='restrict',
        index=True)
    child_ids = fields.One2many(
        'library.book.category', 'parent_id',
        string='Child Categories')
```

3. To enable the special hierarchy support, also add the following:

```
_parent_store = True
parent_left = fields.Integer(index=True)
parent_right = fields.Integer(index=True)
```

4. To add a check preventing looping relations, add the following line to the model:

```
@api.constrains('parent_id')
def _check_hierarchy(self):
    if not self._check_recursion():
        raise models.ValidationError(
            'Error! You cannot create recursive categories.')
```

Finally, a module upgrade will make these changes effective.

How it works...

Steps 1 and 2 create the new model with hierarchic relations. The `Many2one` relation adds a field to reference the parent record. For faster child record discovery, this field is indexed in the database using the `index=True` parameter. The `parent_id` field must have `ondelete` set to either `'cascade'` or `'restrict'`.

At this point, we have all that is required to have a hierarchic structure, but there are a few more additions we can make to enhance it.

The `One2many` relation does not add any additional fields to the database, but provides a shortcut to access all the records with this record as their parent.

In step 3, we activate the special support for hierarchies. This is useful for high-read but low-write instructions, since it brings faster data browsing at the expense of costlier write operations. It is done by adding two helper fields, `parent_left` and `parent_right`, and setting the model attribute to `_parent_store=True`. When this attribute is enabled, the two helper fields will be used to store data in searches in the hierarchic tree.

By default, it is assumed that the field for the record's Parent is called `parent_id`, but a different name can be used. In that case, the correct field name should be indicated using the additional model attribute—`_parent_name`. The default is as follows:

```
_parent_name = 'parent_id'
```

Step 4 is advised in order to prevent cyclic dependencies in the hierarchy, that is, having a record both in the ascending and descending trees. This is dangerous for programs that navigate through the tree, since they can get into an infinite loop. The `models.Model` provides a utility method for this (`_check_recursion`) that we have reused here.

There's more...

The technique shown here should be used for "static" hierarchies, which are read and queried often but updated seldom. Book categories are a good example, since the library will not be continuously creating new categories, but readers will often be restricting their searches to a category and all its children categories. The reason for this lies in the implementation of the Nested Set Model in the database, which requires an update of the `parent_left` and `parent_right` columns (and the related database indexes) for all records whenever a category is inserted, removed, or moved. This can be a very expensive operation, especially when multiple editions are being performed in parallel transactions.

> If you are dealing with a very dynamic hierarchical structure, the standard `parent_id` and `child_ids` relations will often result in better performance by avoiding table-level locks.

Adding constraint validations to a Model

Models can have validations preventing them from entering undesired conditions.

Two different types of constraints can be used:

- The ones checked at the database level
- The ones checked at the server level

Database-level constraints are limited to the constraints supported by PostgreSQL. The most commonly used ones are the `UNIQUE` constraints, but the `CHECK` and `EXCLUDE` constraints can also be used. If these are not enough for our needs, we can use Odoo server-level constraints written in Python code.

We will use the Library Book model created in `Chapter 4`, *Creating Odoo Addon Modules*, and add a couple of constraints to it. We will add a database constraint preventing duplicate book titles, and a Python model constraint preventing release dates in the future.

Getting ready

We will reuse the `my_module` addon module from `Chapter 4`, *Creating Odoo Addon Modules*.

We expect it to contain at least the following:

```
from odoo import models, fields
class LibraryBook(models.Model):
    _name = 'library.book'
    name = fields.Char('Title', required=True)
    date_release = fields.Date('Release Date')
```

How to do it...

We will edit the `LibraryBook` class in the `models/library_book_categ.py` Python file:

1. To create the database constraint, add a `model` attribute:

```
class LibraryBook(models.Model):
    # ...
    _sql_constraints = [
        ('name_uniq',
         'UNIQUE (name)',
         'Book title must be unique.')
    ]
```

2. To create the Python code constraint, add a `model` method:

```
from odoo import api
class LibraryBook(models.Model):
    # ...
    @api.constrains('date_release')
    def _check_release_date(self):
    for record in self:
        if (record.date_release and
                record.date_release > fields.Date.today()):
            raise models.ValidationError(
                'Release date must be in the past')
```

After these changes are made to the code file, an addon module upgrade and server restart are needed.

How it works...

The first step has a database constraint created on the model's table. It is enforced at the database level. The `_sql_constraints` model attribute accepts a list of constraints to create. Each constraint is defined by a three-element tuple; they are listed as follows:

- A suffix to use for the constraint identifier. In our example, we used `name_uniq`, and the resulting constraint name is `library_book_name_uniq`.
- The SQL to use in the PostgreSQL instruction to alter or create the database table.
- A message to report to the user when the constraint is violated.

As mentioned earlier, other database table constraints can be used. Note that column constraints, such as NOT NULL, can't be added this way. For more information on PostgreSQL constraints in general and table constraints in particular, take a look at http://www.postgresql.org/docs/current/static/ddl-constraints.html.

In the second step, we added a method to perform Python code validation. It is decorated with @api.constrains, meaning that it should be executed to run checks when one of the fields in the argument list is changed. If the check fails, a ValidationError exception will be raised.

> The _constraints model attribute is still available, but has been deprecated since version 8.0. Instead, we should use methods with the new @api.constrains decorator.

Adding computed fields to a Model

Sometimes, we need to have a field that has a value calculated or derived from other fields in the same record or in related records. A typical example is the total amount that is calculated by multiplying a unit price with a quantity. In Odoo models, this can be achieved using computed fields.

To show how computed fields work, we will add one to the Library Books model to calculate the days since the book's release date.

It is also possible to make computed fields editable and searchable. We will also implement this in our example.

Getting ready

We will reuse the my_module addon module from Chapter 4, *Creating Odoo Addon Modules*.

How to do it...

We will edit the `models/library_book.py` code file to add a new field and the methods supporting its logic:

1. Start by adding the new field to the `Library Books` model:

```
class LibraryBook(models.Model):
    # ...
    age_days = fields.Float(
        string='Days Since Release',
        compute='_compute_age',
        inverse='_inverse_age',
        search='_search_age',
        store=False,
        compute_sudo=False,
    )
```

2. Next, add the method with the value computation logic:

```
# ...
from odoo import api  # if not already imported
from odoo.fields import Date as fDate
# ...
class LibraryBook(models.Model):
    # ...
    @api.depends('date_release')
    def _compute_age(self):
        today = fDate.from_string(fDate.today())
        for book in self.filtered('date_release'):
            delta = (today -
                     fDate.from_string(book.date_release))
            book.age_days = delta.days
```

3. To add the method implementing the logic to write on the computed field, use the following code:

```
from datetime import timedelta
# ...
class LibraryBook(models.Model):
    # ...
    def _inverse_age(self):
        today = fDate.from_string(fDate.context_today(self))
        for book in self.filtered('date_release'):
            d = today - timedelta(days=book.age_days)
            book.date_release = fDate.to_string(d)
```

4. To implement the logic allowing you to search on the computed field, use the following code:

```
# from datetime import timedelta
class LibraryBook(models.Model):
    # ...
    def _search_age(self, operator, value):
        today = fDate.from_string(fDate.context_today(self))
        value_days = timedelta(days=value)
        value_date = fDate.to_string(today - value_days)
        # convert the operator:
        # book with age > value have a date < value_date
        operator_map = {
            '>': '<', '>=': '<=',
            '<': '>', '<=': '>=',
        }
        new_op = operator_map.get(operator, operator)
        return [('date_release', new_op, value_date)]
```

An Odoo restart followed by a module upgrade should be needed to correctly activate these new additions.

How it works...

The definition of a computed field is the same as the one for a regular field, except that a `compute` attribute is added to specify the name of the method to use for its computation.

The similarity can be deceptive, since computed fields are internally quite different from regular fields. Computed fields are dynamically calculated at runtime, and unless you specifically add that support yourself, they are not writeable or searchable.

The computation function is dynamically calculated at runtime, but the ORM uses caching to avoid inefficiently recalculating it every time its value is accessed. So, it needs to know what other fields it depends on, using the `@depends` decorator to detect when its cached values should be invalidated and recalculated.

 Ensure that the `compute` function always sets a value on the computed field. Otherwise, an error will be raised. This can happen when you have `if` conditions in your code that sometimes fail to set a value on the computed field, and can be tricky to debug.

Write support can be added by implementing the `inverse` function; it uses the value assigned to the computed field to update the origin fields. Of course, this only makes sense for simpler calculations; nevertheless, there are still cases where it can be useful. In our example, we make it possible to set the book release date by editing the **Days Since Release** computed field.

It is also possible to make searchable a non-stored computed field by setting the `search` attribute to the method name to use (similar to `compute` and `inverse`).

However, this method is not expected to implement the actual search. Instead, it receives as parameters the operator and value used to search on the field, and is expected to return a domain with the replacement search conditions to use. In our example, we translate a search of the **Days Since Release** field into an equivalent search condition on the **Release Date** field.

The optional `store=True` flag makes the field stored in the database. In this case, after being computed, the field values are stored in the database, and from there on, they are retrieved like regular fields instead of being recomputed at runtime. Thanks to the `@api.depends` decorator, the ORM will know when these stored values need to be recomputed and updated. You can think of it as a persistent cache. It also has the advantage of making the field usable for search conditions, sorting and grouping by operations, without the need to implement the `search` method.

The `compute_sudo=True` flag is to be used in the cases where the computations need to be done with elevated privileges. This can be the case when the computation needs to use data that may not be accessible to the end user.

 Be careful when using this, as it will bypass all security rules, including the company separation rules in a multi-company setup. Ensure that you double-check the domains you use in the computation for possible issues related to this.

Exposing related fields stored in other Models

When reading data from the server, Odoo clients can only get values for the fields available in the model being queried. Client-side code can't use dot notation to access data in the related tables like server-side code can.

However, those fields can be made available there by adding them as related fields. We will do this to make the publisher's city available in the Library Book model.

Getting ready

We will reuse the `my_module` addon module from `Chapter 4`, *Creating Odoo Addon Modules*.

How to do it...

Edit the `models/library_book.py` file to add the new "related" field:

1. Ensure that we have a field for the book publisher:

```
class LibraryBook(models.Model):
    # ...
    publisher_id = fields.Many2one(
        'res.partner', string='Publisher')
```

2. Now, add the related field for the publisher's city:

```
# class LibraryBook(models.Model):
    # ...
    publisher_city = fields.Char(
        'Publisher City',
        related='publisher_id.city',
        readonly=True)
```

Finally, we need to upgrade the addon module for the new fields to be available in the Model.

How it works...

Related fields are just like regular fields, but they have the additional attribute, `related`, with a string for the separated chain of fields to traverse.

In our case, we access the publisher related record through `publisher_id`, and then read its `city` field. We can also have longer chains, such as `publisher_id.country_id.country_code`.

Note that in the recipe, we set the related field as `readonly`. If we don't do that, the field will be writable, and the user may change its value. This will have the effect of changing the value of the `city` field of the related publisher. While this can be a useful side effect, caution needs to be exercised; all the books published by the same publisher will have their `publisher_city` field updated, which may not be what the user expected.

There's more...

Related fields are in fact computed fields. They just provide a convenient shortcut syntax to read field values from related models. As a computed field, this means that the `store` attribute is also available to them. As a shortcut, they also have all the attributes from the referenced field, such as `name`, `translatable`, and `required`.

Additionally, they support a `related_sudo` flag similar to `compute_sudo`; when set to `True`, the field chain is traversed without checking user access rights.

Using related fields in a `create()` method can harm performance, as the computation of theses fields is delayed until the end of the creation. So, if you have a `One2many` relation, such as in the `sale.order` and `sale.order.line` models, and you have a related field on the line model referring to a field on the 'order' model, you should explicitly read the field on the order model during record creation instead of using the related field shortcut, especially if there are a lot of lines.

Adding dynamic relations using Reference fields

With relational fields, we need to decide beforehand the relation's target model (or comodel). However, sometimes we may need to leave that decision to the user and first choose the model we want and then the record we want to link to.

With Odoo, this can be achieved using Reference fields.

Getting ready

We will reuse the `my_module` addon module from Chapter 4, *Creating Odoo Addon Modules*.

How to do it...

Edit the `models/library_book.py` file to add the new related field:

1. We first add a helper method to dynamically build the list of selectable target models:

```
from odoo import models, fields, api
class LibraryBook(models.Model):
    # ...
    @api.model
    def _referencable_models(self):
        models = self.env['res.request.link'].search([])
        return [(x.object, x.name) for x in models]
```

2. Then, we add the Reference field and use the previous function to provide the list of selectable models:

```
ref_doc_id = fields.Reference(
    selection='_referencable_models',
    string='Reference Document')
```

Since we are changing the model's structure, a module upgrade is needed to activate these changes.

How it works...

Reference fields are similar to many-to-one fields, except that they allow the user to select the model to link to.

The target model is selectable from a list provided by the `selection` attribute. The `selection` attribute must be a list of two element tuples, where the first is the model internal identifier, and the second is a text description for it.

Here's an example:

```
[('res.users', 'User'), ('res.partner', 'Partner')]
```

However, rather than providing a fixed list, we can use a model list configurable by end users. That is the purpose of the built-in **Referenceable Models** available in the **Settings | Technical | Database Structure** menu option. This model's internal identifier is `res.request.link`.

Our recipe started with providing a function to browse all the Model records that can be referenced to dynamically build a list to be provided to the `selection` attribute. Although both forms are allowed, we declared the function name inside quotes, instead of a direct reference to the function without quotes. This is more flexible, and for example, allows for the referenced function to be defined only later in the code, which is something that is not possible when using a direct reference.

The function needs the `@api.model` decorator because it operates on the model level, not on the recordset level.

 While this feature looks nice, it comes with a significant execution overhead. Displaying the Reference fields for a large number of records, for instance, in a list view, can create heavy database loads as each value has to be looked up in a separate query. It is also unable to take advantage of database referential integrity, like regular relation fields can.

Adding features to a Model using inheritance

One of the most important Odoo features is the ability of module addons extending features defined in other module addons without having to edit the code of the original feature. This might be to add fields or methods, modify the existing fields, or extend the existing methods to perform additional logic.

It is the most frequently used method of inheritance and is referred to by the official documentation as **traditional inheritance** or **classical inheritance**.

We will extend the built-in Partner model to add it to a computed field with the authored book count. This involves adding a field and a method to an existing model.

Getting ready

We will reuse the `my_module` addon module from `Chapter 4`, *Creating Odoo Addon Modules*.

How to do it...

We will be extending the built-in Partner model. We should do this in its own Python code file, but to keep the explanation as simple we can, we will reuse the `models/library_book.py` code file:

1. First, we ensure that the `authored_book_ids` inverse relation is in the Partner model and add the computed field:

```
class ResPartner(models.Model):
    _inherit = 'res.partner'
    _order = 'name'
    authored_book_ids = fields.Many2many(
        'library.book', string='Authored Books')
    count_books = fields.Integer(
        'Number of Authored Books',
        compute='_compute_count_books'
        )
```

2. Next, add the method needed to compute the book count:

```
# ...
from odoo import api  # if not already imported
# class ResPartner(models.Model):
    # ...
    @api.depends('authored_book_ids')
    def _compute_count_books(self):
        for r in self:
            r.count_books = len(r.authored_book_ids)
```

Finally, we need to upgrade the addon module for the modifications to take effect.

How it works...

When a model class is defined with the `_inherit` attribute, it adds modifications to the inherited model rather than replacing it.

This means that fields defined in the inheriting class are added or changed on the parent model. At the database layer, it is adding fields on the same database table.

Fields are also incrementally modified. This means that if the field already exists in the superclass, only the attributes declared in the inherited class are modified; the other ones are kept as in the parent class.

Methods defined in the inheriting class replace the method in the parent class. So, unless they include a call to the parent's version of the method, we will lose features. Due to this, when we want to add logic to the existing methods, they should include a statement with `super` to call its version in the parent class. This is discussed in more detail in `Chapter 6`, *Basic Server-Side Development*.

There's more...

With the `_inherit` traditional inheritance, it's also possible to copy the parent model's features into a completely new model. This is done by simply adding a `_name` class attribute with a different identifier. Here's an example:

```
class LibraryMember(models.Model):
    _inherit = 'res.partner'
    _name = 'library.member'
```

The new model has its own database table with its own data totally independent from the `res.partner` parent model. Since it still inherits from the Partner model, any later modifications to it will also affect the new model.

In the official documentation, this is called **prototype inheritance**, but in practice, it is seldom used. The reason is that delegation inheritance usually answers to that need in a more efficient way, without the need to duplicate data structures. For more information on it, you can refer to the *Using Delegation inheritance to copy features to another Model* recipe.

Using abstract Models for reusable Model features

Sometimes, there is a particular feature that we want to be able to add to several different models. Repeating the same code in different files is bad programming practice, so it would be nice to be able to implement it once and be able to reuse it many times.

Abstract models allow us to just create a generic model that implements some feature that can then be inherited by regular models in order to make that feature available in them.

As an example, we will implement a simple `Archive` feature. It adds the `active` field to the model (if it doesn't exist already) and makes an archive method available to toggle the `active` flag. This works because `active` is a magic field; if present in a model by default, the records with `active=False` will be filtered out from queries.

We will then add it to the Library Book model.

Getting ready

We will reuse the `my_module` addon module from `Chapter 4`, *Creating Odoo Addon Modules*.

How to do it...

The archive feature will certainly deserve its own addon module, or at least its own Python code file. However, to keep the explanation as simple as possible, we will cram it into the `models/library_book.py` file:

1. Add the abstract model for the archive feature. It must be defined in the Library Book model, where it will be used:

```
class BaseArchive(models.AbstractModel):
    _name = 'base.archive'
    active = fields.Boolean(default=True)

    def do_archive(self):
        for record in self:
            record.active = not record.active
```

2. Now, we will edit the Library Book model to inherit the Archive model:

```
class LibraryBook(models.Model):
    _name = 'library.book'
    _inherit = ['base.archive']
    # ...
```

An upgrade to the addon module is needed for the changes to be activated.

How it works...

An Abstract model is created by a class based on `models.AbstractModel` instead of the usual `models.Model`. It has all the attributes and capabilities of regular models; the difference is that the ORM will not create an actual representation for it in the database. So, it can have no data stored in it. It serves only as a template for a reusable feature that is to be added to regular models.

Our Archive abstract model is quite simple; it just adds the `active` field and a method to toggle the value of the `active` flag, which we expect to later be used via a button on the user interface.

When a model class is defined with the `_inherit` attribute, it inherits the attribute methods of those classes, and what is defined in our class adds modifications to these inherited features.

The mechanism at play here is the same as that for a regular model extension (as per the *Adding features to a Model using inheritance* recipe). You may have noticed that here, `_inherit` uses a list of model identifiers instead of a string with one model identifier. In fact, `_inherit` can have both forms. Using the list form allows us to inherit from multiple (usually Abstract) classes. In this case, we are inheriting just one, so a text string would be fine. A list was used instead to underline that a list can be used.

There's more...

A noteworthy built-in abstract model is `mail.thread`, provided by the `mail` (Discuss) addon module. It enables, on models, the discussion features that power the message wall seen at the bottom of many forms.

Other than `AbstractModel`, a third model type is available, which is `models.TransientModel`.

It has database representation like `models.Model`, but the records created there are supposed to be temporary and regularly purged by a server-scheduled job. Other than that, Transient models work just like regular models.

They are useful for more complex user interactions known as wizards, for example, to request the user some input to then run a process or a report. In `Chapter 9`, *Advanced Server-Side Development Techniques*, we explore how to use them for advanced user interaction.

Using delegation inheritance to copy features to another Model

Traditional inheritance using `_inherit` performs in-place modification to extend the model's features.

However, there are cases where rather than modifying an existing model, we want to create a new model based on an existing one to leverage the features it already has. This is one with Odoo's **delegation inheritance** that uses the _inherits model attribute (note the additional s).

Traditional inheritance is quite different than the concept in object-oriented programming. Delegation inheritance, in turn, is similar in that a new model can be created to include the features from a parent model. It also supports polymorphic inheritance, where we inherit from two or more other models.

We have a library with books. It's about time for our library to also have members. For a library member, we need all the identification and address data found in the Partner model, and we also want it to keep some information regarding the membership: a start date, termination date, and card number.

Adding those fields to the Partner model is not the best solution since they will be not be used for Partners that are not members. It would be great to extend the Partner model to a new model with some additional fields.

Getting ready

We will reuse the my_module addon module from Chapter 4, *Creating Odoo Addon Modules*.

How to do it...

The new Library Member model should be in its own Python code file, but to keep the explanation as simple as possible, we will reuse the models/library_book.py file:

1. Add the new model, inheriting from res.partner:

```
# from odoo import models, fields  # if not done yet
class LibraryMember(models.Model):
    _name = 'library.member'
    _inherits = {'res.partner': 'partner_id'}
    partner_id = fields.Many2one(
        'res.partner',
        ondelete='cascade')
```

2. Next, we add the fields that are specific to Library Members:

```
# class LibraryMember(models.Model):
    # ...
    date_start = fields.Date('Member Since')
    date_end = fields.Date('Termination Date')
    member_number = fields.Char()
    date_of_birth = fields.Date('Date of birth')
```

Now, we should upgrade the addon module to have the changes activated.

How it works...

The `_inherits` model attribute sets the parent models that we want to inherit from. In this case, just one—`res.partner`. Its value is a key-value dictionary where the keys are the inherited models, and the values are the field names used to link to them. These are `Many2one` fields that we must also define in the model. In our example, `partner_id` is the field that will be used to link with the `Partner` parent model.

To better understand how it works, let's look at what happens on the database level when we create a new Member:

- A new record is created in the `res_partner` table
- A new record is created in the `library_member` table
- The `partner_id` field of the `library_member` table is set to the `id` of the `res_partner` record that is created for it

The Member record is automatically linked to a new Partner record. It's just a many-to-one relation, but the delegation mechanism adds some magic so that the Partner's fields are seen as if belonging to the Member record, and a new Partner record is also automatically created with the new Member.

You might like to know that this automatically created Partner record has nothing special about it. It's a regular Partner, and if you browse the Partner model, you will be able to find that record (without the additional Member data, of course). All Members are at the same time Partners, but only some Partners are also Members.

So, what happens if you delete a Partner record that is also a Member? You decide by choosing the `ondelete` value for the relation field. For `partner_id`, we used `cascade`. This means that deleting the Partner will also delete the corresponding Member. We could have used the more conservative setting `restrict` to forbid deleting the Partner while it has a linked Member. In this case, only deleting the Member will work.

It's important to note that delegation inheritance only works for fields and not for methods. So, if the Partner model has a `do_something()` method, the Members model will not automatically inherit it.

There's more...

A noteworthy case of delegation inheritance is the Users model, `res.users`. It inherits from Partners (`res.partner`). This means that some of the fields that you can see on the User are actually stored in the Partner model (notably, the `name` field). When a new User is created, we also get a new automatically created Partner.

We should also mention that traditional inheritance with `_inherit` can also copy features into a new model, although in a less efficient way. This was discussed in the *Adding features to a Model using inheritance* recipe.

6

Basic Server-Side Development

In this chapter, we will cover the following topics:

- Defining model methods and using the API decorators
- Reporting errors to the user
- Obtaining an empty recordset for a different model
- Creating new records
- Updating values of recordset records
- Searching for records
- Combining recordsets
- Filtering recordsets
- Traversing recordset relations
- Extending the business logic defined in a Model
- Extending write() and create()
- Customizing how records are searched

Introduction

In Chapter 5, *Application Models*, we saw how to declare or extend business models in custom modules. The recipes in that chapter cover writing methods for computed fields as well as methods to constrain the values of fields. This chapter focuses on the basics of server-side development in Odoo-method definitions, recordset manipulation, and extending inherited methods.

Defining model methods and using the API decorators

The model classes defining custom data models declare fields for the data processed by the model. They can also define custom behavior by defining methods on the model class.

In this recipe, we will see how to write a method that can be called by a button in the user interface, or by some other piece of code in our application. This method will act on `LibraryBooks` and perform the required actions to change the state of a selection of books.

Getting ready

This recipe assumes that you have an instance ready, with the `my_module` addon module available, as described in Chapter 4, *Creating Odoo Addon Modules*. You will need to add a state field to the `LibraryBook` model, defined as follows:

```
from odoo import models, fields, api
class LibraryBook(models.Model):
    # [...]
    state = fields.Selection([('draft', 'Unavailable'),
                              ('available', 'Available'),
                              ('borrowed', 'Borrowed'),
                              ('lost', 'Lost')],
                             'State')
```

Refer to the recipe *Adding models* in Chapter 4, *Creating Odoo Addon Modules* for more clarity.

How to do it...

For defining a method on `Library Book` to allow changing the state of a selection of books, you need to add the following code to the model definition:

1. Add a helper method to check whether a state transition is allowed:

```
@api.model
def is_allowed_transition(self, old_state, new_state):
    allowed = [('draft', 'available'),
               ('available', 'borrowed'),
               ('borrowed', 'available'),
               ('available', 'lost'),
```

```
                    ('borrowed', 'lost'),
                    ('lost', 'available')]
        return (old_state, new_state) in allowed
```

2. Add a method to change the state of some books to a new one passed as an argument:

```
@api.multi
def change_state(self, new_state):
    for book in self:
        if book.is_allowed_transition(book.state,
                                      new_state):
            book.state = new_state
        else:
            continue
```

How it works...

The code in the recipe defines two methods. They are normal Python methods, having `self` as their first argument, and can have additional arguments as well. The methods are decorated with **decorators** from the `odoo.api` module.

> A number of these decorators were initially introduced in Odoo 9.0 to ensure that the conversion of calls is made using the **old** or **traditional** API to the **new** API. As of Odoo 10.0, the old API is no longer supported, but the decorators are a core part of the new API.

When writing a new method, you will generally use `@api.multi`. This decorator indicates that the method is meant to be executed on a recordset. In such methods, `self` is a recordset that can refer to an arbitrary number of database records (this includes empty recordsets), and the code will often loop over the records in `self` to do something on each individual record.

The `@api.model` decorator is similar, but it's used on methods for which only the model is important, not the contents of the recordset, which is not acted upon by the method. The concept is similar to Python's `@classmethod` decorator.

Here's an example code snippet calling the `change_state()` method from the recipe:

```
# returned_book_ids is a list of book ids to return
books = self.env['library.book']
books.browse(returned_book_ids).change_state('available')
```

When `change_state()` is called, `self` is a (possibly empty) recordset containing records of the `library.book` model. The body of the `change_state()` method loops over `self` to process each book in the recordset. Looping on `self` looks strange at first, but you will get used to this pattern very quickly.

Inside the loop, `change_state()` calls `is_allowed_transition()`. The call is made using the `book` local variable, but it can be made on any recordset for the `library.book` model, including, for example, `self`, since `is_allowed_transition()` is decorated with `@api.model`. If the transition is allowed, `change_state()` assigns the new state to the book by assigning a value to the attribute of the recordset. This is only valid on recordsets of length `1`, which is guaranteed to be the case when iterating over `self`.

There's more...

You may encounter the `@api.one` decorator while reading source code. This decorator is **deprecated** because its behavior can be confusing at first glance; also, knowing of `@api.multi`, it looks like this decorator allows the method to be called only on recordsets of size `1`, but it does not. When it comes to recordset length, `@api.one` is similar to `@api.multi`, but it does a `for` loop on the recordset outside the method and aggregates the returned value of each iteration of the loop in a list, which is returned to the caller.

 Avoid using `@api.one` in your code. You may want to check out the `foreach` decorator defined in the **oca-decorators** project (`https://github.com/OCA/oca-decorators`), which serves a similar purpose but with clearer semantics.

See also

Refer to the *Adding buttons to form* recipe in `Chapter 10`, *Backend Views*, to learn how to call such a method from the user interface.

Reporting errors to the user

During method execution, it is sometimes necessary to abort the processing because an error condition was met. This recipe shows how to do this so that a helpful error message is displayed to the user when a method that writes a file to disk encounters an error.

Getting ready

To use this recipe, you need a method with an error condition. We will use the following one:

```
import os
from odoo import models, fields, api

class SomeModel(models.Model):
    _name = 'some.model'
    data = fields.Text('Data')

    @api.multi
    def save(self, filename):
        path = os.path.join('/opt/exports', filename)
        with open(path, 'w') as fobj:
            for record in self:
                fobj.write(record.data)
                fobj.write('\n')
```

This method can fail because of permission issues, or a full disk, or an illegal name, which will cause an IOError or an OSError exception to be raised.

How to do it...

To display an error message to the user when an error condition is encountered, you need to take the following steps:

1. Add the following import at the beginning of the Python file:

```
from odoo.exceptions import UserError
from odoo.tools.translate import _
```

2. Modify the method to catch the exception raised and raise a UserError exception:

```
@api.multi
def save(self, filename):
    if '/' in filename or '\\' in filename:
        raise UserError('Illegal filename %s' % filename)
    path = os.path.join('/opt/exports', filename)
    try:
        with open(path, 'w') as fobj:
            for record in self:
                fobj.write(record.data)
```

```
                    fobj.write('\n')
        except (IOError, OSError) as exc:
            message = _('Unable to save file: %s') % exc
            raise UserError(message)
```

How it works...

When an exception is raised in Python, it propagates up the call stack until it is processed. In Odoo, the RPC layer that answers the calls made by the web client catches all exceptions and, depending on the exception class, it will trigger different possible behaviors on the web client.

Any exception not defined in odoo.exceptions will be handled as an Internal Server Error (**HTTP status 500**), with the stack trace. A UserError will display an error message in the user interface. The code of the recipe changes the OSError to a UserError to ensure that the message is displayed in a friendly way. In all cases, the current database transaction is rolled back.

Of course, it is not required to catch an exception with a try..except, construct to raise a UserError exception. It is perfectly okay to test for some condition, such as the presence of illegal characters in a filename, and to raise the exception when that test is True. This will prevent further processing of the user request.

We are using a function with a strange name, _(), defined in odoo.tools.translate. This function is used to mark a string as translatable, and to retrieve the translated string at runtime, given the language of the end user found in the execution context. More information is available in Chapter 12, *Internationalization*.

When using the _() function, ensure that you pass it the string with the interpolation placeholder, not the interpolated string:

```
_('Warning: could not find %s') % value
```
is correct, but
```
_('Warning: could not find %s' % value)
```
is not.

This last version will certainly not find the string with the substituted value in the translation database.

There's more...

There are a few more exception classes defined in odoo.exceptions, all deriving the base legacy except_orm exception class. Most of them are only used internally, apart from the following:

- Warning: In Odoo 8.0, odoo.exceptions.Warning played the role of UserError in 9.0 and later. It is now deprecated because the name was deceptive (it is an error, not a warning) and it collided with the Python built-in Warning class. It is kept for backward compatibility only, and you should use UserError in your code.

- ValidationError: This exception is raised when a Python constraint on a field is not respected. In Chapter 5, *Application Models*, refer to the *Adding constraint validations to a Model* recipe for more information.

Obtaining an empty recordset for a different model

When writing Odoo code, the methods of the current model are available via self. If you need to work on a different model, it is not possible to directly instantiate the class of that model; you need to get a recordset for that model to start working.

This recipe shows how to get an empty recordset for any model registered in Odoo inside a model method.

Getting ready

This recipe will reuse the setup of the library example in the my_module addon module.

We will write a small method in the library.book model searching for all library.members. To do this, we need to get an empty recordset for library.members.

How to do it...

To get a recordset for `library.members` in a method of `library.book`, you need to take the following steps:

1. In the `LibraryBook` class, write a method called `get_all_library_members`:

```
class LibraryBook(models.Model):
    # ...
    @api.model
    def get_all_library_members(self):
        # ...
```

2. In the body of the method, use the following code:

```
library_member_model = self.env['library.member']
return library_member_model.search([])
```

How it works...

At start up, Odoo loads all the modules and combines the various classes deriving from `Model` and defining or extending a given model. These classes are stored in the Odoo **registry** indexed by name. The `env` attribute of any recordset, available as `self.env`, is an instance of the `Environment` class defined in the `odoo.api` module. This class plays a central role in Odoo development:

- It provides a a shortcut access to the registry by emulating a Python dictionary; if you know the name of the model you're looking for, `self.env[model_name]` will get you an empty recordset for that model. Moreover, the recordset will share the environment of `self`.
- It has a `cr` attribute that is a database cursor you may use to pass raw SQL query. Refer to the *Execute raw SQL queries* recipe in `Chapter 9`, *Advanced Server-Side Development Techniques*, for more on this.
- It has a `user` attribute that is a reference to the current user performing the call. Take a look at `Chapter 9`, *Advanced Server-Side Development Techniques*; for more on this, refer to the *Changing the user performing an action* recipe.
- It has a `context` attribute that is a dictionary containing the context of the call. This includes information about the language of the user, the timezone, the current selection of records, and many more. Refer to the *Call a method with a modified context* recipe in `Chapter 9`, *Advanced Server-Side Development Techniques* for more on this.

The call to `search()` is explained in the *Searching for records* recipe later.

See also

The *Changing the user performing an action* and *Calling a method with a modified environment* recipes in `Chapter 9`, *Advanced Server-Side Development Techniques*, deal with modifying `self.env` at runtime.

Creating new records

A frequent need when writing business logic methods is to create new records. This recipe explains how to create records of the `res.partner` model, which is defined in Odoo's `base` addon module. We will create a new partner representing a company, with some contacts.

Getting ready

You need to know the structure of the models for which you want to create a record, especially their names and types as well as any constraints existing on these fields (for example, whether some of them are mandatory). The `res.partner` model defined in Odoo has a very large number of fields, and to keep things simple, we will only use a few of these. To help you follow the recipe, here's a restricted definition of the model we will use in this recipe:

```
class ResPartner(models.Model):
    _name = 'res.partner'
    name = fields.Char('Name', required=True)
    email = fields.Char('Email')
    date = fields.Date('Date')
    is_company = fields.Boolean(
        'Is a company',
        help="Check if the contact is a company, "
                "otherwise it is a person"
    )
    parent_id = fields.Many2one('res.partner', 'Related Company')
    child_ids = fields.One2many('res.partner', 'parent_id',
                                 'Contacts')
```

How to do it...

In order to create a partner with some contacts, you need to take the following steps:

1. Inside the method that needs to create a new partner, get the current date formatted as a string expected by `create()`:

```
def some_method(self):
    today_str = fields.Date.context_today(self)
```

2. Prepare a dictionary of values for the fields of the first contact:

```
val1 = {'name': 'Eric Idle',
        'email': 'eric.idle@example.com'
        'date': today_str}
```

3. Prepare a dictionary of values for the fields of the second contact:

```
val2 = {'name': 'John Cleese',
        'email': 'john.cleese@example.com',
        'date': today_str}
```

4. Prepare a dictionary of values for the fields of the company:

```
partner_val = {
    'name': 'Flying Circus',
    'email': 'm.python@example.com',
    'date': today_str,
    'is_company': True,
    'child_ids': [(0, 0, val1),
                  (0, 0, val2),
                  ]
}
```

5. Call the `create()` method to create the new records:

```
record = self.env['res.partner'].create(partner_val)
```

How it works...

To create a new record for a model, we can call the `create(values)` method on any recordset related to the model. This method returns a new recordset of length 1 containing the new record, with field values specified in the `values` dictionary.

In the dictionary, the keys give the name of the fields, and the corresponding values correspond to the value of the field. Depending on the field type, you need to pass different Python type for the values:

- `Text` field values are given with Python strings.
- `Float` and `Integer` field values are given using Python floats or integers.
- `Boolean` field values are given, preferably using Python booleans or integer.
- `Date` (respectively `Datetime`) field values are given as Python strings (expressed in UTC for `Datetime` fields). Use `fields.Date.to_string()` (respectively `fields.Datetime.to_string()`) to convert a Python `datetime.date` (respectively `datetime.datetime`) object to the expected format.
- `Binary` field values are passed as a Base64 encoded string. The `base64` module from the Python standard library provides methods such as `encodebytes(bytestring)` to encode a string in Base64.
- `Many2one` field values are given with an integer, which has to be the database ID of the related record.
- `One2many` and `Many2many` fields use a special syntax. The value is a list containing tuples of three elements, as follows:

Tuple	Effect
`(0, 0, dict_val)`	Create a new record that will be related to the main record.
`(6, 0, id_list)`	Create a relation between the record being created and existing records, whose IDs are in the Python list `id_list`. Caution: when used on a `One2many`, this will remove the records from any previous relation.

In the recipe, we create the dictionaries for two contacts in the company we want to create, and then we use these dictionaries in the `child_ids` entry of the dictionary for the company being created, using the `(0, 0, dict_val)` syntax explained earlier.

When `create()` is called in step 5, three records are created:

- One for the main partner company, which is returned by `create`
- One for each of the two contacts, which are available in `record.child_ids`

There's more...

If the model defined some **default values** for some fields, nothing special needs to be done; `create()` will take care of computing the default values for the fields not present in the supplied dictionary.

On the other hand, `onchange` methods are not called by `create()`, because they are called by the web client during the initial edition of the record. Some of these methods compute default values for fields related to a given field. When creating records by hand, you have to do the work yourself, either by providing explicit values or by calling the onchange methods. The *Calling onchange methods on the server side* recipe in `Chapter 9`, *Advanced Server-Side Development Techniques*, explains how to do this.

Updating values of recordset records

Business logic often means updating records by changing the values of some of their fields. This recipe shows how to add a contact for a partner and modify the date field of the partner as we go.

Getting ready

This recipe will use the same simplified `res.partner` definition as the *Creating new records* recipe. You may refer to this simplified definition to know the fields.

The `date` field of `res.partner` has no defined meaning in Odoo. In order to illustrate our purpose, we will use this to record an activity date on the partner, so creating a new contact should update the date of the partner.

How to do it...

To update a partner, you can write a new method called `add_contact()`, defined like this:

```
@api.model
def add_contacts(self, partner, contacts):
    partner.ensure_one()
    if contacts:
        partner.date = fields.Date.context_today(self)
        partner.child_ids |= contacts
```

How it works...

The method starts by checking whether the partner passed as an argument contains exactly one record by calling `ensure_one()`. This method will raise an exception if this is not the case, and the processing will abort. This is needed, because we cannot add the same contacts to several partners at the same time.

Then, the method checks that the `contacts` recordset is not empty, because we don't want to update the `date` of the partner if we are not modifying it.

Finally, the method modifies the values of the attributes of the partner record. Since `child_ids` is a `One2many` relation, its value is a recordset. We use `|=` to compute the union of the current contacts of the partner and the new contacts passed to the method. Refer to the *Combining recordsets* recipe for more information on these operators.

Note that no assumption is made on `self`. This method can be defined on any model class.

There's more...

There are three options available if you want to write new values to the fields of records:

- Option 1 is the one explained in the recipe, and it works in all contexts, assigning values directly on the attribute representing the field of the record. It is not possible to assign a value to all recordset elements in one go, so you need to iterate on the recordset, unless you are certain that you are only handling a single record.

- Option 2 is to use the update() method by passing a dictionary mapping field names to the values you want to set. This also only works for recordsets of length 1. It can save some typing when you need to update the values of several fields at once on the same record. Here's step 2 of the recipe, rewritten to use this option:

```
@api.model
def add_contacts(self, partner, contacts):
    partner.ensure_one()
    if contacts:
        today = fields.Date.context_today(self)
        partner.update(
            {'date': today,
             'child_ids': partner.child_ids | contacts}
        )
```

- Option 3 is to call the write() method, passing a dictionary mapping field names to the values you want to set. This method works for recordsets of arbitrary size and will update all records with the specified values in one single database operation when the two previous options perform one database call per record and per field. However, it has some limitations:
  - It does not work if the records are not yet present in the database (refer to the *Writing onchange methods* recipe in Chapter 9, *Advanced Server-Side Development Techniques*, for more information on this)

- It requires using a special format when writing relational fields, similar to the one used by the `create()` method:

Tuple	Effect
`(0, 0, dict_val)`	This creates a new record that will be related to the main record.
`(1, id, dict_val)`	This updates the related record with the specified ID with the supplied values.
`(2, id)`	This removes the record with the specified ID from the related records and deletes it from the database.
`(3, id)`	This removes the record with the specified ID from the related records. The record is not deleted from the database.
`(4, id)`	This adds an existing record with the supplied ID to the list of related records.
`(5, )`	This removes all the related records, equivalent to calling `(3, id)` for each related `id`.
`(6, 0, id_list)`	This creates a relation between the record being updated and the existing record, whose IDs are in the Python list `id_list`.

At the time of writing, the official documentation is outdated and mentions that the operation numbers 3, 4, 5, and 6 are not available on `One2many` fields, which is no longer true. However, some of these may not work with `One2many` fields, depending on constraints on the models; for instance, if the reverse `Many2one` relation is required, then operation 3 will fail because it will result in an unset `Many2one` relation.

Searching for records

Searching for records is also a common operation in business logic methods. This recipe shows us how to find all the `Partner` companies and their contacts by company name.

Getting ready

This recipe will use the same simplified `res.partner` definition as the *Creating new records* recipe previously. You may refer to this simplified definition to know the fields.

We will write the code in a method called `find_partners_and_contact(self, name)`.

How to do it...

In order to find the partners, you need to perform the following steps:

1. Get an empty recordset for `res.partner`:

```
@api.model
def find_partners_and_contacts(self, name):
    partner = self.env['res.partner']
```

2. Write the search domain for your criteria:

```
domain = ['|',
          '&',
          ('is_company', '=', True),
          ('name', 'like', name),
          '&',
          ('is_company', '=', False),
          ('parent_id.name', 'like', name)
          ]
```

3. Call the `search()` method with the domain and return the recordset:

```
return partner.search(domain)
```

How it works...

Step 1 defines the method. Since we are not using the contents of `self`, we decorate it with `@api.model`, but this is not linked to the purpose of this recipe. Then, we get an empty recordset for the `res.partner` model because we need it to search the `res.partner` records.

Step 2 creates a search domain in a local variable. Often, you'll see this creation inlined in the call to search, but with complex domains, it is a good practice to define it separately.

For a full explanation of the **search domain** syntax, refer to the *Defining filters on record lists: Domain* recipe in `Chapter 10`, *Backend Views*.

Step 3 calls the `search()` method with the domain. The method returns a recordset containing all records matching the domain, which can then be further processed. In the recipe, we call the method with just the domain, but the following keyword arguments are also supported:

- `offset=N`: This is used to skip the `N` first records that match the query. This can be used along with `limit` to implement pagination or to reduce memory consumption when processing a very large number of records. It defaults to `0`.
- `limit=N`: Return at most `N` records. By default, there is no limit.
- `order=sort_specification`: This is used to force the order on the returned recordset. By default, the order is given by the `_order` attribute of the model class.
- `count=boolean`: If `True`, this returns the number of records instead of the recordset. It defaults to `False`.

 We recommend using the `search_count(domain)` method rather than `search(domain, count=True)`, as the name of the method conveys the behavior in a much clearer way; both will give the same result.

There's more...

We said that the `search()` method returned all the records matching the domain. This is not completely true. The method ensures that only records to which the user performing the search has access are returned. Additionally, if the model has a `boolean` field called **active** and no term of the search domain is specifying a condition on that field, then an implicit condition is added by search to only return `active=True` records. So, if you expect a search to return something but you only get empty recordsets, ensure that you check the value of the `active` field (if present) and to check for **record rules**.

Refer to the *Calling a method with a different context* recipe in Chapter 9, *Advanced Server-Side Development Techniques*, for a way to not have the implicit `active = True` condition added. Take a look at the *Limit record access using record rules* recipe in Chapter 11, *Access Security*, for more information about record-level access rules.

If for some reason, you find yourself writing raw SQL queries to find record IDs, ensure that you use `self.env['record.model'].search([('id', 'in', tuple(ids))]).ids` after retrieving the IDs to ensure that security rules are applied. This is especially important in **multicompany** Odoo instances where record rules are used to ensure proper discrimination between companies.

Combining recordsets

Sometimes, you will find that you have obtained recordsets that are not exactly what you need. This recipe shows various ways of combining them.

Getting ready

To use this recipe, you need to have two or more recordsets for the same model.

How to do it...

Here's the way to achieve common operations on recordsets:

1. To merge two recordsets into one while preserving their order, use the following operation:

   ```
   result = recordset1 + recordset2
   ```

2. To merge two recordsets into one while ensuring that there are no duplicates in the result, use the following operation:

   ```
   result = recordset1 | recordset2
   ```

3. To find the records that are common to two recordsets, use the following operation:

   ```
   result = recordset1 & recordset2
   ```

How it works...

The class for recordsets implements various Python operator redefinitions, which are used here. Here's a summary table of the most useful Python operators that can be used on recordsets:

Operator	Action performed
R1 + R2	This returns a new recordset containing the records from R1, followed by the records from R2. This can generate duplicate records in the recordset.
R1 – R2	This returns a new recordset consisting of the records from R1, which are not in R2. The order is preserved.
R1 & R2	This returns a new recordset with all the records that belong to both R1 and R2 (intersection of recordsets). The order is *not* preserved here.
R1 | R2	This returns a new recordset with the records belonging to either R1 or R2 (union of recordsets). The order is *not* preserved, but there are no duplicates.
R1 == R2	True if both recordsets contain the same records.
R1 <= R2 R1 in R2	True if all records in R1 are also in R2. Both syntaxes are equivalent.
R1 >= R2 R2 in R1	True if all records in R2 are also in R1. Both syntaxes are equivalent.
R1 != R2	True if R1 and R2 do not contain the same records.

There are also in-place operators +=, –=, &=, and |=, which modify the left-hand side operand instead of creating a new recordset. These are very useful when updating a record's One2many or Many2many fields. Refer to the *Updating values of recordset records* recipe previously for an example.

There's more...

The sorted() method will sort the records in a recordset. Called without arguments, the _order attribute of the model will be used. Otherwise, a function can be passed to compute a comparison key in the same fashion as the Python built-in sorted(sequence, key) function. The reverse keyword argument is also supported.

A note about performance
When the default `_order` parameter of the model is used, the sorting is delegated to the database and a new `SELECT` function is performed to get the order. Otherwise, the sorting is performed by Odoo. Depending on what is being manipulated, and depending on the size of the recordsets, there can be some important performance differences.

Filtering recordsets

In some cases, you already have a recordset, but you need to operate only on some records. You can, of course, iterate on the recordset, checking for the condition on each iteration and acting depending on the result of the check. It can be easier, and in some cases, more efficient, to construct a new recordset containing only the interesting records and calling a single operation on that recordset.

This recipe shows how to use the `filter()` method to extract a recordset from another one.

Getting ready

We will reuse the simplified `res.partner` model shown in the *Creating new records* recipe previously. This recipe defines a method to extract partners having an email address from a supplied recordset.

How to do it...

In order to extract records with an email address from a recordset, you need to perform the following steps:

1. Define the method accepting the original recordset:

```
@api.model
def partners_with_email(self, partners):
```

2. Define an inner predicate function:

```
def predicate(partner):
    if partner.email:
        return True
    return False
```

3. Call `filter()`, as follows:

```
return partners.filter(predicate)
```

How it works...

The implementation of the `filter()` method of recordsets creates an empty recordset in which it adds all the records for which the predicate function evaluates to `True`. The new recordset is finally returned. The order of records in the original recordset is preserved.

The preceding recipe used a named internal function. For such simple predicates, you will often find an anonymous lambda function used:

```
@api.model
def partners_with_email(self, partners):
    return partners.filter(lambda p: p.email)
```

Actually, to filter a recordset based on the fact that the value of a field is *truthy* in the Python sense (non-empty strings, non-zero numbers, non-empty containers, and so on), you can pass the field name to filter like this `partners.filter('email')`.

There's more...

Keep in mind that `filter()` operates in the memory. If you are trying to optimize the performance of a method on the critical path, you may want to use a search domain or even move to SQL, at the cost of readability.

Traversing recordset relations

When working with a recordset of length 1, the various fields are available as record attributes. Relational attributes (One2many, Many2one, and Many2many) are also available with values that are recordsets too. When working with recordsets with more than one record, the attributes cannot be used.

This recipe shows you how to use the `mapped()` method to traverse recordset relations; we will write two methods performing the following operations:

- Retrieving the emails of all contacts of one or more companies passed as an argument
- Retrieving the various companies to which some contact partners are related

Getting ready

We will reuse the simplified Partner model shown in the *Create new records* recipe of this chapter.

How to do it...

To write the partner manipulation methods, you need to perform the following steps:

1. Define a method called `get_email_addresses()`:

```
@api.model
def get_email_addresses(self, partner):
```

2. Call `mapped()` to get the email addresses of the contacts of the partner:

```
return partner.mapped('child_ids.email')
```

3. Define a method called `get_companies()`:

```
@api.model
def get_companies(self, partners):
```

4. Call `mapped()` to get the different companies of the partners:

```
return partners.mapped('parent_id')
```

How it works...

Step 1 and 3 are straightforward. Let's jump straight to the interesting parts of the recipe. In step 2 and step 4, we call the mapped(path) method to traverse the fields of the recordset; path is a string containing field names separated by dots. For each field in the path, mapped() produces a new recordset containing all the records related by this field to all elements in the current recordset and then applies the next element in the path on that new recordset. If the last field in the path is a relational field, mapped() will return a recordset; otherwise, a Python list is returned.

The mapped() method has two remarkable properties:

- If the path is a single scalar field name, then the returned list is in the same order as the processed recordset
- If the path contains a relational field, then order is not preserved, but duplicates are removed from the result

 This second property is very useful in a method decorated with @api.multi, where you want to perform an operation on all the records pointed by a Many2many field of all records in self, but need to ensure that the action is performed only once (even if two records of self share the same target record).

There's more...

When using mapped(), keep in mind that it operates in the memory inside the Odoo server by repeatedly traversing relations and therefore making SQL queries, which may not be efficient; however, the code is terse and expressive. If you are trying to optimize a method on the critical path of the performance of your instance, you may want to rewrite the call to mapped() and express it as a search() with the appropriate domain, or even move to SQL (at the cost of readability).

The mapped() method can also be called with a function as argument. In this case, it returns a list containing the result of the function applied to each record of self, or the union of the recordsets returned by the function, if the function returns a recordset.

See also

- The *Searching for records* recipe
- The *Executing raw SQL queries* recipe in `Chapter 9`, *Advanced Server-Side Development Techniques*

Extending the business logic defined in a Model

When defining a model that extends another model, it is often necessary to customize the behavior of some methods defined on the original model. This is a very easy task in Odoo, and one of the most powerful features of the underlying framework.

We will demonstrate this by extending a method that creates records to add a new field in the created records.

Getting ready

If you want to follow the recipe, ensure that you have the `my_module` addon from `Chapter 4`, *Creating Odoo addon Modules*, with the loan wizard defined in the *Writing a wizard to guide the user* recipe from `Chapter 9`, *Advanced Server-Side Development Techniques*.

Create a new addon module called `library_loan_return_date` that depends on `my_module`. In this module, extend the `library.book.loan` model, as follows:

```
class LibraryBookLoan(models.Model):
    _inherit = 'library.book.loan'
    expected_return_date = fields.Date('Due for', required=True)
```

Extend the `library.member` model, as follows:

```
class LibraryMember(models.Model):
    _inherit = 'library.member'
    loan_duration = fields.Integer('Loan duration',
                                   default=15,
                                   required=True)
```

Since the `expected_return_date` field is required and no default is provided, the wizard to record loans will cease functioning because it does not provide a value for that field when it creates loans.

How to do it...

To extend the business logic in the `library.loan.wizard` model, you need to perform the following steps:

1. In `my_module`, modify the `record_loans()` method in the `LibraryLoanWizard` class. The original code is in the *Writing a wizard to guide the user* recipe in `Chapter` 9, *Advanced Server-Side Development Techniques*. The new version is as shown:

```
@api.multi
def record_loans(self):
    for wizard in self:
        books = wizard.book_ids
        loan = self.env['library.book.loan']
        for book in wizard.book_ids:
            values = wizard._prepare_loan(book)
            loan.create(values)
@api.multi
def _prepare_loan(self, book):
    return {'member_id': self.member_id.id,
            'book_id': book.id}
```

2. In `library_loan_return_date`, create a class that extends `library.loan.wizard` and defines the `_prepare_loan` method, as follows:

```
from datetime import timedelta
from odoo import models, fields, api
class LibraryLoanWizard(models.TransientModel):
    _inherit = 'library.load.wizard'

    def _prepare_loan(self, book):
        values = super(LibraryLoanWizard,
                       self
                       )._prepare_loan(book)
        loan_duration = self.member_id.loan_duration
        today_str = fields.Date.context_today(self)
        today = fields.Date.from_string(today_str)
        expected = today + timedelta(days=loan_duration)
        values.update(
```

```
                    {'expected_return_date':
                        fields.Date.to_string(expected)}
        )
        return values
```

How it works...

In step 1, we refactor the code from the *Writing a wizard to guide the user* recipe in `Chapter 9,` *Advanced Server-Side Development Techniques,* to use a very common and useful coding pattern to create the `library.book.loan` records. The creation of the dictionary of values is extracted in a separate method rather than hard-coded in the method calling `create()`. This eases extending the addon module in case new values have to be passed at creation time, which is exactly the case we are facing.

Step 2 then does the extension of the business logic. We define a model that extends `library.loan.wizard` and redefines the `_prepare_loan()` method. The redefinition starts by calling the implementation from the parent class:

```
    values = super(LibraryLoanWizard, self)._prepare_loan(book)
```

In the case of Odoo models, the parent class is not what you'd expect by looking at the Python class definition. The framework has dynamically generated a class hierarchy for our recordset, and the parent class is the definition of the model from the modules on which we depend. So, the call to `super()` brings back the implementation of `library.loan.wizard` from `my_module`. In this implementation, `_prepare_loan()` returns a dictionary of values with `'member_id'` and `'book_id'`. We update this dictionary by adding the `'expected_return_date'` key before returning it.

There's more...

In this recipe, we chose to extend the behavior by calling the normal implementation and modifying the returned result *afterward*. It is also possible to perform some actions *before* calling the normal implementation, and of course, we can also do both.

However, what we saw in this recipe is that it is more difficult to change the behavior of the middle of a method. We had to refactor the code to extract an extension point to a separate method and override this new method in the extension module.

You may be tempted to completely rewrite a method. Always be very cautious when doing so; if you do not call the super() implementation of your method, you are breaking the extension mechanism and potentially breaking addons for which their extension of the same method will never be called.

Unless you are working in a controlled environment in which you know exactly which addons are installed and you've checked that you are not breaking them, avoid doing this. Also, if you have to, ensure that you document what you are doing in a very visible way.

What can you do before and after calling the original implementation of the method? There are lots of things, including (but not limited to) those listed:

- Modifying the arguments that are passed to the original implementation (before)
- Modifying the context that is passed to the original implementation (before)
- Modifying the result that is returned by the original implementation (after)
- Calling another method (before, after)
- Creating records (before, after)
- Raising a UserError to cancel the execution in forbidden cases (before, after)
- Splitting self in smaller recordsets, and calling the original implementation on each of the subsets in a different way (before)

Extending write() and create()

The *Extending the business logic defined in a Model* recipe showed how to extend methods defined on a model class. If you think about it, methods defined on the parent class of the model are also part of the model. This means that all the base methods defined on models.Model (actually on models.BaseModel, which is the parent class of models.Model) are also available and can be extended.

This recipe shows how to extend create() and write() to control access to some fields of the records.

Getting ready

We will extend on the library example from the my_module addon module in Chapter 4, *Creating Odoo addon Modules*.

You will also need the security groups defined in the *Creating security Groups and assigning them to Users* recipe and the access rights defined in the *Adding security access to models* recipe from `Chapter 11`, *Access Security*.

Modify the `security/ir.model.access.csv` file to give write access to library users to books:

```
id,name,model_id:id,group_id:id,perm_read,perm_write,perm_create,perm_unlin
k
access_library_book_user,library.book.user,model_library_book,base.group_us
er,1,1,0,0
access_library_book_admin,library.book.admin,model_library_book,base.group_
system,1,0,0,0
```

Add a `manager_remarks` field to the `library.book` model. We want only members of the `Library Managers` group to be able to write to that field:

```
from odoo import models, api, exceptions
class LibraryBook(models.Model):
    _name = 'library.book'
    manager_remarks = fields.Text('Manager Remarks')
```

How to do it...

In order to prevent users who are not members of the **Library Managers** group from modifying the value of `manager_remarks`, you need to perform the following steps:

1. Extend the `create()` method, like this:

```
@api.model
def create(self, values):
    if not self.user_has_groups(
            'library.group_library_manager'):
        if 'manager_remarks' in values:
            raise exceptions.UserError(
                'You are not allowed to modify '
                'manager_remarks'
            )
    return super(LibraryBook, self).create(values)
```

2. Extend the `write()` method, as follows:

```
@api.multi
def write(self, values):
    if not self.user_has_groups(
            'library.group_library_manager'):
        if 'manager_remarks' in values:
            raise exceptions.UserError(
                'You are not allowed to modify '
                'manager_remarks'
            )
    return super(LibraryBook, self).write(values)
```

3. Extend the `fields_get()` method, as follows:

```
@api.model
def fields_get(self,
               allfields=None,
               attributes=None):
    fields = super(LibraryBook, self).fields_get(
        allfields=allfields,
        attributes=attributes
    )
    if not self.user_has_groups(
            'library.group_library_manager'):
        if 'manager_remarks' in fields:
            fields['manager_remarks']['readonly'] = True
```

How it works...

Step 1 redefines the `create()` method. Before calling the base implementation of `create()`, our method uses the `user_has_groups()` method to check whether the user belongs to the `library.group_library_manager` group (this is the XML ID of the group). If this is not the case and a value is passed for `manager_remarks`, a `UserError` exception is raised, preventing the creation of the record. This check is performed before the base implementation is called.

Step 2 does the same thing for the `write()` method; before writing, we check the group and the presence of the field in the values to write and raise `UserError` if there is a problem.

Step 3 is a small bonus; the `fields_get()` method is used by the web client to query for the fields of the model and their properties. It returns a Python dictionary mapping field names to a dictionary of field attributes, such as the `display` or the `help` string. What interests us is the `readonly` attribute, which we force to `True` if the user is not a library manager. This will make the field read only in the web client, which will avoid unauthorized users from trying to edit it only to be faced with an error message.

Having the field set to read only in the web client does not prevent RPC calls from writing it. This is why we also extend `create()` and `write()`.

There's more...

When extending `write()`, note that before calling the `super()` implementation of `write()`, `self` is still unmodified. You can use this to compare the current values of the fields to the ones in the values dictionary.

In the recipe, we chose to raise an exception, but we could have also chosen to remove the offending field from the values dictionary and silently skipped updating that field in the record:

```
@api.multi
def write(self, values):
    if not self.user_has_groups(
            'library.group_library_manager'):
        if 'manager_remarks' in values:
            del values['manager_remarks']
    return super(LibraryBook, self).write(values)
```

After calling `super().write()`, if you want to perform additional actions, you have to be wary of anything that can cause another call to `write()`, or you will create an infinite recursion loop. The workaround is to put a marker in the context to be checked to break the recursion:

```
class MyModel(models.Model):
    @api.multi
    def write(self, values):
        super(MyModel, self).write(values)
        if self.env.context.get('MyModelLoopBreaker'):
            return
        self = self.with_context(MyModelLoopBreaker=True)
        self.compute_things() # can cause calls to writes
```

Customizing how records are searched

The *Defining the Model representation and order* recipe in `Chapter 4`, *Creating Odoo addon Modules*, introduced the `name_get()` method, which is used to compute a representation of the record in various places, including in the widget used to display `Many2one` relations in the web client.

This recipe shows us how to allow searching for a book in the `Many2one` widget by title, author, or ISBN by redefining `name_search`.

Getting ready

For this recipe, we will use the following model definition:

```
class LibraryBook(models.Model):
    _name = 'library.book'
    name = fields.Char('Title')
    isbn = fields.Char('ISBN')
    author_ids = fields.Many2many('res.partner', 'Authors')

    @api.multi
    def name_get(self):
        result = []
        for book in self:
        authors = book.author_ids.mapped('name')
            name = '%s (%s)' % (book.name, ', '.join(authors))
            result.append((book.id, name))
            return result
```

When using this model, a book in a `Many2one` widget is displayed as **Book Title (Author1, Author2...)**. Users expect to be able to type in an author's name and find the list filtered according to this name, but this will not work as the default implementation of `name_search` only uses the attribute referred to by the `_rec_name` attribute of the model class, in our case, `'name'`. As a service to the advanced users, we also want to allow filtering by ISBN number.

How to do it...

In order to allow searching `library.book` either by book title, one of the authors, or ISBN, you need to define the `_name_search()` method in the `LibraryBook` class, as follows:

```
@api.model
def _name_search(self, name='', args=None, operator='ilike',
                 limit=100, name_get_uid=None):
    args = [] if args is None else args.copy()
    if not(name == '' and operator == 'ilike'):
        args += ['|', '|',
                 ('name', operator, name),
                 ('isbn', operator, name),
                 ('author_ids.name', operator, name)
                 ]
    return super(LibraryBook, self)._name_search(
        name='', args=args, operator='ilike',
        limit=limit, name_get_uid=name_get_uid)
```

How it works...

The default implementation of `name_search()` actually only calls the `_name_search()` method, which does the real job. This `_name_search()` method has an additional argument, `name_get_uid`, which is used in some corner cases to compute the results using `sudo()`.

We pass most of the arguments that we receive unchanged to the `super()` implementation of the method:

- `name` is a string containing the value the user has typed so far.
- `args` is either `None` or a search domain used as a prefilter for the possible records (it can come from the domain parameter of the `Many2one` relation, for instance).
- `operator` is a string containing the match operator. Generally, you will have `'ilike'` or `'='`.
- `limit` is the maximum number of rows to retrieve.
- `name_get_uid` can be used to specify a different user when calling `name_get()` in the end to compute the strings to display in the widget.

Our implementation of the method does the following:

1. It generates a new empty list if `args` is `None`, and makes a copy of `args` otherwise. We make a copy to avoid our modifications to the list having side effects on the caller.

2. Then, we check whether `name` is not an empty string or if `operator` is not `'ilike'`. This is to avoid generating a dumb domain `[('name', ilike, '')]` that does not filter anything. In this case, we jump straight to the call to the `super()` implementation.

3. If we have a `name`, or if the `operator` is not `'ilike'`, then we add some filtering criteria to `args`. In our case, we add clauses that will search for the supplied name in the title of the books, or in their ISBN, or in the author's names.

4. Finally, we call the `super()` implementation with the modified domain in `args` and force `name` to `''` and `operator` to `ilike`. We do this to force the default implementation of `_name_search()` to not alter the domain it receives, so the one we specified is to be used.

There's more...

We mentioned in the introduction that this method is used in the `Many2one` widget. For completeness, it is also used in the following parts of Odoo:

- When using the `in` operator on `One2many` and `Many2many` fields in the domain
- To search for records in the `many2many_tags` widget
- To search for records in the CSV file import

See also

The *Define the Model Representation and Order* recipe in `Chapter 4`, *Creating Odoo addon Modules*, presents how to define the `name_get()` method, which is used to create a text representation of a record.

The *Defining filters on record lists: Domain* recipe in `Chapter 10`, *Backend Views*, provides more information about search domain syntax.

7
Module Data

In this chapter, we will cover the following topics:

- Using external IDs and namespaces
- Loading data using XML files
- Using the noupdate and forcecreate flags
- Loading data using CSV files
- Loading data using YAML files
- Addons updates and data migration

In order not to have to repeat a lot of code, we'll make use of the models defined in `Chapter 5`, *Application Models*. So, in order to follow the examples, grab this chapter's code.

Introduction

In this chapter, we'll look at how addon modules can provide data at installation time. This is useful for providing default values and adding metadata such as view descriptions, menus, or actions. Another important usage is providing demonstration data, which is loaded when the database is created with the **Load demonstration data** checkbox checked.

Using external IDs and namespaces

There was a lot of talk about XML IDs already, without specifying what an XML ID is. This recipe will give a deeper understanding of this.

How to do it...

We write into the already existing records to demonstrate how to use cross-module references:

1. Add a data file to your module manifest:

```
'data': [
    'data/res_partner.xml',
],
```

2. Change the name of our main company:

```
<record id="base.main_company" model="res.company">
    <field name="name">Packt publishing</field>
</record>
```

3. Set our main company's partner as publisher:

```
<record id="book_cookbook" model="library.book">
    <field name="publisher_id" ref="base.main_partner" />
</record>
```

On installation of this module, the company will be renamed and the book from the next recipe will be assigned to our partner. On subsequent updates of our module, only the publisher will be assigned, but the company's name will be left untouched.

How it works...

An XML ID is a string referring to a record in the database. The IDs themselves are records of model `ir.model.data`. This table's rows contain the module declaring the XML ID in the first place, the identifier string, the referred model, and the referred ID. Every time an XML ID has to be written to, Odoo checks whether the string is namespaced already (that is, it contains exactly one dot), and if not, it adds the current module name as namespace. Then, it looks up whether there is already a record in `ir.model.data` with the specified name. If so, an UPDATE statement for the listed fields is executed; if not, a CREATE statement is executed. This is why you can give partial data when a record already exists, as we did earlier.

A widespread application for partial data, apart from changing records defined by other modules, is using a shortcut element to create a record in a convenient way and writing a `field` on this record, which is not supported by the shortcut element:

```
<act_window id="my_action" name="My action"
 model="res.partner" />
<record id="my_action" model="ir.actions.act_window">
<field name="auto_search" eval="False" />
</record>
```

The `ref` function, as used in the *Loading data using XML files* recipe, also adds the current module as namespace if appropriate, but raises an error if the resulting XML ID does not exist already. This also applies to the `id` attribute if it is not namespaced already.

There's more...

You probably need to access records with an XML ID from your code sooner or later. Use the `self.env.ref()` function in those cases, which returns a browse record of the referenced record. Note that here, you always have to pass the full XML ID.

See also

Consult the *Using the noupdate and forcecreate flags* recipe to find out why the company's name is changed only on installation of the module.

Loading data using XML files

Using the data model in Chapter 5, *Application Models*, we'll add a book and an author as demonstration data, while we add a well-known publisher as normal data in our module.

How to do it...

Create two XML files and link them in your __manifest__.py file:

1. Add in a file called data/demo.xml to your manifest, in the demo section:

```
'demo': [
    'data/demo.xml',
],
```

2. Add content to this file:

```xml
<odoo>
    <record id="author_af" model="res.partner">
        <field name="name">Alexandre Fayolle</field>
    </record>
    <record id="author_dr" model="res.partner">
        <field name="name">Daniel Reis</field>
    </record>
    <record id="author_hb" model="res.partner">
        <field name="name">Holger Brunn</field>
    </record>
    <record id="book_cookbook" model="library.book">
        <field name="name">Odoo Cookbook</field>
        <field name="short_name">cookbook</field>
        <field name="date_release">2016-03-01</field>
        <field name="author_ids"
                eval="[(6, 0, [ref('author_af'), ref('author_dr'),
                            ref('author_hb')])]"
                                                        />
        <field name="publisher_id" ref="res_partner_packt" />
    </record>
</odoo>
```

3. Add a file called data/res_partner.xml to your manifest, in the data section:

```
'data': [
    'data/res_partner.xml',
],
```

4. Add content to this file:

```xml
<odoo>
    <record id="res_partner_packt" model="res.partner">
        <field name="name">Packt Publishing</field>
        <field name="city">Birmingham</field>
        <field name="country_id" ref="base.uk" />
```

```
        </record>
    </odoo>
```

When you update your module now, you'll see in any case the publisher we created, and if your database has demo data enabled, as pointed out in `Chapter 2`, *Creating Odoo Modules*, you'll also find this book and its authors.

How it works...

As you saw earlier, demo data is technically just the same as normal data. The only difference is that the first is pulled by the **demo** key in the manifest, and the latter by the **data** key.

To create a record, use the record element, which has the mandatory attributes—id and `model`. For the `id` attribute, consult the *Using external IDs and namespaces* recipe; the model attribute refers to a model's `_name` property.

Then, you use the `field` element to fill columns in the database as defined by the model you named. The model also decides which are the mandatory fields to fill and also possibly defines default values, in which case you don't need to give those fields a value explicitly.

As shown earlier, the field element can contain its value as simple text in case of scalar values.

If you need to pass the content of a file (for setting an image, for example), use the **file** attribute on the `field` element, and pass the file's name relative to the addons path.

For setting up references, there are two possibilities. The simplest is using the `ref` attribute, which works for many2one fields and just contains the XML ID of the record to be referenced.

For one2many and many2many fields, we need to resort to the `eval` attribute. This is a general purpose attribute that can be used to evaluate Python code to use as the field's value; think of `strftime('%Y-01-01')` as an example to populate a date field. X2many fields expect to be populated by a list of 3-tuples, where the first value of the tuple determines the operation to be carried out. Within an `eval` attribute, we have access to a function called `ref`, which returns the database ID of an XML ID given as a string. This allows us to refer to a record without knowing its concrete ID, which is probably different per database, as explained here:

- (2, id, False) deletes the linked record with `id` from the database; the third element of the tuple is ignored.

- (3, id, False) only cuts the link to a record with id, but leaves the existing record as it is. Here also, the last element of the tuple is ignored.
- (4, id, False) adds a link to the existing record id; the last element of the tuple is ignored too. This should be what you use most of the time, usually accompanied using the ref function to get the database ID of a record known by its XML ID.
- (5, False, False) cuts all links, but keeps the linked records intact.
- (6, False, [id, ...]) first clears out currently referenced records to replace them with the ones mentioned in the list of IDs. The second element of the tuple is ignored.

Note that order matters in data files and that records within data files can only refer to records defined in data files earlier in the list. This is why you should always check whether your module installs in an empty database, because during development, it often happens that you add records all over the place, which works because the records defined afterward are already in the database from an earlier update.

Demo data is always loaded after the files from the data key, which is why the reference in the example works.

There's more...

While you can do basically anything with the record element, there are shortcut elements defined that make it more convenient for the developer to create certain kinds of records. Examples are **menu item**, **template**, or **act window**. Refer to Chapter 10, *Backend Views*, and Chapter 16, *CMS Website Development*, for information about those.

A field element can also contain the function element, which calls a function defined on a model to provide a field's value. Refer to the *Using the noupdate and forcecreate flags* recipe for an application where we simply call a function to directly write to the database, circumventing the loading mechanism.

The preceding list misses out entries for 0 and 1, because they are not very useful when loading data. They are entered, as follows, for the sake of completeness:

- (0, False, {'key': value}) creates a new record of the referenced model, with its fields filled from the dictionary at position three. The second element of the tuple is ignored. As those records don't have an XML ID and are evaluated every time the module is updated, leading to double entries, it's better to avoid this in general, create the record in its own record element, and link it as explained earlier.
- (1, id, {'key': value}) can be used to write on an existing linked record. For the same reasons as mentioned earlier, you should avoid this syntax in your XML files.

These syntaxes are the same as the one explained in the *Creating new records* and *Updating values of records* recipes in Chapter 6, *Basic Server-Side Development*.

Using the noupdate and forcecreate flags

Most addon modules have different types of data. Some data simply needs to exist for the module to work properly, other data shouldn't even be changed by the user, while most data is meant to be changed as per the user's pleasure and is only provided as a convenience. This recipe will detail how to address the different types. First, we'll write a field in an already existing record, and then we'll create a record that is supposed to be recreated during a module update.

How to do it...

We can enforce different behaviors from Odoo when loading data by setting certain attributes on the enclosing <odoo> element or the <record> element itself:

1. Add a publisher only created at installation time, but not updated on subsequent updates. However, if the user deletes it, it will be recreated:

```
<odoo noupdate="1">
    <record id="res_partner_packt" model="res.partner">
        <field name="name">Packt publishing</field>
    </record>
</odoo>
```

2. Add a book category that is not changed during addon updates and not recreated if the user deletes it:

```
<odoo noupdate="1">
    <record id="book_category_all" model="library.book.category"
            forcecreate="false">
        <field name="name">All books</field>
    </record>
</odoo>
```

How it works...

The `<odoo>` element can have a `noupdate` attribute, which is propagated to the `ir.model.data` records created when reading the enclosed data records for the first time, ending up as a column in this table.

When Odoo installs an addon (called `init` mode), all noupdate records are written. When you update an addon (called `update` mode), the existing XML IDs are checked to see whether they have the `noupdate` flag set, and if so, elements trying to write to this XML ID are ignored. This is not the case if the record in question was deleted by the user, which is why you can force not recreating noupdate records also in `update` mode by setting the flag **forcecreate** on the record to `false`.

In legacy addons (<= 8.0), you'll often find an `<openerp>` element enclosing a `<data>` element, which contains the `<record>` and other elements. This is still possible, but deprecated. By now, `<odoo>`, `<openerp>`, and `<data>` have exactly the same semantics; they are meant as a bracket to enclose XML data.

There's more...

You can force *init* mode by starting your Odoo server with the `--init=your_addon` parameter, overwriting all the existing noupdate records. This will also cause deleted records to be recreated. Note that this can cause double records and related installation errors if a module circumvents the XML ID mechanism, for example, by creating records in Python code called by YAML files.

For modules you write from scratch, you don't need to worry too much about noupdate records in either your own addon or other ones, as long as you only install it after all development is done. But, imagine you add a new feature to an existing module that is already out in the wild. Then, you might need to set a specific value on, for example, the main partner, which is a noupdate record. For users with a previous version already installed, this data update will never be executed! You can work around this using the <function> element to temporarily unset the record to noupdate, as follows:

```
<function name="write" model="ir.model.data">
    <function name="search" model="ir.model.data">
        <value eval="[('module', '=', 'base'),
                      ('name', '=', 'main_partner')]" />
    </function>
    <value eval="{'noupdate': False}" />
</function>
<record id="base.main_partner" model="res.partner">
    <field name="book_ids" eval="[(4, ref('book_cookbook'))]"
</record>
<function name="write" model="ir.model.data">
    <function name="search" model="ir.model.data">
        <value eval="[('module', '=', 'base'),
                      ('name', '=', 'main_partner')]" />
    </function>
    <value eval="{'noupdate': True}" />
</function>
```

With this code, you can circumvent any noupdate flag, but ensure that this is really what you want. Another option for solving the scenario sketched here is to write a migration script, as outlined in the *Addon updates and data migration* recipe.

See also

Odoo also uses XML IDs to keep track of which data is to be deleted after an addon update. If a record had an XML ID from the module's namespace before the update, but the XML ID is not reinstated during the update, the record and its XML ID will be deleted from the database because they're considered obsolete. For a deeper discussion of this mechanism, refer to the *Addon updates and data migration* recipe.

Loading data using CSV files

While you can do everything you need with XML files, this format is not the most convenient when you need to provide larger amounts of data, especially given that many people are more comfortable preprocessing data in Calc or some other spreadsheet software. Another advantage of this format is that it is what you get when you use the standard export function. In this recipe, we'll take a look at importing table-like data.

How to do it...

Traditionally, **access control lists** (**ACLs**), (refer to `Chapter 11`, *Access Security*) are a type of data that is loaded via CSV files:

1. Add `security/ir.model.access.csv` to your data files:

```
'data': [
    ...
    'security/ir.model.access.csv',
],
```

2. Add an ACL for our books in this file:

```
"id","name","model_id:id","group_id:id","perm_read",
"perm_write","perm_create","perm_unlink"
"access_library_book_user","ACL for books",
"model_library_book","base.group_user",1,0,0,0
```

Now, we have an ACL that permits normal users to read book records, but does not allow them to edit, create, or delete them.

How it works...

You simply drop all your data files in your manifest's **data** list. Odoo will use the file extension to decide which type of file it is. A specialty of CSV files is that their file name must match the name of the model to be imported, in our case, `ir.model.access`. The first line needs to be a header with column names that match the model's field names exactly.

For scalar values, you can use a quoted (if necessary, because the string contains quotes or commas itself) or an unquoted string.

When writing many2one fields with a CSV file, Odoo first tries to interpret the column value as XML ID. If there's no dot, add the current module name as a namespace, and look up the result in `ir.model.data`. In case this fails, the model's `name_search` function is called with the column's value as a parameter and the first result returned wins. When this also fails, the line is considered invalid and Odoo raises an error.

 Note that data read from CSV files is always `noupdate=False` and there's no convenient way around this. This means subsequent updates of your addon will always overwrite possible changes made by the user.
If you need to load huge amounts of data and the noupdate is a problem for you, load a CSV file from an init hook.

There's more...

Importing one2many and many2many fields with CSV files is possible, but a bit tricky. In general, you're better off creating the records separately and setting up the relation with an XML file afterward, or working with a second CSV file that sets up the relationship.

If you really need to create related records within the same file, order your columns so that all scalar fields are to the left and fields of the linked model are to the right, with a column header consisting of the linking field's name and the linked model's field, separated by a colon:

```
"id","name","model_id:id","perm_read","perm_read", "group_id:name"
"access_library_book_user","ACL for books","model_library_book",1,
"my group"
```

This will create a group called `my group`; you can write more fields in the group record by adding columns to the right. If you need to link multiple records, repeat the line and only change the right-hand side columns as appropriate. Given that Odoo fills empty columns with the previous line's value, you don't need to copy all data, but simply add a line with empty values save for the fields of the linked model you want to fill.

For x2m fields, just list the XML IDs of the records to be linked.

Loading data using YAML files

A third format for data import is YAML, which gives you less overhead than XML, but still more control than CSV. Traditionally, it was used for tests rather than for data import, which is why you have more possibilities to call code here.

How to do it...

Take the following steps to translate the first recipe in this chapter to YAML:

1. Add a file called `data/demo.yml` to your manifest, in the demo section:

```
'demo': [
    'data/demo.yml',
],
```

2. Add content to this file:

```
-
    !record {id: author_af, model: res.partner}
        name: Alexandre Fayolle
-
    !record {id: author_dr, model: res.partner}
        name: Daniel Reis
-
    !record {id: author_hb, model: res.partner}
        name: Holger Brunn
-
    !record {id: book_cookbook, model: library.book}
        name: Odoo cookbook
        short_name: cookbook
        date_release: 2016-03-01
        author_ids: [(6, 0, [ref('author_af'), ref('author_dr'),
                             ref('author_hb')])]
        publisher_id: res_partner_packt
```

3. Add a file called `data/res_partner.yml` to your manifest, in the data section:

```
'data': [
    'data/res_partner.yml',
],
```

4. Add content to this file:

```
-
    !record {id: res_partner_packt, model: res.partner}
        name: Packt publishing
        city: Birmingham
        country_id: base.uk
```

We did the same as in the first recipe, but in YAML syntax. Note that YAML files need the `.yml` extension to be recognized correctly.

How it works...

Odoo introduces a YAML datatype `record`, which is where most of the Odoo-specific behavior is implemented. As with XML, a **record** needs an **ID** and a **model** set in order to do something useful.

For field values, you use YAML's standard notation, which means you don't need quoting for strings. When filling `many2one` fields, Odoo will simply presuppose that what you give here is a XML ID, so there is no need for extra marking here either.

There's more...

We've seen that linking `one2many` and `many2many` fields is a bit awkward with XML and CSV, and in the preceding example, we used the same syntax to do the linking. In YAML, you could have done it more elegantly by simply writing the following:

```
!record {id: book_cookbook, model: library.book}
    name: Odoo cookbook
    short_name: cookbook
    date_release: 2016-03-01
    author_ids:
    -    name: Alexandre Fayolle
    -    name: Daniel Reis
    -    name: Holger Brunn
```

This way, you created three records of the `res.partner` type, linked in the `author_ids` field. Note that here also, creating records inline means that they have no XML ID, which makes it difficult to refer to them from other places.

Also, note that as with CSV, we can't influence the `noupdate` flag with YAML files.

See also

This recipe focused on using YAML files to load data. If you're interested in testing using YAML files, refer to `Chapter 8`, *Debugging and Automated Testing*.

Addon updates and data migration

The data model you choose when writing an addon module might turn out to have some weaknesses, so you may need to adjust it during the life cycle of your addon module. In order to allow that without a lot of hacks, Odoo supports versioning in addon modules and running migrations if necessary.

How to do it...

We assume that in an earlier version of our module, the `date_release` field was a character field, where people wrote whatever they saw fit as the date. Now we realize that we need this field for comparisons and aggregations, which is why we want to change its type to `Date`. Odoo does a great job at type conversions, but, in this case, we're on our own, which is why we need to provide instructions on how to transform a database with the previous version of our module installed to a database where the current version can run:

1. Bump the version in your `__manifest__.py`:

```
'version': '11.0.1.0.1',
```

2. Provide premigration code in `migrations/11.0.1.0.1/pre-migrate.py`:

```
def migrate(cr, version):
    cr.execute('ALTER TABLE library_book RENAME COLUMN date_release
                                       TO date_release_char')
```

3. Provide post migration code in `migrations/11.0.1.0.1/post-migrate.py`:

```
from odoo import fields
from datetime import date

def migrate(cr, version):
    cr.execute('SELECT id, date_release_char FROM library_book')
    for record_id, old_date in cr.fetchall():
        # check if the field happens to be set in Odoo's internal
        # format
        new_date = None
        try:
            new_date = fields.Date.from_string(old_date)
        except ValueError:
            if len(old_date) == 4 and old_date.isdigit():
                # probably a year
                new_date = date(int(old_date), 1, 1)
```

```
            else:
                # try some separators, play with day/month/year
                # order ...
                pass
        if new_date:
            cr.execute('UPDATE library_book SET date_release=%s',
                    (new_date,))
```

Without this code, Odoo would have renamed the old `date_release` column to `date_release_moved` and created a new one, because there's no automatic conversion from character fields to date fields. From the point of view of the user, the data in `date_release` will simply be gone.

How it works...

The first crucial point is that you increase the version number of your addon, as migrations run only between different versions. During every update, Odoo writes the version number from the manifest at the time of the update into the `ir_module_module` table. The version number is prefixed with Odoo's major and minor version, if the version number has three or fewer components. In the preceding example, we also explicitly named Odoo's major and minor version, which is good practice, but a value of `1.0.1` would have had the same effect, because, internally, Odoo prefixes short version numbers for addons with its own major and minor version number. Generally, using the long notation is a good thing because you can see with just a glance at the manifest file, for which version of Odoo an addon is meant.

The two migration files are just code files that don't need to be registered anywhere. When updating an addon, Odoo compares the addon's version as noted in `ir_module_module` with the version in the addon's manifest. If the manifest's version is higher (after possibly adding Odoo's major and minor version), this addon's `migrations` folder will be searched if it contains folders with the version(s) in between, up to, and including the version that is currently updated.

Then, within the folders found, it searches for Python files whose names start with `pre-`, loads them, and expects them to define a function called `migrate`, which has two parameters. This function is called with a database cursor as the first argument and the currently installed version as the second argument. This happens before Odoo even looks at the rest of the code the addon defines, so you can assume that nothing changed in your database layout compared to the previous version.

After all `pre-migrate` functions run successfully, Odoo loads the models and data declared in the addon, which can cause changes in the database layout. Given that we renamed `date_release` in `pre-migrate.py`, Odoo will just create a new column with that name, but with the correct data type.

After that, with the same search algorithm, `post-migrate` files will be searched and executed if found. In our case, we need to look at every value and see whether we can make something usable out of it; otherwise, we keep `NULL` as data. Don't write scripts iterating over a whole table yourself if not absolutely necessary; in this case, we should have written a very big unreadable SQL switch that does what we want.

 If you simply want to rename a column, you don't need a migration script. In this case, you can set the `oldname` parameter of the field in question to the field's original column name; Odoo then takes care of the renaming itself.

There's more...

In both the pre- and post-migration steps, you only have access to a cursor, which is not very convenient if you're used to Odoo environments. It can lead to unexpected results to use models at this stage, because in the pre-step, the addon's models are not yet loaded and also, in the post-step, models defined by addons depending on the current addon are not yet loaded too. However, if this is not a problem for you, either because you want to use a model your addon doesn't touch or a model for which you know that the aforementioned is not a problem, you can create the environment you're used to by writing the following:

```
from odoo import api, SUPERUSER_ID

def migrate(cr, version):
    env = api.Environment(cr, SUPERUSER_ID, {})
    # env holds all currently loaded models
```

See also

When writing migration scripts, you'll often be confronted with repetitive tasks such as checking whether a column or table exists, renaming things, or mapping some old values to new values. It's frustrating and error-prone to reinvent the wheel here; consider using `https://github.com/OCA/openupgradelib` if you can afford the extra dependency.

8

Debugging and Automated Testing

In this chapter, we will cover the following topics:

- Producing server logs to help debug methods
- Using the Odoo shell to interactively call methods
- Using the Python debugger to trace method execution
- Writing tests for your module using Python unit tests
- Running server tests
- Using the Odoo Community Association maintainer quality tools

Introduction

We saw in Chapter 6, *Basic Server-Side Development*, how to write model methods to implement the logic of our module. However, a responsible developer not only writes the implementation, but also provides automated tests for this implementation. The recipes in this chapter cover the debugging and testing of server-side methods.

Producing server logs to help debug methods

Server logs are a nice help when trying to figure out what has been happening at runtime before a crash. They can also be added to provide additional information when debugging an issue. This recipe shows how to add logging to an existing method.

Getting ready

We will add some logging statements to the following method, which saves the stock levels of products to a file:

```python
from os.path import join
from odoo import models, api, exceptions
EXPORTS_DIR = '/srv/exports'

class ProductProduct(models.Model):
    _inherit = 'product.product'
    @api.model
    def export_stock_level(self, stock_location):
        products = self.with_context(
            location=stock_location.id
        ).search([])
        products = products.filtered('qty_available')
        fname = join(EXPORTS_DIR, 'stock_level.txt')
        try:
            with open(fname, 'w') as fobj:
                for prod in products:
                    fobj.write('%s\t%f\n' % (prod.name,
                                             prod.qty_available))
        except IOError:
            raise exceptions.UserError('unable to save file')
```

How to do it...

In order to get some logs when this method is being executed, perform the following steps:

1. At the beginning of the code, import the `logging` module:

```python
import logging
```

2. Before the definition of the model class, get a logger for the module:

```
_logger = logging.getLogger(__name__)
```

3. Modify the code of the `export_stock_level()` method, as follows:

```
@api.model
def export_stock_level(self, stock_location):
    _logger.info('export stock level for %s',
                    stock_location.name)
    products = self.with_context(
        location=stock_location.id).search([])
    products = products.filtered('qty_available')
    _logger.debug('%d products in the location',
                    len(products))
    fname = join(EXPORTS_DIR, 'stock_level.txt')
    try:
        with open(fname, 'w') as fobj:
            for prod in products:
                fobj.write('%s\t%f\n' % (
                    prod.name, prod.qty_available))
    except IOError:
        _logger.exception(
            'Error while writing to %s in %s',
            'stock_level.txt', EXPORTS_DIR)
        raise exceptions.UserError('unable to save file')
```

How it works...

Step 1 imports the module `logging` from the Python standard library. Odoo uses this module to manage its logs.

Step 2 sets up a logger for the Python module. We use a common idiom in Odoo using the `__name__` automatic variable for the logger name and calling the logger `_logger`.

The `__name__` variable is set automatically by the Python interpreter at module import time, and its value is the full name of the module. Since Odoo does a little trick with the imports, the addon modules are seen by Python as belonging to the `odoo.addons` Python package. So, if the code of the recipe is in `my_module/models/book.py`, `__name__` will be `odoo.addons.my_module.models.book`.

By doing this, we get two benefits:

- The global logging configuration set on the odoo logger is applied to our logger, because of the hierarchical structure of loggers in the logging module
- The logs will be prefixed with the full module path, which is a great help when trying to find where a given log line is produced

Step 3 uses the logger to produce log messages. Available methods for this are (by increasing log level) debug, info, warning, error, and critical. All these methods accept a message in which you can have % substitutions and additional arguments to be inserted into the message. You should not do the % substitution yourself; the logging module is smart enough to perform this operation only if the log has to be produced. If you are running with log level of INFO, then DEBUG logs will avoid doing the substitution that is CPU consuming in the long run.

Another useful method shown in the recipe is _logger.exception(), which can be used in an exception handler. The message will be logged with a level of ERROR, and the stack trace is also printed in the application log.

There's more...

You can control the **logging level** of the application from the command line or from the configuration file. There are two main ways of doing this:

- To control the log level globally, you can use the --log-level command-line options. Refer to Chapter 1, *Managing Odoo Server Instances* for more information.
- To set the log level for a given logger, you can use --log-handler=prefix:level. In this case, prefix is a piece of the path of the logger name, and level is one of DEBUG, INFO, WARNING, ERROR, or CRITICAL. If you omit prefix, then you set the default level for all loggers. For instance, to set the logging level of my_module loggers to DEBUG and keep the default log level for the other addons, you can start Odoo like this:

  ```
  $ python odoo.py --log-handler=odoo.addons.my_module:DEBUG
  ```

- It is possible to specify --log-handler multiple times on the command line.

- You can also configure the **log handler** in the configuration file of your Odoo instance. In that case, you can use a comma-separated list of `prefix:level` pairs. For example, the following line is a sane configuration for minimal logging output, still keeping the most important messages; we keep error messages by default, except for messages produced by `werkzeug`, for which we only want critical messages, and `odoo.service.server` for which we keep info level messages (this includes the notification of server startup):

```
log_handler = :ERROR,werkzeug:CRITICAL,odoo.service.server:INFO
```

See also

The *Call a method with a modified context* recipe in `Chapter 9`, *Advanced Server-Side Development Techniques*.

Using the Odoo shell to interactively call methods

The Odoo web interface is meant for end users, although the developer mode unlocks a number of powerful features. However, testing and debugging through the web interface is not the easiest way to do things, as you need to manually prepare data, navigate in the menus to perform actions, and so on. The Odoo shell is a **command-line interface**, which you can use to issue calls. This recipe shows how to start the Odoo shell and perform actions such as calling a method inside the shell.

Getting ready

We will reuse the same code as in the previous recipe to produce server logs to help debug methods; this enables the `product.product` model to add a new method. We assume that you have an instance with the addon installed and available. In the recipe, we expect that you have an Odoo configuration file for this instance called `project.conf`.

How to do it...

In order to call the `export_stock_level()` method from the Odoo shell, you need to perform the following steps:

1. Start the Odoo shell specifying your project configuration file:

```
$ ./odoo-bin shell -c project.conf --log-level=error
```

2. Check for error messages, and read the information text displayed before the usual Python command-line prompt:

```
env: <odoo.api.Environment object at 0x7fac2ac2d990>
odoo: <module 'odoo' from '/home/cookbook/odoo/odoo/__init__.pyc'>
openerp: <module 'odoo' from '/home/cookbook/odoo/odoo/__init__.pyc'>
self: res.users(1,)
Python 3.5.2 (default, Sep 14 2017, 22:51:06)
[GCC 5.4.0 20160609] on linux
Type "help", "copyright", "credits" or "license" for more information.
>>>
```

3. Get a recordset for `product.product`:

```
>>> product = env['product.product']
```

4. Get the main stock location record:

```
>>> location_stock = env.ref('stock.stock_location_stock')
```

5. Call the `export_stock_level()` method:

```
>>> product.export_stock_level(location_stock)
```

6. Commit the transaction before exiting:

```
>>> env.cr.commit()
```

7. Exit the shell by pressing *Ctrl + D*

How it works...

Step 1 uses `odoo-bin shell` to start the Odoo shell. All the usual command-line arguments are available. We use `-c` to specify a project configuration file and `--log-level` to reduce the verbosity of the logs. When debugging, you may want to have a logging level of `DEBUG` only for some specific addons.

Before providing you with a Python command-line prompt, `odoo-bin shell` starts an Odoo instance that does not listen on the network and initializes some global variables, which are mentioned in the output:

- env is an environment connected to the database specified on the command line or in the configuration file.
- odoo is the odoo package imported for you. You get access to all the Python modules within that package to do what you want.
- openerp is an alias for the odoo package for backward compatibility.
- self is a recordset of res.users containing a single record for the Odoo superuser (Administrator), which is linked to the environment env.

Steps 3 and 4 use env to get an empty recordset and find a record by XML ID. Step 5 calls the method on the product.product recordset. These operations are identical to what you would use inside a method, with the small difference that we use env and not self.env (although we can have both, as they are identical). Take a look at Chapter 6, *Basic Server-Side Development*, for more information on what is available.

Step 6 commits the database transaction. This is not strictly necessary here because we did not modify any record in database, but if we had done so and wanted these changes to persist, this is necessary; when you use Odoo through the web interface, each RPC call runs in its own database transaction, and Odoo manages these for you. When running in the shell mode, this no longer happens and you have to call env.cr.commit() or env.cr.rollback() yourself. Otherwise, when you exit the shell, any transaction in progress is automatically rolled back. When testing, this is fine, but if you use the shell, for example, to script the configuration of an instance, don't forget to commit your work!

Using the Python debugger to trace method execution

Sometimes, application logs are not enough to figure out what is going wrong. Fortunately, we have the Python **debugger** available to us. This recipe shows how to insert a break point in a method and trace the execution by hand.

Getting ready

We will reuse the export_stock_level() method shown in the two previous recipes. Ensure that you have a copy at hand.

How to do it...

In order to trace the execution of export_stock_level() with pdb, perform the following steps:

1. Edit the code of the method, and insert the line highlighted here:

```
def export_stock_level(self, stock_location):
    import pdb; pdb.set_trace()
    products = self.with_context(
        location=stock_location.id
    ).search([])
    fname = join(EXPORTS_DIR, 'stock_level.txt')
    try:
        with open(fname, 'w') as fobj:
            for prod in products.filtered('qty_available'):
                fobj.write('%s\t%f\n' % (
                    prod.name, prod.qty_available))
    except IOError:
        raise exceptions.UserError('unable to save file')
```

2. Run the method. We will use the Odoo shell, as explained in the *Use the Odoo shell to interactively call methods* recipe earlier:

```
$ ./odoo-bin shell -c project.cfg --log-level=error
[...]
>>> product = env['product.product']
>>> location_stock = env.ref('stock.stock_location_stock')
>>> product.export_stock_level(location_stock)
> /home/cookbook/stock_level/models.py(18)export_stock_level()
-> products = self.with_context(
(Pdb)
```

3. At the (Pdb) prompt, issue the args (shortcut a) command to get the values of the arguments passed to the method:

```
(Pdb) a
self = product.product()
stock_location = stock.location(14,)
```

4. Enter the list command to check where in the code you are standing:

```
(Pdb) list
 13        @api.model
 14        def export_stock_level(self, stock_location):
 15            _logger.info('export stock level for %s',
```

```
 16                    stock_location.name)
 17         import pdb; pdb.set_trace()
 18 ->      products = self.with_context(
 19         location=stock_location.id).search([])
 20         products = products.filtered('qty_available')
 21         _logger.debug('%d products in the location',
 22                     len(products))
 23         fname = join(EXPORTS_DIR, 'stock_level.txt')
(Pdb)
```

5. Enter the `next` command three times to walk through the first lines of the method. You may also use n, which is a shortcut:

```
(Pdb) next
> /home/cookbook/stock_level/models.py(19)export_stock_level()
-> location=stock_location.id).search([])
(Pdb) n
> /home/cookbook/stock_level/models.py(20)export_stock_level()
-> products = products.filtered('qty_available')
(Pdb) n
> /home/cookbook/stock_level/models.py(21)export_stock_level()
-> _logger.debug('%d products in the location',
(Pdb) n
> /home/cookbook/stock_level/models.py(22)export_stock_level()
-> len(products))
(Pdb) n
> /home/cookbook/stock_level/models.py(23)export_stock_level()
-> fname = join(EXPORTS_DIR, 'stock_level.txt')
(Pdb) n
> /home/cookbook/stock_level/models.py(24)export_stock_level()
-> try:
```

6. Use the p command to display the values of the `products` and `fname` variables:

```
(Pdb) p products
product.product(32, 14, 17, 19, 21, 22, 23, 29, 34, 33, 26, 27, 42)
(Pdb) p fname
'/srv/exports/stock_level.txt'
```

7. Change the value of `fname` to point to the `/tmp` directory:

```
(Pdb) !fname = '/tmp/stock_level.txt'    superuser (Administrator), which
is linked to the environment env.
```

8. Use the `return` (shortcut `r`) command to execute the current function to its end:

```
(Pdb) return
--Return--
> /home/cookbook/stock_level/models.py(26)export_stock_level()->None
-> for product in products:
```

9. Use the `cont` (shortcut `c`) command to resume execution of the program:

```
(Pdb) c
>>>
```

How it works...

In step 1, we hard code a break point in the source code of the method by calling the `set_trace()` method of the `pdb` module from the Python standard library. When this method is executed, the normal flow of the program stops, and you get a (`Pdb`) prompt in which you can enter `pdb` commands.

Step 2 calls the `stock_level_export()` method using the shell mode. It is also possible to restart the server normally and to use the web interface to generate a call to the method you need to trace by clicking on the appropriate elements of the user interface.

When you need to manually step through some code using the Python debugger, here are a few tips that will make your life easier:

- Reduce the logging level to avoid having too many log lines polluting the output of the debugger. Starting at the ERROR level is generally fine. You may want to enable some specific loggers with a higher verbosity, which you can do using the `--log-handler` command-line option (refer to the *Produce server logs to help debug methods* recipe).
- Run the server with `--workers=0` to avoid any multiprocessing issues that can cause the same break point to be reached twice in two different processes.
- Run the server with `--max-cron-threads=0` to disable the processing of `ir.cron` periodic tasks, which may otherwise trigger while you are stepping through the method, producing unwanted logs and side effects.

Steps 3 to 8 use several `pdb` commands to step through the execution of the method. Here's a summary of the main commands of `pdb`. Most of them are also available using the first letter as a shortcut. We indicate this by having the optional letters between parenthesis:

- `h(elp)`: This displays help on the `pdb` commands.
- `a(rgs)`: This shows the value of the arguments of the current function/methods.
- `l(ist)`: This displays the source code being executed by chunks of 11 lines, initially centered on the current line. Successive calls will move further in the source code file. Optionally, you can pass two integers at the start and end, specifying the region to display.
- `p`: This prints a variable.
- `pp`: This pretty-prints a variable (useful with lists and dictionaries).
- `w(here)`: This shows the call stack, with the current line at the bottom and the Python interpreter at the top.
- `u(p)`: This moves up one level in the call stack.
- `d(own)`: This moves down one level in the call stack.
- `n(ext)`: This executes the current line of code and then stops.
- `s(tep)`: This is to step inside the execution of a method call.
- `r(eturn)`: This resumes the execution of the current method until it returns.
- `c(ont(inue))`: This resumes the execution of the program until the next break point is hit.
- `b(reak) <args>`: This creates a new break point and displays its identifier; `args` can be one of the following:
    - `<empty>`: This lists all break points
    - `line_number`: This breaks at the specified line in the current file
    - `filename:line_number`: This breaks at the specified line of the specified file (which is searched for in the directories of `sys.path`)
    - `function_name`: This breaks at the first line of the specified function
- `tbreak <args>`: This is similar to break, but the break point will be canceled after it has been reached, so successive execution of the line won't trigger it twice.
- `disable bp_id`: This disables a break point by ID.
- `enable bl_id`: This enables a disabled break point by ID.
- `j(ump) lineno`: The next line to execute will be the one specified. This can be used to rerun or to skip some lines.

- `(!)` `statement`: This executes a Python statement. The `!` character can be omitted if the command does not look like a `pdb` command; for instance, you need it if you want to set the value of a variable named `a`, because `a` is the shortcut for the `args` command.

There's more...

In the recipe, we inserted a `pdb.set_trace()` statement to break into `pdb`. We can also start `pdb` directly from within the Odoo shell, which is very useful when you cannot easily modify the code of the project using `pdb.runcall()`. This function takes a method as the first argument and the arguments to pass to the function as the next arguments. So, inside the Odoo shell, you do this:

```
>>> import pdb
>>> product = env['product.product']
>>> location_stock = env.ref('stock.stock_location_stock')
>>> pdb.runcall(product.export_stock_level, location_stock)
> /home/cookbook/stock_level/models.py(16)export_stock_level()
-> products = self.with_context(
(Pdb)
```

In this recipe, we focused on the Python debugger from the Python standard library, `pdb`. It is very useful to know that tool because it is guaranteed to be available on any Python distribution. There are other Python debuggers available, such as `ipdb` (`https://pypi.python.org/pypi/ipdb`) and `pudb` (`https://pypi.python.org/pypi/pudb`), which can be used as drop-in replacements for `pdb`. They share the same API and most commands seen in this recipe are unchanged. Also, of course, if you develop for Odoo using a Python IDE, you certainly have access to a debugger integrated with it.

See also

- For the full documentation of `pdb`, refer to `https://docs.python.org/3.5/library/pdb.html`.

Writing tests for your module using Python unit tests

Odoo supports different ways of writing addon module tests, YAML tests, and Python tests. Writing YAML tests for new modules is not encouraged by the editors, and it is quite possible that the support will be dropped altogether in a future version. Therefore, we will not cover these in this book, and we will instead focus on Python unit tests.

If you are familiar with the Python unit testing tools, you will be pleased to know that these are also available within the Odoo framework.

In this recipe, we will see how to write Python **unit tests** for the my_module methods we wrote in the *Define Model methods and use the API decorators* recipe in Chapter 6, *Basic Server-Side Development*.

Getting ready

This recipe assumes that you have an instance ready with the code for the my_module module defined in Chapter 4, *Creating Odoo Modules*, and the code in the *Define Model methods and use the API decorators* recipe from Chapter 6, *Basic Server-Side Development*.

This recipe also depends on the security rules defined in the *Adding Access Security* recipe from Chapter 4, *Creating Odoo Modules*.

How to do it...

In order to write unit tests for the module, perform the following steps:

1. Create a subdirectory called tests inside the addon module directory:

```
$ mkdir my_module/tests
```

2. Create an __init__.py file in that directory with the following contents:

```
from . import test_library
```

3. Create a test_library.py file in tests/ subdirectory. Inside the test_library.py file, import the Odoo test base class:

```
from odoo.tests.common import TransactionCase
```

4. Create a `TestCase` class:

```
class LibraryTestCase(TransactionCase):
```

5. Add a `setUp` method that creates a book:

```
def setUp(self):
    super(LibraryTestCase, self).setUp()
    demo_user = self.env.ref('base.user_demo')
    demo_user.groups_id |=\
        self.env.ref('my_module.group_librarian')
    book_model = self.env['library.book'].sudo(demo_user)
    self.book = book_model.create(
        {'name': 'Test book', 'state': 'draft'}
    )
```

6. Add a `test` method changing the state:

```
def test_change_draft_available(self):
    '''test changing state from draft to available'''
    self.book.change_state('available')
    self.assertEqual(self.book.state, 'available')
```

7. Add a second `test` method trying to make an illegal state change:

```
def test_change_available_draft_no_effect(self):
    '''test forbidden state change from available to draft'''
    self.book.change_state('available')
    self.book.change_state('draft')
    self.assertEqual(
        self.book.state,
        'available',
        'the state cannot change from available to %s' % \
        self.book.state
    )
```

How it works...

We create a Python subpackage in our module called `tests` and add a test module with a name starting with `test_`. This is the convention used by Odoo for **test discovery**.

In this file, we import the base test class, `TransactionCase` from `odoo.tests.common`. This class extends the `unittest.TestCase` class from the Python standard library to make it suitable for use in Odoo by overloading the `setUp()` and `tearDown()` methods of `unittest.TestCase`:

- The `setUp()` method initializes the `self.env` attribute that you can use to perform the usual operations (refer to the recipes in Chapter 6, *Basic Server-Side Development*)
- The `tearDown()` method rolls back the database transaction so that the tests are run in insulation

 If your test case redefines these two methods, ensure that you call the `super()` implementation.

The tests are defined in methods named with a `test` prefix. The test runner will then run one after the other with a call to `setUp()` before each test method and a call to `tearDown()` after each. Inside the method, you can use all the usual assertion methods from `unittest.TestCase`. Here are the most commonly used ones:

Method	Checks that
`assertEqual(a, b)`	`a == b`
`assertNotEqual(a, b)`	`a != b`
`assertTrue(x)`	`bool(x) is True`
`assertFalse(x)`	`bool(x) is False`
`assertIn(a, b)`	`a in b`
`assertNotIn(a, b)`	`a not in b`
`assertRaises(exc, fun, *args, **kwargs)`	`fun(*args, **kwargs)` raises exc

All these methods except `assertRaises()` accept an optional `msg` argument, which will be displayed in the error message when the assertion is not true. Otherwise, a standard error message is used.

`assertRaises` is best used as a context manager. Suppose you want to test that modifying a record raises a `UserError` exception. You can write the following test:

```
class TestCase(TransactionCase):
    # setUp method defines self.record
    def testWriteRaisesUserError(self):
        with self.assertRaises(UserError):
            self.record.write({'some_field': some_value})
```

The test will succeed if the exception passed to `assertRaises` is generated by the block of code, otherwise it will fail.

For more information on unit tests in Python, refer to the standard library documentation at `https://docs.python.org/3.5/library/unittest.html#test-cases`.

 Note that in the `setUp()` method, we use `sudo()` to change the user in the environment of `self.book_model`. This ensures that the tests will not run using the administrator user, which bypasses the access rules and that the security rules we set up in our module are getting exercised.

Refer to the *Run server tests* recipe to see how to run the test.

There's more...

The `odoo.tests.common` module defines several classes that can be used as base classes for test cases:

- `TransactionCase`: Each test method is run independently, and the database transaction is rolled back after each. This means that any changes made in one test method are not seen by the other test methods. You can use the traditional `setUp()` and `tearDown()` methods to perform test initialization and cleanup.
- `SingleTransactionCase`: All the test methods are run in the same transaction, which is only rolled back after the last method. If you need to perform initialization and cleanup for the test case, you need to extend the `setUpClass()` and `tearDownClass()` methods. Don't forget to decorate these with `@classmethod`, or you will get strange errors when calling the `super()` implementation.

- `SavePointCase`: It is an extension of `SingleTransactionCase` that creates the database `SAVEPOINT` before running test methods and restores them after the test is run. The net effect is that you can run your tests in isolation as with `TransactionCase`, without having to pay the price of a costly `setUp()` method recreating all the data between all tests; the initialization is performed in `setUpClass()`, and we roll back the transaction to the saved state after each test.

The module also defines two decorators: `at_install(bool)` and `post_install(bool)`. By default, the tests for a given addon module are run just after the module is initialized, before initializing the next addon module; this corresponds to decorating the test methods with both `@at_install(True)` and `@post_install(False)`. Sometimes, you may need to change this. A typical case is the following: both `module_a` and `module_b` extend the same model, but they do not depend on one another. Both add a required field to the models `field_a` and `field_b`, and provide a default value for that field. In the tests of these modules, new records are created. If both modules are installed when the tests are run, the tests will fail, whereas if only `module_a` or `module_b` is installed, the tests will pass. The reason is that if, for instance, `module_a` is loaded first, when the tests create a new record, the default value for `field_b` is not computed because `module_b` is not loaded yet. However, the database `NOT NULL` constraint for `field_b` is present and will prevent the record from being created. A solution is to decorate the test methods of both modules with `@at_install(False)` and `@post_install(True)`, which will force the tests to be run after all modules have been initialized.

Running server tests

Now that you know how to write tests, let's see how you can run them!

Getting ready

We will reuse the tests for the `my_module` module from one of the previous recipes. You will need an instance with the addon installed. In this recipe, we assume that the instance configuration file is in `project.cfg`.

How to do it...

To run the tests for my module addon, install the module with demo data:

```
$ ./odoo-bin -c project.cfg --without-demo=False --stop-after-init \
-i my_module
```

Then, run the following command:

```
$ ./odoo-bin -c project.cfg --test-enable --log-level=error \
--stop-after-init -u my_module
```

How it works...

The key part in this recipe is the `--test-enable` command-line flag that tells Odoo to run the tests. The `--stop-after-init` flag will stop the instance after the tests have run, and `-u` will update the specified module. When an update (or install) is performed with tests enabled, all the affected addon modules' tests are run (this includes dependencies automatically installed or reverse dependencies automatically updated; refer to the *Install and upgrade local addon modules* recipe in `Chapter 2`, *Managing Odoo Server Instances*, for more information on this).

If the tests are not run, check that you have demo data enabled for the module; in the configuration file, the `without_demo` parameter should be `False`. In doubt, you can force this in the database by running the `UPDATE ir_module_module SET demo=true WHERE name='my_module';` query.

You can run the tests using the `--log-level=error --log-handler=odoo.modules.loading:INFO` log configuration. This allows us to have information about the various test's files being processed but not the details of the logs of the operations, only the error messages.

How do you know that the tests ran successfully? The exit status of Odoo will be equal to the number of failed tests, so if it is not `0`, then at least one test has failed. You will get more information about the failures in the server log messages.

There's more...

The main drawback of this way of running tests is that you have to run all the tests for a given addon module, even if you know that they all pass but the one you are trying to fix, and you also have to update the addon (which can be a costly operation in itself).

There is a way around this. If you want to run the tests in `my_module/tests/test_library.py`, you can use the following command:

```
$ odoo-bin -c project.cfg --log-level=error --stop-after-init \
--test-file my_module/tests/test_library.py
```

This will run only the tests defined in that file. Since it skips updating the module, it will not work if you have changed the model structure by adding new fields or modified the data files of the addon since the last time the module was updated.

One final note about tests:

Always be suspicious if your tests are not in error on the first run. There are good chances that this means you made a mistake. A typical goof is to forget to import the test file in `tests/__init__.py`. It is always a good idea when tests are passing on the first run to force a failure, for instance, adding `assert False` on the first line of a method and to run them again.

Using the Odoo Community Association maintainer quality tools

The **Odoo Community Association** (**OCA**) manages a large number of Odoo projects using the GitHub infrastructure. The association projects use Travis CI for continuous integration. This recipe shows how you can use the maintainer QA tools developed by the community in your own GitHub repositories.

Getting ready

To use this recipe, you need to have a public GitHub repository with your modules. At the time of writing this, the OCA tools expect that this repository contains several addons in subdirectories.

How to do it...

To integrate the OCA `maintainer-quality-tools` with your repository, you need to perform the following steps:

1. Connect to `https://travis-ci.org/`:

2. To sign in, choose **Sign in with Github**.

3. Click on your name in the top-right corner to access your profile's settings, as shown in the following screenshot:

4. Click on the **Sync** button to load the information about all your public repositories in Travis. This can take a couple of minutes depending on how many repositories you have.

5. For all the repositories you want to use **Travis on**, enable them by toggling the grey cross to a green check mark.

6. You can click on the cogwheel to access each repositories, settings, but the defaults are okay too.

7. Inside a local clone of your repository, create a file called `.travis.yml` with the following content:

```
language: python
sudo: false
cache:
  apt: true
  directories:
    - $HOME/.cache/pip
python:
  - "3.5"
addons:
  apt:
    packages:
      - expect-dev  # provides unbuffer utility
      - python-lxml  # because pip installation is slow
      - python-simplejson
      - python-serial
      - python-yaml
virtualenv:
  system_site_packages: true
env:
  global:
    - VERSION="11.0" TESTS="0" LINT_CHECK="0"
  matrix:
    - LINT_CHECK="1"
    - TESTS="1" ODOO_REPO="odoo/odoo"
    - TESTS="1" ODOO_REPO="OCA/OCB"
install:
  - git clone --depth=1
https://github.com/OCA/maintainer-quality-tools.git ${HOME}/maintainer-
quality-tools
  - export PATH=${HOME}/maintainer-quality-tools/travis:${PATH}
  - travis_install_nightly
script:
  - travis_run_tests
after_success:
  - travis_after_tests_success
```

8. Commit the file and push it to GitHub:

```
$ git add .travis.yml
$ git commit -m "add travis configuration"
$ git push origin
```

9. Go to your `travis-ci.org` page and click on your project's name. You should see a first build in progress. If your code follows the OCA coding standard, it may even be green on the first run:

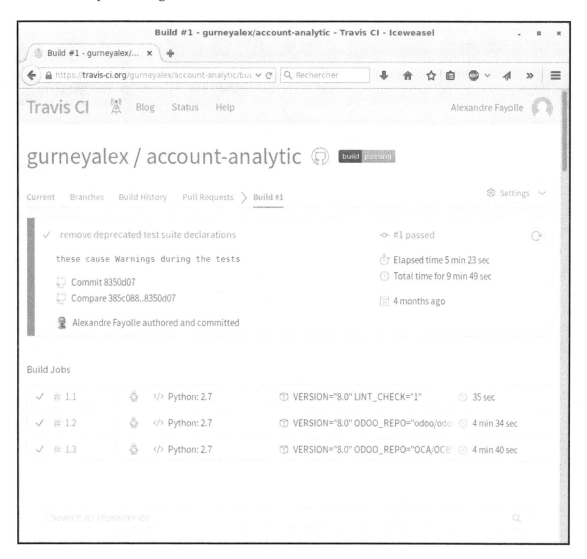

How it works...

When you enable Travis CI on a repository, Travis registers a hook on GitHub. By default, the hook will trigger a Travis CI build for each push to a branch of the repository and for each pull request. Pull requests are built on a temporary merge of the PR to ensure that the merged branches pass the tests.

The Travis CI configuration file proposed here is fairly advanced and very close to the one found in the `sample_files` subdirectory of the maintainer-quality-tools project you can find at `https://github.com/OCA/maintainer-quality-tools` (we removed the transifex configuration used to manage module translations). Here's an explanation of the customized sections in the file:

- `addons`: This has nothing to do with Odoo addon modules. It's used to ask Travis to install some Ubuntu packages using distribution packages in the testing environment. This saves us from installing Python packages such as `python-lxml` from source, which takes a lot of time.
- `env`: This section defines environment variables and the build matrix. The maintainer quality tools use these environment variables to know what to test, and will run each `env` line in a separate test run:
    - `VERSION`: This is the Odoo version to test against.
    - `LINT_CHECK`: Use `0` for a build with no `flake8` or `Pylint` tests, and `1` otherwise. In the matrix, we set the first build to perform the lint check, as this is fast and we want rapid feedback if the coding standards are not met or if the linter finds errors.
    - `TESTS`: Use `0` for a build in which the module tests are not run, otherwise use `1`.
    - `ODOO_REPO`: It is the GitHub repository for Odoo to test against when `TESTS` is `1`. In the recipe, we set up a build against both the official `https://github.com/odoo/odoo` repository and the community backports repository `https://github.com/OCA/OCB`. If unset, only the official repository is used.
- `install`: This section downloads the `maintainer-quality-tools` in the build environment and call the `travis_install_nightly` utility, which will set up Odoo in Travis.
- `script`: This section calls the `travis_run_tests` from the maintainer-quality-tools. This is the script in charge of checking the environment variables form the build matrix and performing the appropriate actions.

- `after_success`: After the tests in the script section have run successfully, the `travis_after_test_success` script is run. In the context of the recipe, this script will check the test coverage of the modules using `https://coveralls.io` and produce a report in the build.

There's more...

Maybe you are not interested in the whole setup, which is heavily dependent on Travis-CI, and you would like some lighter tools to help you in your day-to-day work. The good news is that some of the tools behind the setup shown in the recipe can be used individually, especially the **static code checkers** Pylint and Flake8.

Using Pylint to check your code

Pylint (`https://www.pylint.org/`) is a static code checker for Python. There is a very interesting project called pylint-odoo, which provides a Pylint plugin to perform Odoo-specific checks. To install, run the following command, preferably in a virtual environment:

```
$ pip3 install --upgrade --pre pylint-odoo
```

When this is done, you can check your addon module with the following command:

```
$ pylint --load-plugins=pylint_odoo -rn -e epylint
<path_to_the_addon_directory>
```

This will produce an output such as the following:

```
********** Module my_module
C: 1, 0: Missing ./README.rst file. Template here:
https://github.com/OCA/maintainer-tools/blob/master/template/module/README.
rst (missing-readme)
************* Module my_module.__manifest__
C: 2, 0: Missing author required "Odoo Community Association (OCA)" in
manifest file (manifest-required-author)
C: 2, 0: Deprecated key "description" in manifest file (manifest-
deprecated-key)
************* Module my_module.models.library_book
W: 14,12: The attribute string is redundant. String parameter equal to name
of variable (attribute-string-redundant)
```

The README file on `https://github.com/OCA/pylint-odoo/blob/master/README.rst` of the module will give you an up-to-date list of checks performed by the tool. Then, you can use Pylint's command-line options to tune the output. For instance, if you are not interested in the *missing author* check, which is specific to the Odoo Community Association, you can remove the check by checking the message ID in the README (it is C8101) and passing it to the `-d` or `--disable` command-line option like this:

```
$ pylint --load-plugin=pylint_odoo -rn -e epylint -d C8101 \
<path_to_the_addon_directory>
```

It is possible to store the command-line options you pass to Pylint in a configuration file to ease your daily work.

Using Flake8 to check your code

Flake8 `http://flake8.pycqa.org/` is also a popular tool you can use to verify that your code is correctly formatted. Programming text editors and IDEs supporting Python development generally offer a way to run `flake8` as you type, highlighting portions of code that do not match the agreed coding conventions.

To install flake8, run this:

```
$ pip install flake8
```

Here's a flake8 configuration file used for the Odoo Community Association development:

```
[flake8]
# E123,E133,E226,E241,E242 are ignored by default by pep8 and flake8
# F811 is legal in odoo 8 when we implement 2 interfaces for a method
# F999 pylint support this case with expected tests
ignore = E123,E133,E226,E241,E242,F811,F601
max-line-length = 79
exclude = __unported__,__init__.py
```

Save this in a file called `.flake8` at the root of your project, and you should then be able to run the following:

```
$ flake8 <path_to_file_or_directory>
```

Otherwise, better yet, set up your editor to check your code as you type!

9
Advanced Server-Side Development Techniques

In this chapter, we will see how to do the following:

- Changing the user performing an action
- Calling a method with a modified context
- Executing raw SQL queries
- Writing a wizard to guide the user
- Defining onchange methods
- Calling onchange methods on the server side
- Defining a model based on a SQL view

Introduction

In Chapter 6, *Basic Server-Side Development*, we saw how to write methods on a model class, how to extend methods from inherited models, and how to work with recordsets. This chapter deals with more advanced topics such as working with the environment of a recordset and working with on change methods.

Changing the user performing an action

When writing business logic code, you may have to perform some actions with a different security context. A typical case is performing an action with the rights of the Administrator, who bypasses security checks.

This recipe shows us how to let normal users modify the phone number of a company using `sudo()`.

Getting ready

We will work on records of the `res.company` model. By default, only members of the **Administration/Access Rights** user group can modify the records of `res.company`, but in our case, we need to provide an access point to change only the phone number to users who are not necessarily members of that group.

How to do it...

In order to let normal users modify the phone number of a company, you need to perform the following steps:

1. Define a model extending the `res.company` model:

```
class ResCompany(models.Model):
    _inherit = 'res.company'
```

2. Add a method called `update_phone_number()`:

```
@api.multi
def update_phone_number(self, new_number):
```

3. In the method, ensure that we are acting on a single record:

```
self.ensure_one()
```

4. Modify the user of the environment:

```
company_as_superuser = self.sudo()
```

5. Write the new phone number:

```
company_as_superuser.phone = new_number
```

How it works...

In step 4, we call `self.sudo()`. This method returns a new recordset with a new **environment** in which the user is not the same as the one in `self`. When called without an argument, `sudo()` will link the Odoo **superuser**, Administrator, to the environment. All method calls via the returned recordset are made with the new environment and therefore with superuser privileges.

If you need a specific user, you can pass either a recordset containing that user or the database `id` of the user. The following snippet allows you to search books that are visible, using the `public` user:

```
public_user = self.env.ref('base.public_user')
public_book = self.env['library.book'].sudo(public_user)
```

 Caution when using sudo(): There is no traceability of the action; the author of the last modification of the company in our recipe will be the Administrator, not the user originally calling `update_phone_number`. The community addon, `base_suspend_security`, found at `https://github.com/OCA/server-backend/`, can be used to work around this limitation.

There's more...

When using `sudo()` without an argument, you set the user of the context to the Odoo superuser. This superuser bypasses all the security rules of Odoo, both the **access control lists** and the **record rules**. By default, this user also has a `company_id` field set to the main company of the instance (the one with ID 1). This can be problematic in a **multi company** instance:

- If you are not careful, new records created in this environment will be linked to the company of the superuser
- If you are not careful, records searched in this environment may be linked to any company present in the database, which means that you may be leaking information to the real user, or worse, you may be silently corrupting the database by linking together records belonging to different companies

When using `sudo()`, always double-check to ensure that your calls to `search()` don't rely on the standard record rules to filter the results, and ensure that your calls to `create()` do not rely on default values that are computed using some of the current user's field such as `company_id`.

Using `sudo()` also involves creating a new `Environment` instance. This environment will have an initially empty recordset cache, and that cache will evolve independently from the cache of `self.env`. This can cause spurious database queries. In any case, you should avoid creating new environment inside loops, and try to move these environment creations to the outmost possible scope.

See also

- The *Obtain an empty recordset for a model* recipe in `Chapter 6`, *Basic Server-Side Development*, explains what the environment is
- For more information about access control lists and record rules, check `Chapter 11`, *Access Security*

Calling a method with a modified context

The context is part of the environment of a recordset. It is used to pass information such as the timezone and the language of the user from the user interface as well as contextual parameters specified in actions. A number of methods in the standard addons use the context to adapt their behavior to these values. It is sometimes necessary to modify the context on a recordset to get the desired results from a method call or the desired value for a computed field.

This recipe shows you how to read the stock level for all `product.product` models in a given `stock.location`.

Getting ready

This recipe uses the `stock` and `product` addons. For our purposes, here's a simplified version of the `product.product` model:

```
class product.product(models.Model):
    _name = 'product.product'
```

```
name = fields.Char('Name', required=True)
qty_available = fields.Float('Quantity on Hand',
                            compute='_product_available')
def _product_available(self):
    """if context contains a key 'location' linked to a
    database id, then the stock available is computed within
    that location only. Otherwise the stock of all internal
    locations is computed"""
    pass  # read the real source in addons/stock/product.py :)
```

We intentionally don't provide the implementation of the computation, and we skipped a few other keys that are looked for in the context in order to focus on the recipe. You may want to check the full source code of this method in the `stock` standard addon module.

How to do it...

In order to compute the stock levels in a given location for all the products, you need to perform the following steps:

1. Create a model class extending `product.product`:

```
class ProductProduct(models.Model):
    _inherit = 'product.product'
```

2. Add a method called `stock_in_location()`:

```
@api.model
def stock_in_location(self, location):
```

3. In the method, get a `product.product` recordset with a context modified, as follows:

```
product_in_loc = self.with_context(
    location=location.id,
    active_test=False
)
```

4. Search all products:

```
all_products = product_in_loc.search([])
```

5. Create an array with the product name and stock level of all products present in the specified location:

```
stock_levels = []
for product in all_products:
    if product.qty_available:
        stock_levels.append((product.name,
                             product.qty_available))
return stock_levels
```

How it works...

Step 3 calls `self.with_context()` with some keyword arguments. This returns a new version of `self` (which is a `product.product` recordset) with the keys added to the current **context**. We are adding two keys:

- `location`: This one is mentioned in the docstring of the `product.product` method computing the `qty_available` field.
- `active_test`: When this key is present and linked to the `False` value, the `search()` method does not automatically add (`'active'`, `'='`, `True`) to the search domain. Using this ensures that in step 4, we get all the products, including the disabled ones.

When we read the value of `product.qty_available` in step 5, the computation of that field is made using only the specified stock location.

There's more...

It is also possible to pass a dictionary to `self.with_context()`, in which case the dictionary is used as the new context, overwriting the current one. So, step 3 can also be written like this:

```
new_context = self.env.context.copy()
new_context.update({'location': location.id,
                    'active_test': False})
product_in_loc = self.with_context(new_context)
```

Using `with_context()` involves creating a new `Environment` instance. This **environment** will have an initially empty recordset cache, and that cache will evolve independently of the cache of `self.env`. This can cause spurious database queries. In any case, you should avoid creating new environments inside loops and try to move these environment creations to the outmost possible scope.

See also

- The *Obtain an empty recordset for a model* recipe in `Chapter 6`, *Basic Server-Side Development*, explains what the environment is
- The *Passing parameters to forms and actions: Context* recipe in `Chapter 10`, *Backend Views*, explains how to modify the context in action definitions
- The *Search for records* recipe in `Chapter 6`, *Basic Server-Side Development*, explains active records

Executing raw SQL queries

Most of the time, you can perform the operations you want using the `search()` method. However, sometimes, you need more—either you cannot express what you want using the domain syntax, for which some operations are tricky if not downright impossible, or your query requires several calls to `search()`, which ends up being inefficient.

This recipe shows you how to use raw SQL queries to read `res.partner` records grouped by country.

Getting ready

We will use a simplified version of the res.partner model:

```
class ResPartner(models.Model):
    _name = 'res.partner'
    name = fields.Char('Name', required=True)
    email = fields.Char('Email')
    is_company = fields.Boolean('Is a company')
    parent_id = fields.Many2one('res.partner', 'Related Company')
    child_ids = fields.One2many('res.partner', 'parent_id',
                                'Contacts')
    country_id = fields.Many2one('res.country', 'Country')
```

How to do it...

To write a method that returns a dictionary that contains the mapped names of countries to a recordset of all active partners from that country, you need to perform the following steps:

1. Write a class extending res.partner:

```
class ResPartner(models.Model):
    _inherit = 'res.partner'
```

2. Add a method called partners_by_country():

```
@api.model
def partners_by_country(self):
```

3. In the method, write the following SQL query:

```
sql = ('SELECT country_id, array_agg(id) '
       'FROM res_partner '
       'WHERE active=true AND country_id IS NOT NULL '
       'GROUP BY country_id')
```

4. Execute the query:

```
self.env.cr.execute(sql)
```

5. Iterate over the results of the query to populate the result dictionary:

```
country_model = self.env['res.country']
result = {}
for country_id, partner_ids in self.env.cr.fetchall():
    country = country_model.browse(country_id)
    partners = self.search(
        [('id', 'in', tuple(partner_ids))]
    )
    result[country] = partners
return result
```

How it works...

In step 3, we declare a SQL SELECT query. It uses the id field and the country_id foreign key, which refers to the res_country table. We use a GROUP BY statement so that the database does the grouping by country_id for us, and the array_agg aggregation function. This is a very useful PostgreSQL extension to SQL that puts all the values for the group in an array, which Python maps to a list.

Step 4 calls the execute() method on the database cursor stored in self.env.cr. This sends the query to PostgreSQL and executes it.

Step 5 uses the fetchall() method of the cursor to retrieve a list of rows selected by the query. From the form of the query we executed, we know that each row will have exactly two values, the first being country_id and the other one, the list of ids for the partners having that country. We loop over these rows and create recordsets from the values, which we store in the result dictionary.

There's more...

The object in `self.env.cr` is a thin wrapper around a `psycopg2` cursor. The following methods are the ones you will want to use most of the time:

- `execute(query, params)`: This executes the SQL `query` with the parameters marked as `%s` in the query substituted with the values in params, which is a tuple

 Warning: Never do the substitution yourself, as this can make the code vulnerable to SQL injections.

- `fetchone()`: This returns one row from the database, wrapped in a tuple (even if there is only one column selected by the query)
- `fetchall()`: This returns all the rows from the database as a list of tuples
- `fetchalldict()`: This returns all the rows from the database as a list of dictionaries mapping column names to values

Be very careful when dealing with raw SQL queries:

- You are bypassing all the security of the application. Ensure that you call `search([('id', 'in', tuple(ids)])` with any list of `ids` you are retrieving to filter out records to which the user has no access.
- Any modification you are making is bypassing the constraints set by the addon modules, except the `NOT NULL`, `UNIQUE`, and `FOREIGN KEY` constraints, which are enforced at the database level, and so are any computed field recomputation triggers, so you may end up corrupting the database.

See also

- For access rights management, refer to `Chapter 11`, *Access Security*

Writing a wizard to guide the user

In the *Use Abstract Models for reusable Model features* recipe in `Chapter 5`, *Application Models*, the `models.TransientModel` base class was introduced; this class shares a lot with normal `Models`, except that the records of **transient models** are periodically cleaned up in the database, hence the name *transient*. These are used to create **wizards** or dialog boxes, which are filled in the user interface by the users and generally used to perform actions on the persistent records of the database.

This recipe extends the code from `Chapter 4`, *Creating Odoo Modules*, by creating a wizard to record the borrowing of books by a library member.

Getting ready

If you want to follow the recipe, ensure that you have the `my_module` addon module from `Chapter 4`, *Creating Odoo Modules*.

We will also use a simple model to record book loans:

```
class LibraryBookLoan(models.Model):
    _name = 'library.book.loan'
    book_id = fields.Many2one('library.book', 'Book',
                              required=True)
    member_id = fields.Many2one('library.member', 'Borrower',
                              required=True)
    state = fields.Selection([('ongoing', 'Ongoing'),
                              ('done', 'Done')],
                             'State',
                             default='ongoing', required=True)
```

How to do it...

To add a wizard for recording borrowed books to the addon module, you need to perform the following steps:

1. Add a new transient model to the module with the following definition:

```
class LibraryLoanWizard(models.TransientModel):
    _name = 'library.loan.wizard'
    member_id = fields.Many2one('library.member', string='Member')
    book_ids = fields.Many2many('library.book', string='Books')
```

2. Add the callback method performing the action on the transient model. Add the following code to the `LibraryLoanWizard` class:

```
@api.multi
def record_loans(self):
    loan = self.env['library.book.loan']
    for wizard in self:
        member = wizard.member_id
        books = wizard.book_ids
        for book in books:
            loan.create({'member_id': member.id,
                         'book_id': book.id})
```

3. Create a form view for the model. Add the following view definition to the module views:

```
<record id='library_loan_wizard_form' model='ir.ui.view'>
 <field name='name'>library loan wizard form view</field>
 <field name='model'>library.loan.wizard</field>
 <field name='arch' type='xml'>
   <form string="Borrow books">
     <sheet>
       <group>
         <field name='member_id'/>
       </group>
       <group>
         <field name='book_ids'/>
       </group>
     </sheet>
     <footer>
       <button name='record_loans'
               string='OK'
               class='btn-primary'
               type='object'/>
       <button string='Cancel'
               class='btn-default'
               special='cancel'/>
     </footer>
   </form>
 </field>
</record>
```

4. Create an action and a menu entry to display the wizard. Add the following declarations to the module menu file:

```
<act_window id="action_wizard_loan_books"
            name="Record Loans"
```

```
                  res_model="library.loan.wizard"
                  view_mode="form"
                  target="new"
                  />
    <menuitem id="menu_wizard_loan_books"
              parent="library_book_menu"
              action="action_wizard_loan_books"
              sequence="20"
              />
```

How it works...

Step 1 defines a new model. It is no different from other models, apart from the base class, which is `TransientModel` instead of `Model`. Both `TransientModel` and `Model` share a common base class called `BaseModel`, and if you check the source code of Odoo, you will see that 99% of the work is in `BaseModel` and that both `Model` and `TransientModel` are almost empty.

The only things that change for `TransientModel` records are as follows:

- Records are periodically removed from the database, so the tables for transient models don't grow up in size over time.
- You cannot define access rules on `TransientModels`. Anyone is allowed to create a record, but only the user who created a record can read and use it.
- You must not define `One2many` fields on a `TransientModel` that refer to a normal model, as this will add a column on the persistent model linking to transient data. Use `Many2many` relations in this case. You can, of course, define `Many2one` and `One2many` fields for relations between transient models.

We define two fields in the model: one to store the member borrowing the books and one to store the list of books being borrowed. We can add other scalar fields to record a scheduled return date, for instance.

Step 2 adds the code to the wizard class that will be called when the button defined in step 3 is clicked on. This code reads the values from the wizard and creates `library.book.loan` records for each book.

Step 3 defines a view for our wizard. Refer to the *Document-style forms* recipe in `Chapter 10`, *Backend Views*, for details. The important point here is the button in the footer; the type attribute is set to `'object'`, which means that when the user clicks on the button, the method with the name specified by the name attribute of the button will be called.

Step 4 ensures that we have an entry point for our wizard in the menu of the application. We use `target='new'` in the action so that the form view is displayed as a dialog box over the current form. Refer to the *Add a Menu Item and Window Action* recipe in `Chapter 10`, *Backend Views*, for details.

There's more...

Here are a few tips to enhance your wizards.

Using the context to compute default values

The wizard we are presenting requires the user to fill in the name of the member in the form. There is a feature of the web client we can use to save some typing. When an action is executed, the **context** is updated with some values that can be used by wizards:

Key	Value
`active_model`	This is the name of the model related to the action. This is generally the model being displayed on-screen.
`active_id`	This indicates that a single record is active, and provides the ID of that record.
`active_ids`	If several records were selected, this will be a list with the IDs (this happens when several items are selected in a tree view when the action is triggered. In a form view, you get `[active_id]`).
`active_domain`	An additional domain on which the wizard will operate.

These values can be used to compute default values of the model, or even directly in the method called by the button. To improve on the recipe example, if we had a button displayed on the form view of a `library.member` model to launch the wizard, then the context of the creation of the wizard will contain `{'active_model': 'library.member', 'active_id': <member id>}`. In that case, you can define the `member_id` field
to have a default value computed by the following method:

```
def _default_member(self):
    if self.context.get('active_model') == 'library.member':
        return self.context.get('active_id', False)
```

Wizards and code reuse

In step 2, we could have dispensed with the for wizard in self loop, and assumed that `len(self)` is 1, possibly adding a call to `self.ensure_one()` at the beginning of the method, like this:

```
@api.multi
def record_borrows(self):
    self.ensure_one()
    member = self.member_id
    books = self.book_ids
    loan = self.env['library.book.loan']
    for book in books:
        loan.create({'member_id': member.id, 'book_id': book.id})
```

We recommend using the version in the recipe, though, because it allows reusing the wizard from other parts of the code by creating records for the wizard, putting them in a single recordset (refer to the *Combining recordsets* recipe in `Chapter 6`, *Basic Server Side Development*, to see how to do this) and then calling `record_loans()` on the recordset. Granted that here the code is trivial and you don't really need to jump through all those hoops to record that some books were borrowed by different members. However, in an Odoo instance, some operations are much more complex, and it is always nice to have a wizard available that does "the right thing." When using such wizards, ensure that you check the source code for any possible use of the `active_model/active_id/active_ids` keys from the context, in which case, you need to pass a custom context (refer to the *Call a method with a modified context* recipe covered earlier for how to do this).

Redirecting the user

The method in step 2 does not return anything. This will cause the wizard dialog to be closed after the action is performed. Another possibility is to have the method return a dictionary with the fields of an `ir.action`. In this case, the web client will process the action as if a menu entry had been clicked on by the user. The `get_formview_action()` method defined on the `BaseModel` class can be used to achieve this. For instance, if we wanted to display the form view of the member who has just borrowed the books, we could have written the following:

```
@api.multi
def record_borrows(self):
    loan = self.env['library.book.loan']
    for wizard in self:
        member = wizard.member_id
        books = wizard.book_ids
```

```
        for book in books:
            loan.create({'member_id': member.id,
                         'book_id': book.id})
    members = self.mapped('member_id')
    action = members.get_formview_action()
    if len(member_ids) > 1:
        action['domain'] = [('id', 'in', tuple(member_ids))]
        action['view_mode'] = 'tree,form'
    return action
```

This builds a list of members who have borrowed books from this wizard (in practice, there will only be one such member, when the wizard is called from the user interface) and creates a dynamic action, which displays the members with the specified IDs.

This trick can be extended by having a wizard (with several steps to be performed one after the other), or depending on some condition from the preceding steps, by providing a **Next** button that calls a method defined on the wizard. This method will perform the step (maybe using a hidden field and storing the current step number), update some fields on the wizard, and return an action that will redisplay the same updated wizard and get ready for the next step.

Defining onchange methods

When writing Odoo models, it is often the case that some fields are interrelated. We have seen how to specify constraints between fields in the *Adding constraint validations to a Model* recipe in Chapter 5, *Application Models*. This recipe illustrates a slightly different concept—onchange methods are called when a field is modified in the user interface to update the values of other fields of the record in the web client, usually in a form view.

We will illustrate this by providing a wizard similar to the one defined in the *Write a wizard to guide the user* recipe, but which can be used to record loan returns. When the member is set on the wizard, the list of books is updated to the books currently borrowed by the member. While we are demonstrating onchange methods on a TransientModel, these features are also available on normal Models.

Getting ready

If you want to follow the recipe, ensure that you have the my_module addon from Chapter 4, *Creating Odoo Modules*, with the *Write a wizard to guide the user* recipe's changes applied.

You will also want to prepare your work by defining the following transient model for the wizard:

```
class LibraryReturnsWizard(models.TransientModel):
    _name = 'library.returns.wizard'
    member_id = fields.Many2one('library.member', string='Member')
    book_ids = fields.Many2many('library.book', string='Books')
    @api.multi
    def record_returns(self):
        loan = self.env['library.book.loan']
        for rec in self:
            loans = loan.search(
                [('state', '=', 'ongoing'),
                 ('book_id', 'in', rec.book_ids.ids),
                 ('member_id', '=', rec.member_id.id)]
            )
            loans.write({'state': 'done'})
        return True
```

Finally, you will need to define a view, an action, and a menu entry for the wizard. This is left as an exercise.

How to do it...

To automatically populate the list of books to return when the user is changed, you need to add an `onchange` method in the `LibraryReturnsWizard` step with the following definition:

```
@api.onchange('member_id')
def onchange_member(self):
    loan = self.env['library.book.loan']
    loans = loan.search(
        [('state', '=', 'ongoing'),
         ('member_id', '=', self.member_id.id)]
    )
    self.book_ids = loans.mapped('book_id')
```

How it works...

An `onchange` method uses the `@api.onchange` decorator, which is passed the names of the fields that change and thus will trigger the call to the method. In our case, we say that whenever `member_id` is modified in the user interface, the method must be called.

In the body of the method, we search the books currently borrowed by the member, and we use an attribute assignment to update the `book_ids` attribute of the wizard.

 The `@api.onchange` decorator takes care of modifying the view sent to the web client to add an `on_change` attribute to the field. This used to be a manual operation in the "old API".

There's more...

The basic use of `onchange` methods is to compute new values for fields when some other fields are changed in the user interface, as we've seen in the recipe.

Inside the body of the method, you get access to the fields displayed in the current view of the record, but not necessarily all the fields of the model. This is because `onchange` methods can be called while the record is being created in the user interface *before* it is stored in the database! Inside an `onchange` method, `self` is in a special state, denoted by the fact that `self.id` is not an integer, but an instance of `odoo.models.NewId`. Therefore, you must not make any changes to the database in an `onchange` method, because the user may end up canceling the creation of the record, which will not roll back any changes made by `onchange` called during the edition. To check for this, you can use `self.env.in_onchange()` and `self.env.in_draft()`; the former returns `True` if the current context of execution is an `onchange` method, and the latter returns `True` if `self` is not yet committed to the database.

Additionally, `onchange` methods can return a Python dictionary. This dictionary can have the following keys:

- `warning`: The value must be another dictionary with the `title` and `message` keys containing the title and the content of a dialog box respectively, which will be displayed when the `onchange` method is run. This is useful for drawing the attention of the user to inconsistencies or to potential problems.
- `domain`: The value must be another dictionary mapping field names to domains. This is useful when you want to change the domain of a `One2many` field depending on the value of another field.

For instance, suppose we have a fixed value set for `expected_return_date` in our `library.book.loan` model, and we want to display a warning when a member has some books that are late. We also want to restrict the choice of books to the ones currently borrowed by the user. We can rewrite the `onchange` method as follows:

```python
@api.onchange('member_id')
def onchange_member(self):
    loan = self.env['library.book.loan']
    loans = loan.search(
        [('state', '=', 'ongoing'),
         ('member_id', '=', self.member_id.id)]
    )
    self.book_ids = loans.mapped('book_id')
    result = {
        'domain': {'book_ids': [
                    ('id', 'in', self.book_ids.ids)]
                  }
    }
    late_domain = [
        ('id', 'in', loans.ids),
        ('expected_return_date', '<', fields.Date.today())
    ]
    late_loans = loans.search(late_domain)
    if late_loans:
        message = ('Warn the member that the following '
                    'books are late:\n')
        titles = late_loans.mapped('book_id.name')
        result['warning'] = {
            'title': 'Late books',
            'message': message + '\n'.join(titles)
        }
    return result
```

Calling onchange methods on the server side

The *Creating new records* and *Updating values of a recordset record* recipes in Chapter 6, *Basic Server-Side Development*, mentioned that these operations did not call onchange methods automatically. Yet, in a number of cases, it is important that these operations are called, because they update important fields in the created or updated record. Of course, you can do the required computation yourself, but this is not always possible as the onchange method can be added or modified by a third-party addon module installed on the instance that you don't know about.

This recipe explains how to call the onchange methods on a record by manually playing the onchange method before creating a record.

Getting ready

We will reuse the settings from the *Write onchange methods* recipe. The action will take place in a new method of library.member called return_all_books(self).

How to do it...

In this recipe, we will manually create a record of the library.returns.wizard model, and we want the onchange method to compute the returned books for us. To do this, you need to perform the following steps:

1. Create the return_all_books method in the LibraryMember class:

```
@api.multi
def return_all_books(self):
    self.ensure_one()
```

2. Get an empty recordset for library.returns.wizard:

```
wizard = self.env['library.returns.wizard']
```

3. Prepare the values to create a new wizard record:

```
values = {'member_id': self.id, 'book_ids': False}
```

4. Retrieve the onchange specifications for the wizard:

```
specs = wizard._onchange_spec()
```

5. Get the result of the onchange method:

```
updates = wizard.onchange(values, ['member_id'], specs)
```

6. Merge these results with the values of the new wizard:

```
value = updates.get('value', {})
for name, val in value.items():
    if isinstance(val, tuple):
        value[name] = val[0]
values.update(value)
```

7. Create the wizard:

```
wiz = wizard.create(values)
return wiz.record_returns()
```

How it works...

For an explanation of step 1 to step 3, refer to the *Creating new records* recipe in `Chapter 6`, *Basic Server-Side Development*.

Step 4 calls the _onchange_spec method on the model, passing no argument. This method will retrieve the updates that are triggered by the modification of other field. It does this by examining the form view of the model (remember that onchange methods are normally called by the web client).

Step 5 calls the onchange(values, field_name, field_onchange) method of the model with three arguments:

- values: The list of values we want to set on the record. You need to provide a value for all the fields you expect to be modified by the onchange method. In the recipe, we set book_ids to False for this reason.
- field_name: A list of fields for which we want to trigger the onchange methods. You can pass an empty list, and it will use the fields defined in values. However, you will often want to specify that list manually to control the order of evaluation, in case different fields can update a common field.

- `field_onchange`: The `onchange` specifications that were computed in step 4. This method finds out which `onchange` methods must be called and in what order, and returns a dictionary, which can contain the following keys:
  - `value`: This is a dictionary of newly computed field values. This dictionary only features keys that are in the `values` parameter passed to `onchange()`. Note that the `Many2one` fields are mapped to a tuple containing (`id, display_name`) as an optimization for the web client.
  - `warning`: This is a dictionary containing a warning message that the web client will display to the user.
  - <li

      >

  `domain`
    : This is a dictionary mapping field names to new validity domains.

Generally, when manually playing `onchange` methods, we only care about what is in `value`.

Step 6 updates our initial values dictionary with the values computed by the `onchange`. We process the values corresponding to `Many2one` fields to only keep the `id`. To do so, we take advantage of the fact that these fields are only those whose values are returned as a tuple.

Step 7 finally creates the record.

There's more...

If you need to call an `onchange` method after modifying a field, the code is the same. You just need to get a dictionary for the values of the record, which can be obtained using `values = dict(record._cache)` after modifying the field.

See also

- The *Creating new records* and *Updating values of recordset records* recipes in `Chapter 6`, *Basic Server-Side Development*

Defining a model based on a SQL view

When working on the design of an addon module, we model the data in classes that are then mapped to database tables by Odoo. We apply some well-known design principles such as separation of concerns, data normalization, and more. However, at later stages of the module design, it can become meaningful to aggregate data from several models in a single table, and maybe perform some operations on them on the way, especially for reporting or producing dashboards. To ease doing so, and to leverage the full power of the underlying PostgreSQL database engine in Odoo, it is possible to define a read-only model backed by a PostgreSQL view rather than a table.

In this recipe, we will reuse the loan model from the *Write a wizard to guide the user* recipe in this chapter, and create a new model to ease gathering statistics about book turnover, the age of the readers, and the affinity of authors by reader age.

Getting ready

If you want to follow the recipe, ensure that you have the `my_module` addon module from `Chapter 4`, *Creating Odoo Modules*, and the book loan model from the *Write a wizard to guide the user* recipe.

How to do it...

To create a new model backed by a PostgreSQL view, follow these instructions:

1. Start by creating a new model with the `_auto` class attribute set to `False`:

```
from odoo import models, api, fields, tools
class LibraryBookLoanStatistics(models.Model):
    _name = 'library.book.loan.statistics'
    _auto = False
```

2. Declare the fields you want to see in the model, setting them as `readonly`:

```
book_id = fields.Many2one('library.book', 'Book', readonly=True)
loan_id = fields.Many2one('library.book.loan', 'Loan',
                          readonly=True)
author_id = fields.Many2one('res.partner', 'Author', readonly=True)
reader_id = fields.Many2one('library.member', 'Reader',
                            readonly=True)
reader_age = fields.Integer(
    'Reader age', readonly=True,
    group_operator='avg',
    help="the age of the reader when he borrowed the book"
)
```

3. Define the `init()` method to create the view:

```
@api.model_cr
def init(self):
    tools.drop_view_if_exists(self.env.cr, self._table)
    query = """
    CREATE OR REPLACE VIEW library_book_loan_statistics AS (
    SELECT loan_id + author.res_partner_id * (SELECT MAX(id) FROM
                                              library_book_loan)
            AS id,
        loan.book_id AS book_id,
        loan.id AS loan_id,
        author.res_partner_id AS author_id,
        reader.id AS reader_id,
        EXTRACT(YEAR FROM age(loan.create_date,
                              reader.date_of_birth))
            AS reader_age
    FROM library_book_loan AS loan
    JOIN library_book AS book ON (loan.book_id = book.id)
    JOIN library_book_res_partner_rel AS author ON (book.id =
                                      author.library_book_id)
    JOIN library_member as reader ON (loan.member_id = reader.id)
```

```
    )
    """
    self.env.cr.execute(query)
```

4. You can now define views for the new model. A pivot view is especially useful to explore the data (refer to `Chapter 10`, *Backend Views*).

5. Don't forget to define some access rules for the new model (take a look at `Chapter 11`, *Access Security*).

How it works...

Normally, Odoo will create a new table for the model you are defining using the field definitions for the columns. Actually, this is because on the `BaseModel` class, the `_auto` attribute defaults to `True`. In step 1, by positioning this class attribute to `False`, we tell Odoo that we will manage this by ourselves.

In step 2, we define some fields which will be used by Odoo to generate a table. We take care to flag them as `readonly=True` so that the views do not enable modification that you will not be able to save since PostgreSQL views are read-only.

Step 3 defines the `init()` method. This method normally does nothing; it is called after `_auto_init()` (which is responsible for the table creation when `_auto = True`, but does nothing otherwise), and we use it to create a new SQL view (or update the existing view in case of a module upgrade). The view creation query must create a view with column names matching the field names of the Model.

 It is a common mistake in this case to forget to rename the columns in the view definition query, and this will cause a strange error message when Odoo cannot find the column.

Note that we also need to provide an Integer column called ID containing unique values.

There's more...

It is also possible to have some computed and related fields on such models. The only restriction is that the fields cannot be stored (and therefore you cannot use them to group records or to search). However, in the preceding example, we could have made the editor of the book available by adding a column, defined as follows:

```
publisher_id = fields.Many2one('res.partner',
related='book_id.publisher_id', readonly=True)
```

If you need to group by publisher, then you need to *store* the field by adding it in the view definition rather than using a related field.

Computed fields are still very useful to have. For instance, in the preceding view, we are expanding the many-to-many relation between books and authors. This means that if you group by `book_id` and look at the number of loans, a book with two authors will seem to be borrowed twice as much as if it had just one author. If you want to know how many times a book was borrowed and don't wish to write SQL to add a column for this, in the view, you can have a computed field (although to be completely fair, in this specific example, it is much easier to have this in the SQL view):

```
borrow_count = fields.Integer('Borrow count', compute='_get_borrow_count')
@api.depends('book_id')
def _get_borrow_count(self):
    if not self:
        return
    book_ids = self.mapped('book_id').ids
    query = '''SELECT book_id, count(id)
            FROM library_book_loan
            WHERE book_id in %s GROUP BY book_id'''
    self.env.cr.execute(query, (tuple(book_ids),))
    counts = dict(self.env.cr.fetchall())
    for rec in self:
        rec.borrow_count = counts[rec.book_id]
```

10
Backend Views

In this chapter, we will cover the following topics:

- Adding a menu item and window action
- Having an action open a specific view
- Adding content and widgets to a form view
- Adding buttons to forms
- Passing parameters to forms and actions – Context
- Defining filters on record lists – Domain
- List views
- Search views
- Changing existing views – View inheritance
- Document-style forms
- Dynamic form elements using attrs
- Embedded views
- Kanban views
- Showing kanban cards in columns according to their state
- Calendar and gantt views
- Graph and pivot views

Throughout this chapter, we will assume that you have a database with the base addon installed and an empty Odoo addon module where you add XML code from the recipes to a data file referenced in the addon's manifest. Refer to `Chapter 4`, *Creating Odoo Addon Modules*, for how to activate changes in your addon.

Introduction

This chapter covers all the UI elements that users are confronted with when they use anything other than the website part of Odoo. Historically, this was basically all of OpenERP, so also in an Odoo context, it is often just referred to as the web client. To be more specific, we will call this the **backend** as opposed to the website frontend.

Adding a menu item and window action

The most obvious way to make a new feature available to users is by adding a menu item. When you click on a menu item, something happens. This recipe walks you through how to define that something.

We will create a top level menu displaying a sub menu in the left hand menu bar, opening a list of all customers.

This can also be done using the web user interface, via the settings menu, but we prefer to use XML data files since this is what we'll have to use when creating our addon modules.

How to do it...

In an XML data file of our addon module, perform the following steps:

1. Define an action to be executed:

```
<act_window id="action_all_customers"
    name="All customers"
    res_model="res.partner"
    view_mode="list,form"
    domain="[('customer', '=', True)]"
    context="{'default_customer': True}"
    limit="80"
/>
```

2. Create the menu structure:

```
<menuitem id="menu_custom_toplevel"
    name="My custom menu"
/>
<menuitem id="menu_custom_left"
    parent="menu_custom_toplevel"
    name="This will appear in the left bar"
```

```
/>
```

3. Refer to our action in the menu:

```
<menuitem id="menu_all_customers"
    parent="menu_custom_left"
    action="action_all_customers"
    sequence="10"
    groups=""
/>
```

If we now upgrade the module, we will see a top-level menu that opens a submenu in the left menu bar. Clicking on that menu item will open a list of all customers.

How it works...

The first XML element, `act_window`, declares a window action to display a list view with all the customers. We used the most important attributes:

- `name`: To be used as the title for views opened by the action.
- `res_model`: This is the model to be used. We are using `res.partner`, where Odoo stores all the partners and addresses, including customers.
- `view_mode`: This lists the view types to make available. The default value is *list, form*, making list and form views available. Other possible choices are *kanban, graph, pivot*, and *calendar*, which are explained later in this chapter.
- `domain`: This is optional and allows you to set a filter on the records to be made available in the views. In this case, we want to limit the partners to only those who are customers. We will explain this in more detail in a dedicated recipe later.
- `context`: This can set values made available to the opened views, affecting their behavior. In our example, on new records, we want the customer flag's default value to be `True`. This will be covered in more depth in another recipe.
- `limit`: This sets the default amount of records that can be seen on list views. It defaults to `80`.

> In legacy code, you'll find a view mode *tree* quite often. This was the internal name of list views up to and including Odoo 10. Version 11 still accepts this value, but treats it as if you had written *list*.

Next, we create the menu item hierarchy from the top-level menu to the clickable end menu item. The most important attributes for the `menuitem` element are as listed:

- `name`: This is used as the text the menu items display. If your menu item links to an action, you can leave this out, because the action's name will be used in that case.
- `parent` (`parent_id` if using the `record` element): This is the XML ID referencing the parent menu item. Items with no parent are top-level menus.
- `action`: This is the XML ID referencing the action to be called.
- `sequence`: This is used to order sibling menu items.
- `groups` (`groups_id` with the `record` tag): This is an optional list of user groups that can access this menu item. If empty, it will be available to all users.

Window actions automatically determine the view to be used by looking up views for the target model with the intended type (`form`, `tree`, and so on) and picking the one with the lowest sequence number.

`act_window` and `menuitem` are convenient shortcut XML tags that hide what you're actually doing: you create a record of the `ir.actions.act_window` and `ir.ui.menu` models respectively.

> Be aware that names used with the `menuitem` shortcut may not map to the field names used when using a `record` element—`parent` should be `parent_id` and `groups` should be `groups_id`.

To build the menu, the web client reads all the records from `ir.ui.menu` and infers their hierarchy from the `parent_id` field. Menus are also filtered based on user permissions to models and groups assigned to menus and actions. When a user clicks on a menu item, its `action` is executed.

There's more...

Window actions also support a `target` attribute to specify how the view is to be presented. Possible choices are as follows:

- **current**: This is the default and opens the view in the web client main content area
- **new**: This opens the view in a popup
- **inline**: Like current, but opens a form in edit mode and disables the **Action** menu
- **fullscreen**: The action will cover the whole browser window, so this will overlay the menus too

- **main:** Like current, but also clears out the breadcrumb

The window action's `view_type` attribute is mostly obsolete by now. The alternative to the default **form** is **tree**, which causes grouped lists to render a hierarchical tree. Don't confuse this attribute with the `view_mode` attribute used and explained earlier, which actually decides which types of views are used.

There are also some additional attributes available for window actions that are not supported by the `act_window` shortcut tag. So, to use them, we must use the `record` element with the following fields:

- **res_id**: If opening a form, you can have it open a specific record by setting its ID here. This can be useful for multistep wizards, or in cases when you often have to view/edit a specific record.
- **search_view_id**: This specifies a specific search view to use for tree and graph views.
- **auto_search**: This is **True** by default. Set this to **False** if searching for your object is very time and/or resource consuming. This way, the user can review the search parameters and press **Search** when satisfied. With the default, the search is triggered immediately when the action is opened.

Keep in mind that the menu bar at the top and the menu to the left are all made up of the same stuff, menu items. The only difference is that the items in the top bar don't have any parent menus, while the ones on the left bar have the respective menu item from the top bar as parent. In the left bar, the hierarchical structure is more obvious.

Also bear in mind that for design reasons, the first-level menus in the left bar are rendered as kinds of headers, and standard Odoo doesn't assign an action to them very often. So, even if you can technically assign an action to them, your users won't be used to click on them and will probably be confused if you expect them to do so. In any case, Odoo will open the first menu item's action based on the sequence of the child menu items.

See also

You'll find a more detailed discussion of the XML ID reference mechanism in Chapter 7, *Module Data*. For now, just keep in mind that you can set references this way and—very important—that order matters. If the preceding tags were inverted, the addon containing this XML code wouldn't install, because the `menuitem` would refer to an unknown `action`.

This can become a pitfall when you add new data files and new elements during your development process, because then the order in which you add those files and elements does not necessarily reflect the order in which they will be loaded in an empty database. Always check, before deployment, whether your addon installs in an empty database.

The `ir.actions.act_window` action type is the most common one, but a menu can refer to any type of action. Technically, it is just the same if you link to a client action, a server action, or any other model defined in the `ir.actions.*` namespace. It just differs in what the backend makes out of the action.

If you need just a tiny bit more flexibility in the concrete action to be called, look into server actions that return a window action in turn. If you need complete flexibility on what you present, look into client actions (`ir.actions.client`), which allow you to have a completely custom user interface. However, only do so as the last resort as you lose a lot of Odoo's convenient helpers when using them.

Having an action open a specific view

Window actions automatically determine the view to be used if none is given, but sometimes, we want an action to open a specific view.

We will create a basic form view for the partner model and make the window action specifically open it.

How to do it...

1. Define the partner minimal form view:

```
<record id="form_all_customers" model="ir.ui.view">
    <field name="name">All customers</field>
    <field name="model">res.partner</field>
    <field name="arch" type="xml">
        <form>
            <group>
                <field name="name" />
            </group>
        </form>
    </field>
</record>
```

2. Tell the action from the preceding recipe to use it:

```
<record id="action_all_customers_form"
        model="ir.actions.act_window.view">
    <field name="act_window_id" ref="action_all_customers" />
    <field name="view_id" ref="form_all_customers" />
    <field name="view_mode">form</field>
    <field name="sequence">10</field>
</record>
```

Now, if you open your menu and click on some partner in the list, you should see the very minimal form we just defined.

How it works...

This time, we used the generic XML code for any type of record, that is, the `record` element with the required `id` and `model` attributes. As earlier, the `id` attribute is an arbitrary string that must be unique for your addon. The `model` attribute refers to the name of the model you want to create. Given that we want to create a view, we need to create a record of the `ir.ui.view` model. Within this element, you set fields as defined in the model you chose via the `model` attribute. For `ir.ui.view`, the crucial fields are `model` and `arch`. The `model` field contains the model you want to define a view for, while the `arch` field contains the definition of the view itself. We'll come to its contents in a short while.

The `name` field, while not strictly necessary, is helpful when debugging problems with views, so set it to some string that tells you what this view is intended to do. This field's content is not shown to the user, so you can fill in all the technical hints to yourself that you deem sensible. If you set nothing here, you'll get a default containing the model name and view type.

ir.actions.act_window.view

The second record we defined works in unison with `act_window`, which we defined earlier. We already know that by setting the `view_id` field there, we can select which view is used for the first view mode. However, given that we set the `view_mode` field to the default *tree, form*, `view_id` would have to pick a tree view, but we want to set the form view, which comes second here.

If you find yourself in a situation like this, use the `ir.actions.act_window.view` model, which gives you fine-grained control over which views to load for which view type. The first two fields defined here are examples of the generic way to refer to other objects; you keep the element's body empty but add an attribute called `ref`, which contains the XML ID of the object you want to reference. So, what happens here is that we refer to our action from the previous recipe in the `act_window_id` field, and refer to the view we just created in the `view_id` field. Then, though not strictly necessary, we add a sequence number to position this view assignment relatively to the other view assignments for the same action. This is only relevant if you assign views for different view modes by creating multiple `ir.actions.act_window.view` records.

 Once you define the `ir.actions.act_window.view` records, they take precedence over what you filled in the action's `view_mode` field. So, with only the preceding records, you won't see a list at all, but only a form. So, you should add another `ir.actions.act_window.view` record pointing to a list view for the `res.partner` model.

Adding content and widgets to a form view

The preceding recipe showed how to pick a specific view for an action. Now, we'll demonstrate how to make the form we defined earlier more useful.

How to do it...

1. Define the form view basic structure:

```
<record id="form_all_customers" model="ir.ui.view">
    <field name="name">All customers</field>
    <field name="model">res.partner</field>
    <field name="arch" type="xml">
        <form>
            <!--form content goes here -->
        </form>
    </field>
</record>
```

2. To add a head bar usually used for action buttons and stage pipeline, add this inside the form:

```
<header>
<button type="object" name="open_commercial_entity"
        string="Open commercial partner"
class="btn-primary" />
</header>
```

3. Add fields to the form, using `group` tags to visually organize them:

```
<group string="Content" name="my_content">
    <field name="name" />
    <field name="category_id" widget="many2many_tags" />
</group>
```

Now, the form should display a top bar with a button and two vertically-aligned fields.

How it works...

We'll look at the `arch` field of the `ir.ui.view` model. Here, everything that the user sees happens. First, note that views are defined in XML themselves, so you need to pass the `type="xml"` attribute for the arch field, otherwise the parser will be confused. It is also mandatory that your view definition contains well-formed XML, otherwise you'll get in trouble when loading this snippet.

Now, we'll walk through the tags used previously and summarize the others that are available.

Form

When you define a form view, it is mandatory that the first element within the `arch` field is a `form` element. This fact is used internally to derive the record's `type` field, which is why you're not supposed to set this field. You'll see this a lot in legacy code, though.

The `form` element can have two legacy attributes itself, which are `string` and `version`. In previous versions of Odoo, they were used to decide on the title you saw in the breadcrumb and to differentiate between the forms written in pre-7.0 style and afterward, but both can be considered obsolete by now. The title in the breadcrumb is now inferred from the model's `name_get` function, while the version is assumed to be 7.0 or later.

In addition to the elements listed next, you can use arbitrary HTML within the form tag. The algorithm is that every element unknown to Odoo is considered plain HTML and simply passed through to the browser. Be careful with that, as the HTML you fill in can interact with the HTML code the Odoo elements generate, which might distort rendering.

Header

This element is a container for elements that should be shown in a form's header, which is rendered as a white bar. Usually, as in this example, you place action buttons here or a status bar if your model has a state field.

Button

The button element is used to allow the user to trigger an action. Refer to the *Adding buttons to forms* recipe for details.

Group

The group element is Odoo's main means for organizing content. Fields placed within a group element are rendered with their title, and all the fields within the same group are aligned so that there's also a visual indicator that they belong together. You can also nest group elements; this causes Odoo to render the contained fields in adjacent columns.

In general, you should use this mechanism for all of your fields and only revert to other methods (see next) when necessary.

If you assign the string attribute on a group, its content will be rendered as a heading for the group.

You should develop the habit of assigning a name to every logical group of fields, too. This name is not visible to the user, but is very helpful when we override views in the following recipes. Keep the name unique within a form definition to avoid confusion about which group you refer to. Don't use the string attribute for this, because it will change eventually because of translations.

Field

In order to actually show and manipulate data, your form should contain some `field` elements. They have one mandatory attribute called `name`, which refers to the field's name in the model. So earlier, we offer the user to edit the partner's name and categories. If we only want to show one of them, without the user being able to edit the field, we set the `readonly` attribute to `1` or `True`. This attribute may actually contain a small subset of Python code, so `readonly="2>1"` will make the field read-only too. The same applies to the `invisible` attribute, which you use to have the value read from the database, but not shown to the user. We'll see later in which situations we want to have that.

 Take care not to put the same field twice on your form. Odoo is not designed to support this, and the result will be that all but one of those fields will behave as if they were empty; hidden fields especially can be a nasty source of trouble here.

You must have noticed the `widget` attribute on the categories field. It defines how the data in the field is supposed to be presented to the user. Every type of field has its standard widget, so you don't have to explicitly choose a widget. However, several types provide multiple ways of representation, in which case you might opt for something other than the default. As a complete list of available widgets will exceed the scope of this recipe, you'll have to resort to Odoo's source code to try them out and consult `Chapter 15`, *Web Client Development*, for details on how to make your own.

General attributes

On most elements (this includes `group`, `field`, and `button`), you can set the `attrs` and `groups` attributes. While `attrs` is discussed next, the `groups` attribute gives you the possibility to show some elements only to members of certain groups. Simply put the group's full XML ID (separated by commas for multiple groups) in the attribute, and the element will be hidden for everyone who is not a member of at least one of the groups mentioned.

Other tags

There are situations where you might want to deviate from the strict layout groups prescribed. A good example is, if you want the name field of a record to be rendered as a heading, the field's label will interfere with the appearance. In this case, don't put your field into a group element, but for example, into the plain HTML h1 element. Then, before the h1 element, put a label element with the for attribute set to your field name:

```
<label for="name" />
<h1><field name="name" /></h1>
```

This will be rendered with the field's content as a big heading, but the field's name only in small above. That's basically what the standard partner form does.

If you need a line break within a group, use the newline element. It's always empty:

```
<newline />
```

Another useful element is footer. When you open a form as a popup, this is the good place to place the action buttons. It will be rendered as a separate bar too, analogous to the header element.

Don't address XML nodes with their string attribute (or any other translated attribute, for that matter), as being translated before inheritance is applied, your view overrides will break for other languages.

There's more...

Since form views are basically HTML with some extensions, Odoo also makes extensive use of CSS classes. Two very useful ones are oe_read_only and oe_edit_only; they cause elements with these classes applied to be visible only in read/view mode or only in edit mode. So, to have the label visible only in edit mode, use this:

```
<label for="name" class="oe_edit_only" />
```

Another very useful class is oe_inline, which you can use on fields to make them render as an inline element, not causing unwanted line breaks. Use this class when you embed a field into text or other markup.

Further, the `form` element can have the `create`, `edit`, and `delete` attributes. If you set one of those to `false`, the corresponding action won't be available for this form. Without this being explicitly set, the availability of the action is inferred from the user's permissions. Note that this is purely for straightening the UI; don't use this for security.

See also

The widgets described earlier already offer a lot of functionality, but sooner or later, you will encounter cases where they don't do exactly what you want. For defining your own widgets, refer to `Chapter 15`, *Web Client Development*.

Adding buttons to forms

We added a button in the previous form, but there are quite a few different types of buttons to use. This recipe will add another button; also, it will put the following code in the previous recipe's `header` element.

How to do it...

Add a button referring to an action:

```
<button type="action"
 name="%(base.action_partner_category_form)d"
 string="Open partner categories" />
```

How it works...

The button's `type` attribute determines the semantics of the other fields, so we'll first look into the possible values:

- `action`: This makes the button call an action as defined in the `ir.actions.*` namespace. The `name` attribute needs to contain the action's database ID, which you can conveniently have Odoo look up with a Python format string containing the XML ID of the action in question.
- `object`: This calls a method of the current model. The `name` attribute contains the function's name. The function should have the `@api.multi` signature and will act on the currently viewed record.

The `string` attribute is used to assign the text the user sees.

 There used to be a third value—`workflow`—which sent a signal to the by now deprecated and removed workflow engine. If you come across this when migrating code from older versions, you'll probably have to replace it by a method call.

There's more...

Use `btn-primary` CSS classes to render a button that is highlighted (currently purple) and `btn-default` to render a normal button. This is commonly used for cancel buttons in wizards or to offer secondary actions in a visually unobtrusive way. Setting the `oe_link` class causes the button to look like a link.

The call with a button of type **object** can return a dictionary describing an action, which will then be executed on the client side. This way, you can implement multiscreen wizards or just open some other record. Note that clicking on a button always causes the client to issue a `write` or `create` call before running the method.

You can also have content within the `button` tag, replacing the `string` attribute. This is commonly used in button boxes, as described in the *Document style forms* recipe.

Passing parameters to forms and actions – Context

Internally, every method in Odoo has access to a dictionary called **context** that is propagated from every action to the methods involved in delivering that action. The UI also has access to it and can be modified in various ways by setting values in the context. In this recipe, we'll explore some of the applications of this mechanism by toying with the language, default values, and implicit filters.

Getting ready

While not strictly necessary, this recipe will be more fun if you install the French language, in case you didn't start out with this language in the first place. Consult Chapter 12, *Internationalization*, for how to do this. If you have a French database, change **fr_FR** to some other language; **en_US** will do for English. Also, click on the **Active** button (changing to **Archive** when you hover it) on one of your customers in order to archive it and verify that this partner doesn't show up any more in the list.

How to do it...

1. Create a new action, very similar to the one from the first recipe:

```
<act_window id="action_all_customers_fr"
            name="Tous les clients"
            res_model="res.partner"
            domain="[('customer', '=', True)]"
            context="{'lang': 'fr_FR', 'default_lang': 'fr_FR',
                      'active_test': False}" />
```

2. Add a menu that calls this action. This is left as an exercise for the reader.

When you open this menu, the views will show up in French, and if you create a new partner, she will have French as the pre-selected language. A less obvious difference is that you will also see the partner you deactivated earlier.

How it works...

The context dictionary is populated from several sources. First, some values from the current user's record (lang and tz, for the user's language and the user's timezone) are read; then, there are addons that add keys for their own purposes. Further, the UI adds keys about which model and which record we're busy with at the moment (active_id, active_ids, active_model). Also, as seen earlier, we can add our own keys in actions. Those are merged together and passed to the underlying server functions, and also to the client-side UI.

So, by setting the `lang` context key, we force the display language to be French. You will note that this doesn't change the whole UI language, which is because only the list view that we open lies within the scope of this context. The rest of the UI was loaded already with another context that contained the user's original language. However, if you open a record in this list view, it will be presented in French too, and if you open some linked record on the form or press a button that executes an action, the language will be propagated too.

By setting `default_lang`, we set a default value for every record created within the scope of this context. The general pattern is `default_$fieldname: my_default_value`, which enables you to set default values for partners newly created in this case. Given that our menu is about customers, it might have made sense to also set `default_customer: True` to have the **Customer** field checked by default. However, this is a model-wide default for `res.partner` anyway, so this wouldn't have changed anything. For scalar fields, the syntax for this is as you would write it in Python code—string fields go in quotes, numbers just like that, and Boolean fields are either `True` or `False`. For relational fields, the syntax is slightly more complicated; refer to `Chapter 7`, *Module Data*, for how to write those. Note that the default values set in the context override the default values set in the model definition, so you can have different default values in different situations.

The last key is `active_test`, which has very special semantics. For every model that has a field called **active**, Odoo automatically filters out records where this field is `False`. This is why the partner where you unchecked this field disappeared from the list. By setting this key, we can suppress this behavior.

 This is useful for the UI in its own right, but even more useful in your Python code when you need to ensure that some operation is applied to all the records, not just the active ones.

There's more...

While defining a context, you have access to some variables, the most important one being `uid`, which evaluates to the current user's ID. You'll need this for setting default filters (refer to the next recipe, *Defining filters on record lists – Domain*). Further, you have access to the `context_today` function and the `current_date` variable, where the first is a date object representing the current date as seen from the user's time zone and the latter is the current date as seen in UTC, formatted as `YYYY-MM-DD`. For setting a default value for a date field to the current date, use `current_date` and, for default filters, use `context_today()`.

Further, you can do some date calculations with a subset of Python's `datetime`, `time`, and `relativedelta` classes.

> Why the repeated talk about a subset of Python? For various technical reasons, domains have to be evaluated on the client side as well as on the server side. Server-side evaluation existed earlier; there, full Python was available (but is restricted by now too for security reasons). When client-side evaluation was introduced, the best option in order to not break the whole system was to implement a part of Python in JavaScript. So, there is a small JavaScript Python interpreter built into Odoo that works great for simple expressions, and that is usually enough.

> Beware about variables in the context in conjunction with the `<act_window />` shortcut. Those are evaluated at installation time, which is nearly never what you want. If you need variables in your context, use the `<record />` syntax.

The same way that we added some context keys in our action, we can do with buttons. This causes the function or action the button calls to be run in the context given and by now, you know some of the tricks you can pull this way.

Most form element attributes that are evaluated as Python also have access to the context dictionary. The `invisible` and `readonly` attributes are such attributes. So, in cases where you want an element to show up in a form sometimes, but not at other times, you set the `invisible` attribute to `context.get('my_key')`, and for actions that lead to the case where the field is supposed to be invisible, you set the context key `my_key: True`. Such a strategy enables you to adapt your form without having to rewrite it for different occasions.

You can also set a context on relational fields, which influences how the field is loaded. By setting the `form_view_ref` or `tree_view_ref` keys to the full XML ID of a view, you can select a specific view for this field. This is necessary when you have multiple views of the same type for the same object. Without this key, you get the view with the lowest sequence number, which might not always be desirable.

See also

One of the very useful applications of the context is to set default search filters, as described in the *Search views* recipe.

Defining filters on record lists – Domain

We've already seen the first example of a domain in the first action, which was
`[('customer', '=', True)]`. It is a very common use case when you need to display a subset of all available records from an action, or to allow only a subset of possible records to be the target of a `many2one` relation. The way to describe these filters in Odoo is called a domain. This recipe illustrates how to use such a domain to display a selection of partners.

How to do it...

To display a subset of partners from your action, you need to perform the following steps:

1. Add an action for non-French speaking customers:

```
<record id="action_my_customers" model="ir.actions.act_window">
    <field name="name">All my customers who don't speak French</field>
    <field name="res_model">res.partner</field>
    <field name="domain">
        [('customer', '=', True), ('user_id', '=', uid),
        ('lang', '!=', 'fr_FR')]
    </field>
</record>
```

2. Add an action for the customers who are customers or suppliers:

```
<record id="action_customers_or_suppliers"
        model="ir.actions.act_window">
    <field name="name">Customers or suppliers</field>
    <field name="res_model">res.partner</field>
    <field name="domain">['|', ('customer', '=', True),
                              ('supplier', '=', True)]</field>
</record>
```

3. Add menus that call these actions. This is left as an exercise for the reader.

How it works...

The simplest form of a domain is a list of 3-tuples that contain a field name of the model in question as string in the first element, an operator as string in the second element, and the value the field is to be checked against as the third element. This is what we did in the first action, and this is interpreted as "All those conditions have to apply to the records we're interested in." This is actually a shortcut, because the domains know the two prefix operators—& and |—where & is the default. So, in normalized form, the first domain will be written as:

```
['&', '&', ('customer', '=', True), ('user_id', '=', uid),
         ('lang', '!=', 'fr_FR')].
```

While a bit hard to read for bigger expressions, the advantage of prefix operators is that their scope is rigidly defined, which saves you from having to worry about operator precedence and brackets. It's always two expressions: the first & applies to '&', ('customer', '=', True), ('user_id', '=', uid) as the first operand and ('lang', '!=', 'fr_FR') as the second. Then, the second & applies to ('customer', '=', True) as the first operand and ('user_id', '=', uid) as the second.

In the second action, we have to write out the full form because we need the | operator.

There is also a ! operator for negation, but, given logical equivalences and negated comparison operators such as != and not in, it is not really necessary. Note that this is a unary prefix operator, so it only applies to the following expression in the domain and not to everything that follows.

Note that the right operand doesn't need to be a fixed value when you write a domain for a window action or other client-side domains. You can use the same minimal Python as described earlier for contexts, so you can write filters such as *changed last week, my partners,* and more.

There's more...

The preceding domains work only on fields of the model itself, while we often need to filter based on properties of linked records. To do this, you can use the notation also used in @api.depends definitions or related fields: create a dotted path from the current model to the model you want to filter for. To search partners that have a salesperson who is a member of a group starting with the letter G, you would use the [('user_id.groups_id.name', '=like', 'G%')] domain. The path can be arbitrarily long, so you only have to take care that there are relation fields between the current model and the model you want to filter for.

Operators

The following table lists the available operators and their semantics:

Operator (equivalent)	Semantics
=, != (<>)	Exact match, not equal (deprecated notation of not equal).
in, not in	Checks whether the value is one of the values named in a list in the right operand, given as a Python list: [('uid', 'in', [1, 2, 3])].
<, <=	Greater than, greater or equal.
>, >=	Less than, less, or equal.
like, not like	Checks whether the right operand is contained (substring) in the value.
ilike, not ilike	The same as the preceding one, but case insensitive.
=like, =ilike	You can search for patterns here: % matches any string and _ matches one character. This is the equivalent of PostgreSQL's like.
child_of	For models with a parent_id field, this searches for children of the right operand, with the right operand included in the results.
=?	Evaluates to true if the right operand is false; otherwise, it behaves like "="; this is useful when you generate domains programmatically and want to filter for some value if it is set, but ignore it otherwise.

Pitfalls

This all works fine for traditional fields, but a notorious problem is searching for the value of a non-stored function field. It's a problem that people often omit the search function, while this is simple enough to fix by providing the search function in your own code as described in `Chapter 5`, *Application Models*.

Another issue that might baffle developers is Odoo's behavior when searching through `one2many` or `many2many` fields with a negative operator. Imagine that you have a partner with the A tag and you search for `[('category_id.name', '!=', 'B')]`. Your partner shows up in the result and this is what you expected, but if you add the B tag to this partner, it still shows up in your results, because for the search algorithm, it is enough that there is one linked record (A in this case) that does not fulfill the criterion. Now, if you remove the A tag so that B is the only tag, the partner will be filtered out. If you also remove the B tag so that the partner has no tags, it is still filtered out, because conditions on the linked records presuppose the existence of this record. In other situations though, this is the behavior you want, so it is not really an option to change the standard behavior. In case you need a different behavior here, provide a search function of your own that interprets the negation the way you need.

 A small gotcha is that people forget that they are writing XML files when it is about domains. You need to escape the less-than operator. Searching for records that have been created before today will have to be `[('create_date', '&lt;', current_date)]` in XML.

See also

If you ever need to manipulate a domain you didn't create programmatically, use the utility functions provided in `odoo.osv.expression`. Especially, `is_leaf`, `normalize_domain`, `AND`, and `OR` will allow you to combine domains exactly the way Odoo does it. Don't do this yourself, because there are many corner cases you have to take into account and it's very probable that you'll overlook one.

For the standard application of domains, see the *Search views* recipe.

List views

After having spent quite some time on the form view, we'll now take a quick look at how to define list views. Internally, they are called tree views in some places and list views in others, but given that there is another construction within the Odoo view framework called tree, we'll stick to the wording **list** here.

How to do it...

1. Define your list view:

```
<record id="tree_all_customers" model="ir.ui.view">
    <field name="model">res.partner</field>
    <field name="arch" type="xml">
        <tree decoration-bf="customer"
                decoration-danger="supplier"
                decoration-warning="customer and supplier">
            <field name="name" />
            <field name="customer" invisible="1" />
            <field name="supplier" invisible="1" />
        </tree>
    </field>
</record>
```

2. Tell the action from the first recipe to use it:

```
<record id="action_all_customers_tree"
        model="ir.actions.act_window.view">
    <field name="act_window_id" ref="action_all_customers" />
    <field name="view_id" ref="tree_all_customers" />
    <field name="view_mode">tree</field>
    <field name="sequence">5</field>
</record>
```

How it works...

You already know most of what happens here. We define a view, of the `tree` type this time, and attach it to our action with an `ir.actions.act_window.view` element. So, the only thing left to discuss is the `tree` element and its semantics. With a list, you don't have many design choices, so the only valid children of this element are the `field` and `button` elements. They follow the same semantics as earlier, save for the fact that there are a lot less choices for widgets; the only really interesting choices are `progressbar`, `many2onebutton`, and `handle`. The first two behave like their form namesakes. `handle` is specific to list views. It is meant for integer fields and renders a drag handle that the user can use to drag a row to a different position in the list, thereby updating the field's value. This is useful for sequence or priority fields.

What is new here are the decoration-* attributes in the `tree` element. It contains rules as to which font and/or color is chosen for the row, given in the form of `decoration-$name="Python code"`. All matches turn on the corresponding CSS class, so what the previous view does is render partners who are both suppliers and customers in brown, customers in a bold font, and suppliers in red. In your Python code, you can use the fields you named in the view definition, which is why we have to pull the `customer` and `supplier` fields too. We made them invisible because we only need the data and don't want to bother our users with those two extra columns. The possible classes are decoration-bf (bold), decoration-it (italic), and the semantic bootstrap classes decoration-danger, decoration-info, decoration-muted, decoration-primary, decoration-success, and decoration-warning.

There's more...

For numeric fields, you can add a `sum` attribute that causes this column to be summed up with the text you set in the attribute as a tooltip. Less common are the `avg`, `min`, and `max` attributes that display the average, minimum, and maximum, respectively. Note that these four only work on the records currently visible, so you might want to adjust the action's `limit` (covered earlier) in order for the user to see all the records immediately.

A very interesting attribute for the `tree` element is `editable`. If you set this to **top** or **bottom**, the list behaves entirely different than earlier. Without it, clicking on a row opens a form view for the row. With it, clicking on a row makes it editable inline, with the visible fields rendered as form fields. This is particularly useful in embedded list views, which are discussed later in this chapter. The choice is whether new lines will be added on the top or bottom of the list.

By default, records are ordered according to the `_order` property of the displayed model. The user can change ordering by clicking on a column header, but you can also set a different initial order by setting the `default_order` property in the tree element. The syntax is the same as in `_order`.

> Ordering is often a source of frustration for new developers. As Odoo lets PostgreSQL do the work here, you can only order by fields that PostgreSQL knows about and also only the fields that live in the same database table. So, if you want to order by a function or a related field, ensure that you set `store=True`. If you need to order by a field inherited from another model, declare a stored related field.

The `create`, `edit`, and `delete` attributes of the `tree` element work the same as for the `form` element described earlier. They also determine the available controls if the `editable` attribute is set.

Search views

When opening your list view, you'll notice the search field to the upper-right. If you type something there, you get suggestions about what to search for, and there is also a set of predefined filters to choose from. This recipe will walk you through how to define those suggestions and options.

How to do it...

1. Define your search view:

```xml
<record id="search_all_customers" model="ir.ui.view">
    <field name="model">res.partner</field>
    <field name="arch" type="xml">
        <search>
            <field name="name" />
            <field name="category_id"
                    filter_domain="[('category_id', 'child_of', self)]" />
            <field name="bank_ids" widget="many2one" />
            <filter name="suppliers" string="Suppliers"
                    domain="[('supplier', '=', True)]" />
        </search>
    </field>
</record>
```

2. Tell your action to use it:

```
<record id="action_all_customers" model="ir.actions.act_window">
    <field name="name">All customers</field>
    <field name="res_model">res.partner</field>
    <field name="domain">[('customer', '=', True)]</field>
    <field name="search_view_id" ref="search_all_customers" />
</record>
```

When you type something in the search bar now, you'll be offered to search for this term in the name, categories, and bank accounts fields. If your term happens to be a substring of a bank account number in your system, you'll even be offered to search exactly for this bank account.

How it works...

In the case of `name`, we simply listed the field as the one to be offered to the user to search for. We left the semantics at the default, which is a substring search for character fields.

For categories, we do something more interesting. By default, your search term applied to a many2many field triggers `name_search`, which would be a substring search in the category names in this case. However, depending on your category structure, it can be very convenient to search for partners who have the category you're interested in or a child of it. Think about a main category *Newsletter subscribers* with subcategories *Weekly newsletter*, *Monthly newsletter*, and a couple of other newsletter types. Searching for *newsletter subscribers* with the preceding search view definition will give you everyone who is subscribed to any of those newsletters in one go, which is a lot more convenient than searching for every single type and combining the results.

The `filter_domain` attribute can contain an arbitrary domain, so you're neither restricted to searching for the same field you named in the `name` attribute, nor to using only one term. The `self` variable is what the user filled in, and also the only variable you can use here. Here's a more elaborate example from the default search view for partners:

```
<field name="name"
       filter_domain="[
           '|', '|',
           ('display_name', 'ilike', self),
           ('ref', '=', self),
           ('email', 'ilike', self)]"/>
```

This allows the user to not even think a lot about what to search for; just type some letters, press **Enter**, and, with a bit of luck, one of the fields mentioned contains the string we're looking for.

For the `bank_ids` field, we used another trick. The type of field not only decides the default way of searching for the user's input, but it also defines the way Odoo presents the suggestions. Also, given that `many2one` fields are the only ones that offer autocompletion, we force Odoo to do that, even though `bank_ids` is a `one2many` field by setting the `widget` attribute. Without this, the offer will simply be to search in this field, without completion suggestions. The same applies to `many2many` fields. Note that every field with a `many2one` widget set will trigger a search on its model for every one of the user's keystrokes; don't use too many of them.

You should also put the most used fields on the top, because the first field is what is searched if the user just types something and presses Enter. It also seems worth mentioning that the search bar is very well-usable with the keyboard; select a suggestion by pressing the down arrow and open the completion suggestion of a `many2one` by pressing the right arrow. If you educate your users in this and pay attention to a sensible ordering of fields in the search view, they will be much more efficient than by typing something first, grabbing the mouse, and selecting some option.

The `filter` element creates a button that adds the content of the filter's `domain` attribute to the search domain. You should add a logical internal `name` and a `string` attribute to describe the filter to your users.

There's more...

You can group the filters with the `group` tag, which causes them to be rendered slightly closer together than the other filters, but this has semantic implications, too. If you put multiple filters in the same group and activate more than one of them, their domains will be combined with the | operator, while filters and fields not in the same group are combined with the & operator. Cases where you want disjunction for your filters are when they filter for mutually exclusive sets, in which case selecting both of them will always lead to an empty result set. Within the same group, you can achieve the same effect with the `separator` element.

Note that if the user fills in multiple queries for the same field, they will be combined with | too, so you don't need to worry about that.

Apart from the `field`, the `filter` element can have a `context` attribute whose content will be merged with the current context and eventual other context attributes in the search view. This is essential for views that support grouping (refer to recipes about kanban and graph views), because the resulting context determines the field(s) to be grouped with the key `group_by`. We'll look into the details of grouping in the appropriate recipes, but the context has other uses, too. For example, you can write a function field that returns different values depending on the context, and then you can change the values by activating a filter.

The search view itself also responds to context keys. In a very similar way to default values when creating records, you can pass defaults for a search view via the context. If we had set a context of `{'search_default_suppliers': 1}` in our previous action, the suppliers filter would have been preselected in the search view. This works only if the filter has a name though, which is why you should always set it. To set defaults for fields in the search view, use `search_default_$fieldname`.

Further, the `field` and `filter` elements can have a groups property with the same semantics as in the form views in order to make the element only visible for certain groups.

See also

For details about manipulating the context, see the *Passing parameters to forms and actions – Context* recipe.

Users speaking languages with heavy use of diacritical marks will probably want to have Odoo search for **e**, **è**, **é**, and **ê** when filling in the **e** character. This is actually a configuration of the Postgresql server, called unaccent, which Odoo has special support for, but is out of scope for this book.

Changing existing views – View inheritance

Up until now, we ignored the existing views and declared completely new ones. While this is didactically sensible, you'll rarely be in situations where you want to define a new view for an existing model. What you'll rather want to do is to slightly modify the existing views, be it to simply have it show a field you added to the model in your addon, or to customize it to your needs or your customers.

In this recipe, we'll change the default partner form to show the record's last modification date and also allow searching for that. Then, we'll also show this column in the partners' list view.

How to do it...

1. Inject the field in the default form view:

```
<record id="view_partner_form" model="ir.ui.view">
    <field name="model">res.partner</field>
    <field name="inherit_id" ref="base.view_partner_form" />
    <field name="arch" type="xml">
        <field name="website" position="after">
            <field name="write_date" />
        </field>
    </field>
</record>
```

2. Add the field to the default search view:

```
<record id="view_res_partner_filter" model="ir.ui.view">
    <field name="model">res.partner</field>
    <field name="inherit_id" ref="base.view_res_partner_filter" />
    <field name="arch" type="xml">
        <xpath expr="." position="inside">
            <field name="write_date" />
        </xpath>
    </field>
</record>
```

3. Add the field to the default list view:

```
<record id="view_partner_tree" model="ir.ui.view">
    <field name="model">res.partner</field>
    <field name="inherit_id" ref="base.view_partner_tree" />
    <field name="arch" type="xml">
        <field name="email" position="before">
            <field name="write_date" />
        </field>
    </field>
</record>
```

After updating your module, you should see the **Last updated on** extra field beneath the website field on the partner form. When you type in something that looks like a date (a digit or two) in the search box, it should propose to search for partners last modified on this date, and in the partner's list view, you should see the modification date left of the email column.

How it works...

The crucial field here is, as you probably have guessed, `inherit_id`. You need to pass it the XML ID of the view you want to modify (inherit from), and the `arch` field then contains instructions on how to modify the existing XML nodes within the view you're inheriting from. You should actually think of the whole process as quite simple XML processing, because all the semantic parts only come a lot later.

The most canonic instruction within the `arch` field of an inherited view is the `field` element, which has the required attributes `name` and `position`. As you can have every field only once on a form, the name already uniquely identifies a field, and with the `position` attribute, we can place whatever we put within the field element either `before` (1), `inside` (2), or `after` (3) the field we named. The default is **inside**, but for readability, you should always name the position you mean. Remember that we're not talking semantics here; this is about the position in the XML tree relative to the field we have named. How this will be rendered afterward is a completely different matter.

Example 2 demonstrates a different approach. The `xpath` element selects the first element matching the XPath expression named in the `expr` attribute. Also here, the `position` attribute tells the processor where to put the `xpath` element's contents.

XPath might look somewhat scary, but is a very efficient means of selecting the node you need to work on. Take the time to look through some simple expressions; it's worth it. Probably in the tutorials you'll find, you'll stumble upon the term **context node** to which some expressions are relative. In Odoo's view inheritance, that's always the root element of the view you're inheriting from.

For all the other elements found in the `arch` field of an inheriting view, the processor looks for the first element with the same node name and matching attributes (with the attribute position excluded, as this is part of the instruction). Use this only in cases where it is very improbable that this combination is not unique, like a group element combined with a name attribute.

Note that you can have as many instruction elements within the arch field as you need. We only used one per inherited view because there's no more we want to change currently.

There's more...

The position attribute has two other possible values: `replace` and `attributes`. Using `replace` causes the selected element to be replaced with the content of the instruction element. Consequently, if you don't have any content, the selected element is simply removed. The preceding list or form view would cause the email field to be removed:

```
<field name="email" position="replace" />
```

 Removing fields can cause other inheriting views to break and several similarly ugly side effects, so avoid that if possible. If you really need to remove fields, do so in a view that comes late in order of evaluation (refer to the next).

Using `attributes` has a very different semantics from all of the preceding. The processor then expects the element to contain the `attribute` elements with a `name` attribute. Those elements will then be used to set attributes on the selected element. If you want to heed the earlier warning, you'd better set the `invisible` attribute to 1 for the email field:

```
<field name="email" position="attributes">
    <attribute name="invisible">1</attribute>
</field>
```

An `attribute` node can have the `add` and `remove` attributes, which then in turn should contain the value to be removed or added to the space separated list the attribute value is expected to be. This is very useful for the `class` attribute, where you'd add a class (instead of overwriting the whole attribute) by saying the following:

```
<field name="email" position="attributes">
    <attribute name="class" add="oe_inline" />
</field>
```

Order of evaluation in view inheritance

As we have only one parent view and one inheriting view currently, we don't run into any problems with conflicting view overrides. When you have installed a couple of modules, you'll find a lot of overrides for the partner form. This is all fine as long as they change different things in a view, but there are occasions where it is important to understand how overriding works in order to avoid conflicts. Direct descendants of a view are evaluated in ascending order of their `priority` field, so views with a lower priority are applied first. Every step of inheritance is applied to the result of the first, so if a view with priority 3 changes a field and another one with priority 5 removes it, things are fine, but they break if the priorities are reversed.

Then, you can also inherit from a view that is an inheriting view itself. In this case, the second level inheriting view is applied to the result of the view it inherits from. So, if you have four views, A, B, C, and D, where A is a standalone form, B and C inherit from A, and D inherits from B, the order of evaluation is A, B, D, C. Use this to enforce an order without having to rely on priorities; that's safer in general. Especially, if some inheriting view adds a field and you need to apply changes to this field, inherit from the inheriting view and not from the standalone one.

 This kind of inheritance always works on the complete XML tree from the original view, with modifications from the previous inheriting views applied.

See also

For inheriting views, a very useful and not very well-known field is `groups_id`. This field causes the inheritance to take place only if the user requesting the parent view is member of one of the groups mentioned there. This can save you a lot of work when adapting the user interface for different levels of access, because with inheritance, you can have more complex operations than just showing or not showing the elements based on group membership, as is possible with the `groups` attribute on form elements, as discussed earlier. You can, for example, remove elements if the user is member of some group (which is the inverse of what the `groups` attribute does), but also some quite elaborate tricks such as adding attributes based on group membership; think about simple things like making a field read only for certain groups, or more interesting ones such as using different widgets for different groups.

What was described here is the case if the mode field of the original view is set to primary, while the inheriting views have mode extension, which is the default. We'll look into the case that mode of an inheriting view is set to **primary** later, where the rules are slightly different.

Document-style forms

In this recipe, we'll review some design guidelines in order to present a uniform user experience.

How to do it...

1. Start your form with a header element:

```
<header>
    <button name="do_something_with_the_record"
            string="Do something" type="object" class="btn-primary" />
    <button name="do_something_else" string="Second action" />
    <field name="state" widget="statusbar" />
</header>
```

2. Then, add a sheet element for content:

```
<sheet>
```

3. Put some prominent field(s) first:

```
<div class="oe_left oe_title">
    <label for="name" />
    <h1>
        <field name="name" />
    </h1>
</div>
```

4. Put buttons that link to resources relevant for the object in its own box (if applicable):

```
<div class="oe_right oe_button_box" name="buttons">
    <button name="open_something_interesting"
            string="Open some linked record"
            type="object" class="oe_stat_button" />
```

5. Add your content, possibly within a notebook if there are a lot of fields:

```
<group name="some_fields">
    <field name="field1" />
    <field name="field2" />
</group>
```

6. After the sheet, add the chatter widget (if applicable):

```
</sheet>
<div class="oe_chatter">
    <field name="message_follower_ids" widget="mail_followers"/>
    <field name="activity_ids" widget="mail_activity"/>
    <field name="message_ids" widget="mail_thread"/>
</div>
```

How it works...

The header should contain buttons that execute actions on the object the user currently sees. Use the `btn-primary` class to make buttons visually stand out (that's purple at the time of writing), which is a good way to guide the user regarding which would be the most logical action to execute at the moment. Try to have all the highlighted buttons to the left of the non-highlighted buttons and hide the buttons not relevant in the current state (if applicable). If the model has a state, show it in the header using the `statusbar` widget. This will be rendered right aligned in the header.

The sheet element is rendered as a stylized sheet, and the most important fields should be the first thing the user sees when glancing at it. Use the `oe_title` and `oe_left` classes to have them rendered in a prominent place (floating left with slightly adjusted font sizes at the time of writing).

If there are other records of interest concerning the record the user currently sees (such as the partner's invoices on a partner form), put them in an element with the `oe_right` and `oe_button_box` classes; this aligns the buttons in it to the right. On the buttons themselves, use the `oe_stat_button` class to enforce a uniform rendering of the buttons. It's also customary to assign a font awesome class for an icon using the `icon` attribute.

 Even in case you don't like this layout, stick to the element and class names described here, and adjust what you need with CSS and possibly JavaScript. This will make the user interface more compatible with existing addons and allow you to integrate better with core addons.

Dynamic form elements using attrs

So far, we have only looked into changing forms depending on the user's groups (the `groups` attribute on elements and the `groups_id` field on inherited views), but nothing more. This recipe will show you how to change forms based on the content of some fields in it.

How to do it...

1. Define an attribute attrs on some form element:

```
<field name="parent_id"
    attrs="{
        'invisible': [('is_company', '=', True)],
        'required': [('is_company', '=', False)]
    }" />
```

2. Take care that all the fields you refer to are available on your form:

```
<field name="is_company" invisible="True" />
```

This will make the `parent_id` field invisible if the partner is a company, and required if it's not a company.

How it works...

The `attrs` attribute contains a dictionary with the `invisible`, `required`, and `readonly` keys (all of them optional). The values are domains that may refer to the fields existing on the form (and really only those, so no dotted paths), and the whole dictionary is evaluated according to the rules for client-side Python described earlier. So, for example, you can access the context in the right-hand operand.

There's more...

While this mechanism is quite straightforward for scalar fields, it's less obvious how to handle `one2many` and `many2many` fields. In fact, in standard Odoo, you can't do much with those fields within an `attrs` attribute. However, if you only need to check whether such a field is empty or not, use `[[6, False, []]]` as your right-hand operand.

Embedded views

When you show a one2many or a many2many field on a form, you don't have much control over how it is rendered up to now if you haven't used one of the specialized widgets. Also, in the case of many2one fields, it is sometimes desirable to be able to influence the way the linked record is opened. In this recipe, we'll look into how to define private views for those fields.

How to do it...

1. Define your field as usual, but don't close the tag:

```
<field name="child_ids">
```

2. Simply write the view definition(s) into the tag:

```
<tree>
    <field name="name" />
    <field name="email" />
    <field name="phone" />
</tree>
<form>
    <group>
        <field name="name" />
        <field name="function" />
    </group>
</form>
```

3. Close the tag:

```
</field>
```

How it works...

When Odoo loads a form, it first checks for referential fields if there are views embedded as outlined previously. Those embedded views can have the exact same elements as views we defined before. Only if Odoo doesn't find an embedded view of some type does it use the model's default view of this type.

There's more...

While embedded views seem like a great feature in the first place, they complicate view inheritance a lot. For example, as soon as embedded views are involved, field names are not guaranteed to be unique, and you'll usually have to use some quite elaborate XPaths to select elements within an embedded view.

So, in general, you should better define standalone views and use the `form_view_ref` and `tree_view_ref` keys described earlier.

Kanban views

Up until now, we have presented the user with a list of records that can be opened to show a form. While those lists are efficient when presenting a lot of information, they tend to be rather dull, given the lack of design possibilities. In this recipe, we'll take a look at kanban views, which allow us to present lists of records in a more appealing way.

How to do it...

1. Define a view of type kanban:

```
<record id="kanban_all_customers" model="ir.ui.view">
    <field name="model">res.partner</field>
    <field name="arch" type="xml">
        <kanban>
```

2. List the fields you'll use in your view:

```
<field name="name" />
<field name="supplier" />
<field name="customer" />
```

3. Do some design:

```
<templates>
    <t t-name="kanban-box">
        <div class="oe_kanban_card">
            <a type="open">
                <field name="name" />
            </a>
                <t t-if="record.supplier.raw_value or
```

```
                       record.customer.raw_value">
                       is
                       <t t-if="record.customer.raw_value">
                       a customer
                       <t t-if="record.supplier.raw_value"> and </t>
                       </t>
                       <t t-if="record.supplier.raw_value">
                       a supplier
                       </t>
                     </t>
                 </div>
             </t>
       </templates>
```

4. Close all the tags:

```
             </kanban>
         </field>
     </record>
```

5. Add this view to one of your actions. This is left as an exercise for the reader.

How it works...

We need to give a list of fields to load in (2) in order to be able to access them later. The content of the `templates` element must be a single `t` element with the `t-name` attribute set to `kanban-box`.

What you write inside this element will be repeated for each record, with special semantics for `t` elements and `t-*` attributes. For details about that, refer to the *Using client-side QWeb templates* recipe from `Chapter 15`, *Web Client Development*, because technically, kanban views are just an application of QWeb templates.

There are a few modifications that are peculiar to kanban views. You have access to the `read_only_mode`, `record`, and `widget` variables during evaluation. Fields can be accessed using `record.fieldname`, which is an object with the `value` and `raw_value` properties, where `value` is the field's value formatted in a way presentable to the user and `raw_value` is the field's value as it comes from the database.

 Many2many fields make an exception here. You'll only get an ID list via the `record` variable. For a user readable representation, you must use the `field` element.

Note the `type` attribute of the link at the top of the template. This attribute makes Odoo generate a link that opens the record in view mode (**open**) or in the edit mode (**edit**), or it deletes the record (**delete**). The `type` attribute can also be **object** or **action**, which will render links that call a function of the model or an action. In both cases, you need to supplement the attributes for buttons in form views as outlined earlier. Instead of the `a` element, you can also use the `button` element; the `type` attribute has the same semantics there.

There's more...

There are a few more helper functions worth mentioning. If you need to generate a pseudorandom color for some element, use the `kanban_color(some_variable)` function, which will return a CSS class that sets the `background` and `color` properties. This is usually used in `t-att-class` elements.

If you want to display an image stored in a binary field, use `kanban_image(modelname, fieldname, record.id.raw_value)`, which returns a data URI if you included the field in your fields list and the field is set, a placeholder if the field is not set, or a URL that makes Odoo stream the field's contents if you didn't include it in your fields list. Do not include the field in the fields list if you need to display a lot of records simultaneously or you expect very big images. Usually, you'd use this in a `t-att-src` attribute of an `img` element.

Doing design in kanban views can be a bit annoying. What often works better is to generate HTML using a function field of type HTML, and generating this HTML from a Qweb view. This way, you're still doing QWeb, but on the server side, which is a lot more convenient when you need to work on a lot of data.

Showing kanban cards in columns according to their state

This recipe shows you how to set up a kanban view where the user can drag and drop a record from one column to the other, thereby pushing the record in question into another state.

Getting ready

Now and in the rest of this chapter, we'll make use of the project module here as it defines models that lend themselves better to date and state-based views than the ones defined in the base module. So, before proceeding, add `project` to the dependencies list of your addon.

How to do it...

1. Define a kanban view for tasks:

```
<record id="kanban_tasks" model="ir.ui.view">
    <field name="model">project.task</field>
    <field name="arch" type="xml">
        <kanban default_group_by="stage_id">
            <field name="stage_id" />
            <field name="name" />
            <templates>
                <t t-name="kanban-box">
                    <div class="oe_kanban_card">
                        <field name="name" />
                    </div>
                </t>
            </templates>
        </kanban>
    </field>
</record>
```

2. Add a menu and an action using this view. This is left as an exercise for the reader.

How it works...

Kanban views support grouping, which allows you to display records that have the group field in common in the same column. This is commonly used for a `state` or `stage_id` field, because it allows the user to change this field's value for a record by simply dragging it into another column. Set the `default_group_by` attribute on the `kanban` element to the name of the field you want to group by in order to make use of this functionality.

There's more...

If not defined in the dedicated attribute, any search filter can add grouping by setting a context key named `group_by` to the field name(s) to group by.

Calendar and gantt views

This recipe walks you through how to display and edit information about dates and duration in your records in a visual way.

How to do it...

1. Define a calendar view:

```
<record id="calendar_project_task" model="ir.ui.view">
    <field name="model">project.task</field>
    <field name="arch" type="xml">
        <calendar date_start="date_start" date_stop="date_end"
                  color="project_id">
            <field name="name" />
            <field name="user_id" />
        </calendar>
    </field>
</record>
```

2. Add menus and actions using this view. This is left as an exercise for the reader.

How it works...

The calendar view needs to be passed field names in the `date_start` and `date_stop` attributes to indicate which fields to look at when building the visual representation. Use fields of the `Datetime` type, as everything else will get you weird results. While `date_start` is required, you can leave out `date_stop` and set the `date_delay` attribute instead, which is expected to be a `Float` field representing the duration in hours.

The calendar view allows you to give records that have the same value in a field the same (arbitrarily assigned) color. To use this functionality, set the `color` attribute to the name of the field you need. In our example, we can see in one glance which tasks belong to the same project, because we assigned `project_id` as the field to determine the color groups.

The fields you name in the calendar element's body are shown within the block representing the time interval covered, separated by commas.

There's more...

The calendar view has some other helpful attributes. If you want to open calendar entries in a popup instead of the standard form view, set `event_open_popup` to `1`. By default, you create a new entry by just filling in some text, which internally calls the model's `name_create` function to actually create the record. If you want to disable this behavior, set `quick_add` to `0`.

If your model has a notion of covering a whole day, set `all_day` to a field's name that is true if the record covers the whole day, and false otherwise.

Note that this recipe contained information about a legacy view type `gantt`, which has been obsoleted during writing and was removed from the text. The **web_timeline** module from the **web** repository of the OCA introduces a view that can be used if a gantt-style representation is wanted. At the time of writing, this module was not yet available for version 11.

Graph and pivot views

In this recipe, we'll take a look at Odoo's business intelligence views. These are read-only views meant to present data.

Getting ready

We're still making use of the project module here. First, we need some configuration. Activate the **Track time spent on projects and tasks** checkbox in **Configuration** | **Settings** and also install the **hr_timesheet** module in order to be able to record some time on different tasks.

Now, create some projects meant to be umbrella projects for your customers. Then, create a couple of tasks for each customer project. They are meant to model different activities you have per customer. Assign different managers to these projects and activate the **Allow timesheets** box. Finally, create tasks in these projects, give a time estimation per task, and write some work hours on these tasks.

How to do it...

1. Define a graph view using bars:

```xml
<record id="graph_project_task_bar" model="ir.ui.view">
    <field name="model">project.task</field>
    <field name="arch" type="xml">
        <graph type="bar">
            <field name="project_id" type="row" />
            <field name="user_id" type="row" />
            <field name="effective_hours" type="measure" />
        </graph>
    </field>
</record>
```

2. Define a pivot view:

```xml
<record id="graph_project_task_pivot" model="ir.ui.view">
    <field name="model">project.task</field>
    <field name="arch" type="xml">
        <pivot>
            <field name="project_id" type="row" />
            <field name="user_id" type="row" />
            <field name="planned_hours" type="measure" />
            <field name="effective_hours" type="measure" />
        </pivot>
    </field>
</record>
```

3. Add menus and actions using this view. This is left as an exercise for the reader.

If everything went well, you should see graphs that show you how many hours were worked per customer (the projects we defined) under the responsibility of the different project managers.

How it works...

The `type` attribute on a `graph` element determines the initial mode of a graph view. Possible values are **bar**, **line**, and **chart**, while **bar** is the default. The graph view is highly interactive, so the user can switch between the different modes and also add and remove fields. Pivot views have their own root element, `pivot`.

The `field` elements tell Odoo what to display on which axis. For all graph modes, you need at least one field with type `row` and one with type **measure** to see anything useful. Fields of type row determine the grouping, while type measure stands for the value(s) to be shown. Line graphs only support one field of each type, while charts and bars handle two group fields with one measure nicely. The pivot view supports an arbitrary amount of group and measure fields. No worries, things don't break if you switch to a mode that doesn't support the amount of groups and measures you defined. It's just that they'll ignore some of the fields and won't always show a very interesting result.

There's more...

For all graph types, `Datetime` fields are tricky for grouping, because you'll rarely encounter the same field value here. So, if you have a `Datetime` field of type row, also specify the `interval` attribute with one of the following values: **day**, **week**, **month**, **quarter**, or **year**. This will cause the grouping to take place in the given interval.

The pivot table also supports grouping in columns. Use type **col** for the fields you want to have there.

Grouping, like sorting, relies heavily on PostgreSQL. So, here also, the rule applies that a field must live in the database and in the current table in order to be usable.

It is common practice to define database views that collect all the data you need and define a model on top of this view in order to have all the necessary fields available.

Depending on the complexity of your view and the grouping, building the graph can be quite an expensive exercise. Consider setting the `auto_search` attribute to `False` in those cases, so that the user can first adjust all the parameters and only then trigger a search.

11
Access Security

In this chapter, we will see how to carry out the following recipes:

- Creating security groups and assigning them to users
- Adding security access to models
- Limiting access to fields in models
- Limiting record access using record rules
- Using security group to activate features

In order to concisely get the point across, the recipes in this chapter make small additions to an existing module. We chose to use the module created by the recipes in Chapter 4, *Creating Odoo Addon Modules*. To follow the examples better here, you should have that module created and ready to use.

Creating security groups and assigning them to users

Security access in Odoo is configured through security groups: permissions are given to groups and then groups are assigned to users. Each functional area has base security groups provided by a central application.

When addon modules extend an existing *application*, they should add permissions to the corresponding groups, as shown in the *Adding security access to models* recipe later.

When addon modules add a new functional area not yet covered by an existing central *application*, they should add the corresponding security groups. Usually, we should have at least *user* and *manager* roles.

Taking the Library example we introduced in Chapter 4, *Creating Odoo Addon Modules*, it doesn't fit neatly in any of the Odoo core apps, so we add security groups for it.

Getting ready

This recipe assumes that you have an Odoo instance ready, with the my_module available, as described in Chapter 4, *Creating Odoo Addon Modules*.

How to do it...

To add new access security groups to a module, perform the following steps:

1. Ensure that the __manifest__.py addon module manifest has the category key defined:

```
'category': 'Library',
```

2. Add the new security/library_security.xml file to the manifest data key:

```
'data': [
    'security/library_security.xml',
    'views/library_book.xml',
],
```

3. Add the new XML file for the data records at security/library_security.xml, starting with an empty structure:

```
<?xml version="1.0" encoding="utf-8"?>
<odoo>
  <data noupdate="0">
    <!--  Data records go here -->
  </data>
</odoo>
```

4. Add the record tags for the two new groups inside the data XML element:

```
<record id="group_library_user" model="res.groups">
  <field name="name">User</field>
  <field name="category_id" ref="base.module_category_library"/>
  <field name="implied_ids" eval="[(4, ref('base.group_user'))]"/>
</record>

<record id="group_library_manager" model="res.groups">
```

```
    <field name="name">Manager</field>
    <field name="category_id" ref="base.module_category_library"/>
    <field name="implied_ids" eval="[(4, ref('group_library_user'))]"/>
    <field name="users" eval="[(4, ref('base.user_root'))]"/>
</record>
```

If we upgrade the addon module, these two records will be loaded, and we will be able to see them at the **Settings** | **Users** | **Groups** menu option.

How it works...

Addon modules are organized in functional areas, or major *applications*, such as *Accounting & Finance*, *Sales*, or *Human Resources*. These are defined by the `category` key in the manifest file.

If a category name does not exist yet, it will be automatically created. For convenience, a `base.module_category_<category>` XML ID will also be generated for the new category name in lowercase letters, replacing spaces with underscores. This is useful to relate security groups with application categories.

In our example, we used the **Library** category name, and it generated a `base.module_category_library` XML identifier.

By convention, data files adding security related elements should be placed inside a `security` subdirectory.

The order in which files are declared in the `data` key of the module manifest is important, since you can't use an identifier before it has been defined. We may want to use references in views for the security groups we had defined, so it's best to place the security data file at the top of the list before the ACL definition files and other user interface data files.

Security groups should be added using an XML file. It can add records that we want to be customized by the end users. To prevent those possible changes being lost on a module upgrade, we should add those records inside a `<data noupdate="1">` element. This is usually the case for security record rules, discussed in the *Limiting record access using record rules* recipe later.

However, for security groups, the practice used in Odoo core addon modules is to have them defined inside a `<data noupdate="0">` element. This means that they will be rewritten on a module upgrade, and so, should not be directly customized. Customization should instead be done by creating new groups that inherit from the default ones.

Groups are stored in the `res.groups` model, and its most important columns are as follows:

- `name`: This is the group's display name.
- `category_id`: This is a reference to the application category, and is used to organize the groups in the users form.
- `implied_ids`: These are other groups to inherit permissions from.
- `users`: This is the list of users belonging to this group. In new addon modules, usually we want the admin user to conveniently belong to the application's manager group.

The first security group uses as `implied_ids` the `base.group_user` group. This is the Employee user group, and is the basic security group all the backend users are expected to share.

The second security group sets a value on the `users` field to assign it to the administrator user, which has the `base.user_root` XML ID.

Users belonging to a security group will automatically belong to its implied groups. If **Library Manager** has implied the **Library User** group, assigning it to a user will also include her in the **Library User** group.

Also, access permissions granted by security groups are cumulative. A user has some permission if any of the groups they belong to (directly or implied) grants that permission.

Some security groups are shown in the user form as a selection box instead of individual check boxes. This happens when the involved groups are in the same application category and are linearly interrelated through `implied_ids`. For example, Group A has implied Group B, and Group B has implied Group C.

Note that the relations defined in the preceding fields also have reverse relations that can be edited in the related models, such as security groups and users.

Setting values on reference fields, such as `category_id` and `implied_ids`, is done using the related records' XML IDs and some special syntax. This syntax is explained in detail in `Chapter 7`, *Module Data*.

There's more...

Also noteworthy is the special `base.group_no_one` security group called **Extra Rights**. In previous Odoo versions, it was used for advanced features hidden by default, and only made visible when the **Technical Features** flag was activated. Since version 9.0, this has changed, and those features are made visible as long as the **Developer Mode** is activated.

Access permissions granted by security groups are cumulative only. There is no way to deny an access given by some group. This means that a manually created group to customize permissions should inherit from the closest group with fewer permissions than those intended (if any), and then add all the remaining permissions needed.

Groups also have these additional fields available:

- Menus (the `menu_access` field): These are the menu items the group has access to
- Views (the `view_access` field): These are the UI views the group has access to
- Access rights (the `model_access` field): This is the access it has on models, detailed in the *Adding security access to models* recipe
- Rules (the `rule_groups` field): These are the record-level access rules that apply to the group, detailed in the *Limiting record access using record rules* recipe
- Notes (the `comment` field): This is a description or comment text for the group

Adding security access to models

It's common for addon modules to add new models. For example, in the previous chapter, we had examples adding a new Library Books model.

It is easy to miss the creation of security access for new models defined in an addon module if you test it using the convenient `admin` user, because `admin` bypasses all security checks.

However, models with no ACLs will trigger a warning log message on loading, informing about the missing ACL definitions: **The model library.book has no access rules, consider adding one**. To avoid that, you should watch for such messages during tests, and before publishing your code, ensure that you run tests with the `demo` user rather than `admin`.

So, for new models to be usable by non-admin users, we need to define their access control lists so that Odoo knows how it should access them and what operations each user group should be allowed.

Getting ready

We will take the module created in `Chapter 4`, *Creating Odoo Addon Modules* and add the missing ACLs to it.

How to do it...

`my_module` should already contain the `models/library_book.py` Python file creating the `library.book` model. We will now add a data file describing this model's security access control by performing the following steps:

1. Edit the `__manifest__.py` file to declare a new data file:

```
data: [
    # ...Security Groups
    'security/ir.model.access.csv',
    # ...Other data files
]
```

2. Add to the module a new `security/ir.model.access.csv` file, with the following lines:

```
id,name,model_id:id,group_id:id,perm_read,perm_write,perm_create,
perm_unlink
access_library_book_user,library.book.user,model_library_book,
base.group_user,1,0,0,0
access_library_book_admin,library.book.admin,model_library_book,
base.group_system,1,1,1,1
```

We should then upgrade the module to have these ACL records added to our Odoo database. More importantly, if we sign in to a demonstration database using the **demo** user, we should be able to access the **Library** menu option without any security errors.

How it works...

Security access control lists are stored in the core `ir.model.access` model. We just need to add to it the records describing the intended access rights for each user group.

Any type of data file would do, but the common practice is to use a CSV file. The file can be placed anywhere inside the addon module directory, but the convention is to have all the security related files inside a `security` subdirectory.

The first step in our recipe adds this new data file to the manifest and the second adds the file describing the security access control rules. The CSV file must be named after the model where the records will be loaded, so the name used is not just a convention and is mandatory; refer to `Chapter 7`, *Module data*, for details.

If the module also creates new security groups, its data file should be declared in the manifest before the ACLs' data file, since you may want to use them for the ACLs and so, they must already be created when the ACL file is processed.

The columns in the CSV file are as follows:

- `id`: This is the XML ID internal identifier for this rule. Any unique name inside the module would do, but the convention is to use `access_<model>_<group>`.
- `name`: This is a title for the access rule and, by convention, the common practice is to use a `access.<model>.<group>` name.
- `model_id:id`: This is the XML ID for the model. Odoo automatically assigns such an ID to models with a `model_<name>` format, using the model's `_name` with underscores instead of dots. If the model was created in a different addon module, a fully-qualified XML ID is needed, which includes the module name.
- `group_id:id`: This is the XML ID for the user group. If left empty, it applies to all users. The base module provides some basic groups, such as `base.group_user` for all employees and `base.group_system` for the administration user. Other apps can add their own user groups.
- `perm_read`: Members of the preceding group can read the model records (0 or 1).
- `perm_write`: Members of the preceding group can update the model records (0 or 1).
- `perm_create`: Members of the preceding group can add new records of this model (0 or 1).
- `perm_unlink`: Members of the preceding group can delete records of this model (0 or 1).

The CSV file we used adds read-only access to the **Employees | Employee** standard security group, and full write access to the **Administration | Settings** group.

The **Employee** user group, `base.group_user`, is particularly important because the user groups added by the Odoo standard apps inherit from it. This means that if we need a new model to be accessible by all the backend users, regardless of the specific apps they work with, we should add that permission to the **Employee** group.

The resulting ACLs can be viewed from the GUI in debug mode by navigating to **Settings** | **Technical** | **Security** | **Access Controls List**, as shown in the following screenshot:

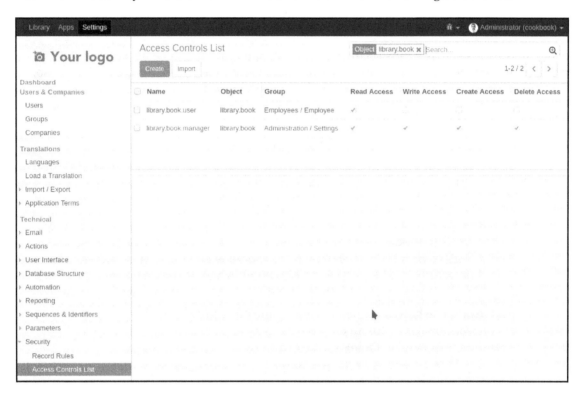

Some people find it easier to use this user interface to define ACLs and then use the export feature to produce a CSV file.

There's more...

It would make sense for us to give this permission to the Library user and Library manager groups defined in the *Creating security groups and assigning them to users* recipe. If you followed that recipe, it's a good exercise to then follow this one, adapting the group identifiers to the Library ones.

It's important to note that access lists provided by addon modules should not be directly customized, since they will be reloaded at the next module upgrade, destroying any customization that could have been done from the GUI.

To customize ACLs, two approaches can be used. One is to create new security groups that inherit from the one provided by the module and add additional permissions on it, but this allows only to add, not to remove. A more flexible approach can be to uncheck the **Active** flag to false on the particular ACL lines, to disable them. It is not visible by default, so we need to edit the tree view to add the `<field name="active" />` column. We can also add new ACL lines for additional or replacement permissions. On a module upgrade, the deactivated ACLs won't be reactivated and the added ACL lines won't be affected.

It's also worth noting that ACLs only apply to regular models and don't need to be defined for *Abstract* or *Transient* models. If defined, these will be disregarded and a warning message will be triggered in the server log.

Limiting access to fields in models

In some cases, we may need more fine-grained access control, and we may also need to limit access to specific fields in a model.

It is possible for a field to be accessible only by specific security groups, using the `groups` attribute. We will show how to add a field with limited access to the Library Books model.

How to do it...

To add a field with access limited to specific security groups, perform the following steps:

1. Edit the model file to add the field:

```
private_notes = fields.Text(groups='base.group_system')
```

2. Edit the view in the XML file to add the field:

```
<field name="private_notes" />
```

That's it. Now, upgrade the addon module for the changes in the model to take place. If you sign in with a user with no system configuration access, such as demo in a database with demonstration data, the Library Books form won't display the field.

How it works...

Fields with the `groups` attribute are specially handled to check whether the user belongs to any of the security groups indicated in the attribute, and if not, removes it from UI views and ORM operations for the user.

Note that this security is not superficial. The field is not only hidden in the user interface, but is also made unavailable to the user in the other ORM operations, such as `read` and `write`. This is also true for the XML-RPC or JSON-RPC calls.

Be careful when using these fields in business logic, or on change UI events (`@api.onchange` methods); they can raise errors for users with no access to the field. One workaround for this is to use privilege elevation, such as the `sudo()` model method or the `compute_sudo` field attribute for computed fields.

The `groups` value is a string containing a comma-separated list of valid XML IDs for security groups. The simplest way to find the XML ID for a particular group is to navigate to its form, at **Settings | Users | Groups**, and then access the **View Metadata** option from the debug menu, as shown in the following screenshot:

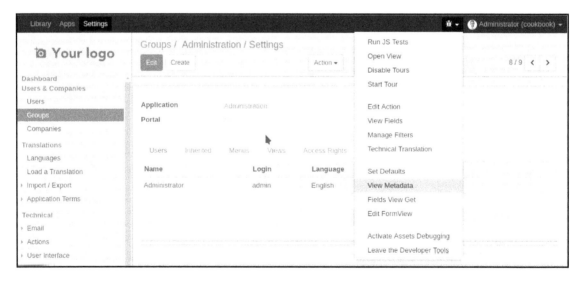

There's more...

In some cases, we need a field to be available or not depending on particular conditions, such as the values in a particular field, like `stage_id` or `state`. This is usually handled at the view level using attributes such as `states` or `attrs`, to dynamically display or hide the field according to certain conditions. You may refer to `Chapter 10`, *Backend Views*, for a detailed description.

Note that these techniques work at the user interface level only and don't provide actual access security. For that, you should add checks in the business logic layer. Either add model methods decorated with `@constrains`, implementing the specific validations intended, or extend the `create`, `write`, or `unlink` methods to add validation logic. You can get more insight on how to do this in `Chapter 6`, *Basic Server-Side Business Logic*.

Limiting record access using record rules

A common need for an application is to be able to limit which records are available to each user on a specific model.

This is achieved using record rules. A record rule is a domain filter expression defined on a model that will then be added on every data query made by the affected users.

As an example, we will add a record rule on the Library Books model so that users in the Employee group will only have access to books they created in the database.

Getting ready

This recipe assumes that you have an instance ready, with `my_module` available, as described in `Chapter 4`, *Creating Odoo Addon Modules*.

How to do it...

Record rules are added using a data XML file. To do so, perform the following steps:

1. Ensure that the `security/library_security.xml` file is referenced by the manifest `data` key:

```
'data': [
    'security/library_security.xml',
```

```
      # ...
   ],
```

2. We should have a `security/library_security.xml` data file, with a `<data>`
   section creating the security group. After it, add this second `<data>` section for
   the record rules:

```xml
<data noupdate="1">
  <record model="ir.rule" id="library_book_user_rule">
      <field name="name">Library: see only own books</field>
      <field name="model_id" ref="model_library_book"/>
      <field name="groups" eval="[(4, ref('base.group_user'))]"/>
      <field name="domain_force">
          [('create_uid', '=', user.id)]
      </field>
  </record>
  <record model="ir.rule" id="library_book_all_rule">
      <field name="name">Library: see all books</field>
      <field name="model_id" ref="model_library_book"/>
      <field name="groups"
              eval="[(4, ref('base.group_system'))]"/>
      <field name="domain_force">[(1, '=', 1)]</field>
  </record>
</data>
```

Upgrading the addon module will load the record rules into the Odoo instance.

To keep the recipe simple, we used the core Employee and settings security groups. We
could have used the Library user and manager groups instead, as defined in the *Adding
security access to models* recipe. It's a good exercise to follow it and modify this module so
that it uses those security groups instead.

How it works...

Record rules are just data records loaded into the `ir.rule` core model. While the file
adding them can be anywhere in the module, the convention is for it to be in the `security`
subdirectory It is common to have a single XML file with both security groups and record
rules.

Unlike groups, in the standard modules, the record rules are loaded in a `data` section with the `noupdate="1"` attribute. With this, those records will not be reloaded on a module upgrade, meaning that manual customizations on them are safe and will survive later upgrades.

To stay consistent with the official modules, we should also have our record rules inside a `<data noupdate="1">` section.

Record rules can be seen from the GUI at the **Settings** | **Technical** | **Security** | **Record Rules** menu option, as shown in the following screenshot:

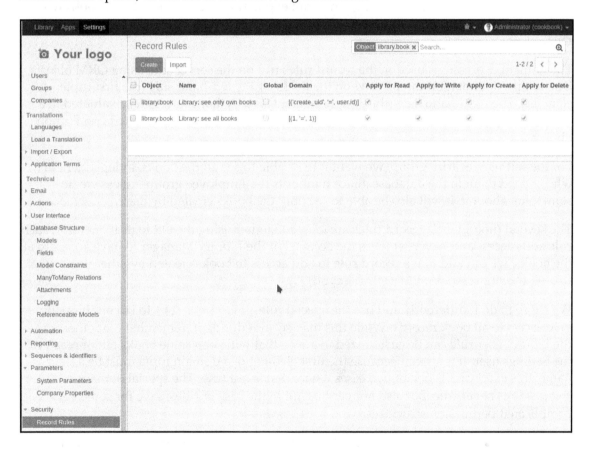

The following are the most important record rule fields used in the example:

- Name (`name`) is a descriptive title for the rule.
- Object (`model_id`) is a reference to the model the rule applies to.
- Groups (`groups`) are the security groups that the rule applies to. If none, the rule is considered *global* and is applied in a different way (more details follow later).
- Rule definition (`domain`) is a domain expression with the record filter to apply.

The first record rule we created was for the Employee security group. It uses the `[('create_uid', '=', user.id)]` domain expression to select only those books where the creation user is the current user. Thus, they will only be able to see the books created by themselves.

The domain expressions used in the record rules run on the server side using ORM objects. Due to this, dot notation can be used on the fields on the left-hand side (the first tuple element). The right-hand side (third tuple element) is a Python expression, evaluated in a context having available the `user` record object, for the current user and the `time` Python library.

For the settings security group, we want it to be able to see all the books, independent of who created them in the database. Since it inherits the Employee group, unless we do something about it, it will also be able to see only the books created by itself.

The several (non-global) record rules are joined together using the OR logical operator; each rule adds access and never removes the access. For the Library Manager to have access to all the books, we can add to it a record rule to add access to books created by other users, like this—`[('create_uid', '!=', user.id)]`.

We chose to do it differently and use the special rule `[(1, '=', 1)]` to unconditionally give access to all book records. While this may seem redundant, remember that otherwise, the Library user rule can be customized in a way that will keep some books out of reach to the Settings user. It is special because the first element of a domain tuple must be a field name; this exact case is one of two cases where that is not true. The special domain `[(1, '=', 0)]` is never true, but also not very useful in the case of rules, save for some very complicated permission structures.

 Record rules are ignored for the built-in `admin` user. When testing your record rules, ensure that you use some other user for that.

There's more...

When a record rule is not assigned to any security group, it is marked as **global** and is handled differently from the other rules.

Global record rules have a stronger effect than group-level record rules, and set access restrictions that those can't override. Technically, they are joined with an AND operator. In standard modules, they are used to implement multi-company security access so that each user can see only their company's data.

In summary, regular non-global record rules are joined together with an OR operator; they are added together and a record is accessible if any of the rules grant that access. Global record rules then add restrictions to the access given by regular record rules, using an AND operator. Restrictions added by global record rules can't be overridden by regular record rules.

Using security groups to activate features

Security groups can restrict some features so that they are accessible only to users belonging to these groups. Security groups can also inherit other groups, so they also grant their permissions.

These two features combined are used to implement a usability feature in Odoo—feature toggling. Security groups can also be used as a way to enable or disable features for some or all the users in an Odoo instance.

This recipe shows how to add options to configuration settings and showcases the two methods to enable additional features, making them visible using security groups or adding them by installing an additional module.

For the first case, we will make the book release dates an optional additional feature and for the second, as an example, we will provide an option to install the Notes module.

Getting ready

This recipe uses my_module described in Chapter 4, *Creating Odoo Addon Modules*. We will need security groups to work with, so you also need to have followed the *Adding security access to models* recipe.

In this recipe, some identifiers need to refer to the addon module's technical name. We will assume that it is `my_module`. In case you are using a different name, replace `my_module` with the actual technical name of your addon module.

How to do it...

To add the configuration options, follow the given steps:

1. To add the needed dependency and the new XML data files, edit the `__manifest__.py` file like this:

```
{   'name': 'Cookbook code',
    'category': 'Library',
    'depends': ['base_setup'],
    'data': [
        'security/ir.model.access.csv',
        'security/library_security.xml',
        'views/library_book.xml',
        'views/res_config_settings.xml',
    ],
}
```

2. To add the new security group used for feature activation, edit the `security/library_book.xml` file and add the following record to it:

```
<record id="group_release_dates" model="res.groups">
    <field name="name">Library: release date feature</field>
    <field name="category_id" ref="base.module_category_hidden" />
</record>
```

3. To make the book release date visible only when this option is enabled, we edit the field definition in the `models/library_book.py` file:

```
class LibraryBook(models.Model):
    # ...
    date_release = fields.Date(
        'Release Date',
        groups='my_module.group_release_dates',
    )
```

4. Edit the `models/__init__.py` file to add a new Python file for the configuration settings model:

```python
from . import library_book
from . import res_config_settings
```

5. To extend the core configuration wizard by adding new options to it, add the `models/res_config_settings.py` file with this code:

```python
from odoo import models, fields

class ConfigSettings(models.TransientModel):
    _inherit = 'res.config.settings'
    group_release_dates = fields.Boolean(
            "Manage book release dates",
            group='base.group_user',
            implied_group='my_module.group_release_dates',
    )
    module_note = fields.Boolean("Install Notes app")
```

6. To make the options available in the UI, add `views/res_config_settings.xml`, extending the form view:

```xml
<?xml version="1.0" encoding="utf-8"?>
<odoo>
    <record id="view_general_config_library" model="ir.ui.view">
        <field name="name">Configuration: add Library options</field>
        <field name="model">res.config.settings</field>
        <field name="inherit_id"
               ref="base_setup.res_config_settings_view_form" />
        <field name="arch" type="xml">
          <div id="business_documents" position="before">
            <div id="my_module">
              <h2>Library</h2>
              <!-- Release Dates option -->
              <div>
                <field name="group_release_dates" class="oe_inline"/>
                <label for="group_release_dates" />
              </div>
              <!-- Notes option -->
              <div>
                <field name="module_note" class="oe_inline"/>
                <label for="module_note" />
              </div>
            </div>
          </div>
        </field>
```

```
            </record>
        </odoo>
```

After upgrading the addon module, the two new configuration options should be available at **Settings** | **General Settings**. The screen should look like this:

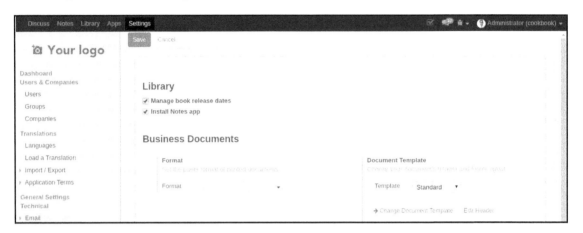

How it works...

The core `base` module provides a `res.config.settings` model, providing the business logic behind option activation. The `base_setup` addon module uses it to provide the several basic configuration options to make available in a new database. It also makes the **Settings** | **General Settings** menu available.

The `base_setup` module adapts `res.config.settings` to some central management dashboard, so we need to extend it to add our own configuration settings.

If we are to decide to create a specific settings form for the Library app, we can still inherit from the `res.config.settings` model with a different `_name`, and then for the new model, provide the menu option and form view for just those settings.

We used two different ways to activate the features: one by enabling a security group, making the feature visible to the user, and the other by installing an addon module providing the feature. The logic to handle both these cases is provided by the base `res.config.settings` model.

The first recipe step adds the `base_setup` addon module to the dependencies, since it provides extensions to the `res.config.settings` model we want to use. It also adds an additional XML data file that we will need to add the new options to the **General Settings** form.

In the second step, we create a new security group, **Library: release date feature**. The feature to activate should be visible only for that group so that it will be hidden until the group is enabled.

In our example, we want the book release date to be available only when the corresponding configuration option is enabled. To achieve this, we use the `groups` attribute on the field so that it is made available only for this security group. We did it at model level so that it is automatically applied to all the UI views where the field is used.

Finally, we extend the `res.config.settings` model to add the new options. Each option is a Boolean field, and its name must begin either by `group_` or `module_`, according to what we want it to do.

The `group_` option field should have an `implied_group` attribute and should be a string containing a comma-separated list of XML IDs for the security groups to activate when it is enabled. The XML IDs must be in the complete form with module name dot identifier name.

We can also provide a `group` attribute to specify for which security groups the feature will be enabled. It will be for all the Employee-based groups if no groups are defined. Thus, they won't apply to portal security groups, since these don't inherit on the Employee base security group, like the other regular security groups.

The mechanism behind the activation is quite simple: it adds the security group in the `group` attribute to the `implied_group`, thus making the related feature visible to the corresponding users.

The `module_` option field does not require any additional attributes. The remaining part of the field name identifies the module to be installed when activating the option. In our example, `module_note` will install the note module.

 Caution: Unchecking the box will uninstall the module without warning, which can cause data loss (models or fields removed and module data removed as a consequence). To avoid unchecking the box by accident, the secure_uninstall community module (from `https://github.com/OCA/server-tools`) prompts for a password before uninstalling the addon module.

The last step of the recipe adds the options to the **General Settings** form view, just before the **Business documents** group, having `id="business_documents"`. It creates its own div with the module name as ID, which is good practice because then other modules extending **my_module** can easily add their own configuration items to this div.

There's more...

Configuration settings can also have fields named with the `default_` prefix. When one of those has a value, it will set it as a global default. The settings field should have a `default_model` attribute to identify the model affected, and the field name after the `default_` prefix identifies the model's field that will have set the default value.

Additionally, fields with none of the three prefixes mentioned can be used for other settings, but you will need to implement the logic to populate their values, using `get_default_` name prefixed methods, and to act when their values are edited, using `set_` name prefixed methods.

For those who would like to go deeper into configuration settings details, the best documentation is in Odoo's source code in `./odoo/addons/base/res/res_config.py`, which is massively commented on with all details explained.

12
Internationalization

In this chapter, we will cover the following recipes:

- Installing a language and configuring user preferences
- Configuring language-related settings
- Translating texts through the web client user interface
- Exporting translation strings to a file
- Using gettext tools to ease translations
- Importing translation files into Odoo

Many of these actions can be done either from the web client user interface or from the command line. Whenever possible, we will show how to use either option.

Installing a language and configuring user preferences

Odoo is localization ready, meaning that it supports several languages and locale settings, such as date and number formats.

When first installed, only the default English language is available. To have other languages and locales available to the users, we need to install them.

Getting ready

We will need to have the **Developer Mode** activated. If it's not, activate it as pointed out in the *Activating the Odoo developer tools* recipe from `Chapter 1`, *Installing the Odoo Development Environment*.

How to do it...

To install a new language in an Odoo instance, follow these steps:

1. Select the **Settings | Translations | Load a Translation** menu option. On the resulting dialog, select the language to install from the list of available languages. If **website** is installed, you will also be given the option to pick the websites where the language will be available:

2. Now, click on the **Load** button and the language will be installed:

3. New languages can also be installed from the command line. The equivalent command for the preceding steps is this:

```
$ ./odoo-bin -d mydb --load-language=es_ES
```

4. To set the language used by a user, go to **Settings** | **Users** | **Users** and, in the **Preferences** tab of the user form, set the **Language** field value. While you are at it, you can use this opportunity to set the user's **Timezone**:

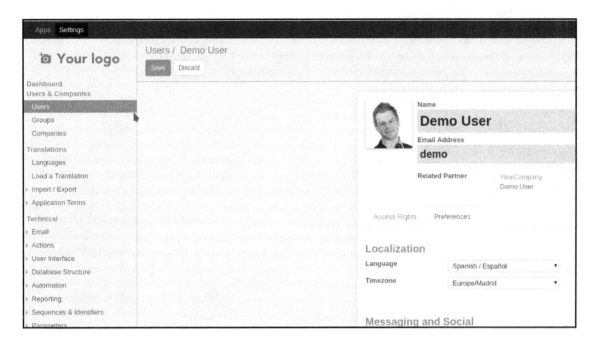

Users can also set these configurations themselves through the **Preferences** menu option, available when they click on the username at the top-right of the web client window.

How it works...

Users can have their own language and timezone preferences. The former is used to translate user interface text into the chosen language and apply local conventions for float and monetary fields. The latter is used to display **datetime** fields in the correct timezone.

Before a language is made available for the users to select, it must be installed with the **Load a Translation** feature. The list of available languages can be seen with the **Settings** | **Translations** | **Languages** menu option, where the ones with the active flag set are installed.

Each Odoo addon module is responsible for providing its own translation resources that should be placed inside an i18n subdirectory. Each language's data should be in a .po file. Following our example, for the Spanish language, the translation data is loaded from the es_ES.po data file.

Odoo also supports the notion of **base language**. For example, if we have an es.po file for Spanish and an es_MX.po file for Mexican Spanish, then es.po is detected as the base language for es_MX.po. When the Mexican Spanish language is installed, both data files are loaded; first the one for the base language and then the specific language is installed. Thus, the specific language translation file only needs to contain the strings that are specific to the language variant, Mexican Spanish in our example.

The i18n subdirectory is also expected to have a <module_name>.pot file, providing a template for translations and containing all the translatable strings. The *Exporting translation strings to a file* recipe explains how to export the translatable strings to generate this file.

When an additional language is installed, the corresponding resources are loaded from all installed addon modules and stored in the **Translated Terms** model. Its data can be viewed (and edited) within the **Settings** | **Translations** | **Application Terms** | **Translated Terms** menu option.

Translation files for the installed languages are also loaded when a new addon module is installed or an existing addon module is upgraded.

There's more...

Translation files can be reloaded without upgrading the addon modules by repeating the **Load a Translation** action. This can be used in case you have updated translation files and don't want to go through the trouble of upgrading the modules (and all their dependencies).

If the **Overwrite Existing Terms** checkbox is left empty, only newly translated strings are loaded. Thus, changed translated strings won't be loaded. Check the box if you want the already existing translations to also be loaded and overwrite the currently loaded translations. Note that this can be potentially disastrous if someone changed translations manually via the interface.

The previous checkbox exists because we can do our specific translations editing **Settings** | **Translations** | **Application Terms** | **Translated Terms**, or using the **Technical Translation** shortcut option in the **Debug** menu. Translations added or modified this way won't be overwritten unless the language is reloaded with the **Overwrite Existing Terms** checkbox enabled.

It can be useful to know that addon modules can also have an `i18n_extra` subdirectory with extra translations. The loading sequence for the translation files is the `.po` files in the `i18n` subdirectory, first for the base language and then for the language; after that, the `.po` files in the `i18n_extra` subdirectory, first for the base language and then for the language. The last string translation loaded is the one that prevails.

Configuring language-related settings

Languages and their variations (such as **es_MX** for Mexican Spanish) also provide locale settings such as date and number formats.

They come with appropriate defaults, so as long as the user is using the correct language, the locale settings should be the correct ones.

However, you might still want to modify a language's settings. For example, you might prefer to have the user interface in the default English, but want to change the American default date and number formats to your needs.

Getting ready

We will need to have the **Developer Mode** activated. If it's not, activate it as pointed out in the *Activating the Odoo developer tools* recipe from `Chapter 1`, *Installing the Odoo Development Environment*.

How to do it...

To modify a language's locale settings, follow these steps:

1. To check the installed languages and their configurations, select the **Settings |
   Translations | Languages** menu option. Clicking on one of the installed
   languages will open a form with the corresponding settings:

2. Edit the language settings. To change the date to the ISO format, change **Date
   Format** to **%Y-%m-%d**, and to change the number format to use a comma as a
   decimal separator, modify the **Decimal Separator** and **Thousands Separator**
   fields accordingly.

How it works...

When signing in and creating a new Odoo user session, the user language is checked in the
user preferences and set in the `lang` context key. This is then used to format the outputs
appropriately: the source texts are translated to the user language, and the dates and
numbers are formatted according to the language's current locale settings.

There's more...

Server-side processes are able to modify the context in which actions are run. For example, to get a record set where the dates are formatted according to the English format independent of the current user's language preference, you can do the following:

```
en_records = self.with_context(lang='en_US').search([])
```

For more details, refer to the *Calling a method with a modified context* recipe from `Chapter 10`, *Advanced Server-Side Development Techniques*.

Translating texts through the web client user interface

The simplest way to translate is to use the translation feature provided by the web client. These translation strings are stored in the database and can later be exported to a `.po` file, either to be included in an addon module or just to later be imported back manually.

Text fields can have translatable content, meaning that their value will depend on the current user's language. We will also see how to set the language-dependent values on these fields.

Getting ready

We will need to have the **Developer Mode** activated. If it's not, activate it as pointed out in *Activating the Odoo developer tools* recipe in `Chapter 1`, *Installing the Odoo Development Environment*.

How to do it...

We will demonstrate how to use translate terms through the web client using the **User Groups** feature as an example:

1. Navigate to the screen to translate. Select the **Settings** top menu and then open **Users & Companies** to open the corresponding view.

2. On the top menu bar, click on the **Debug** menu icon and select the **Technical Translation** option:

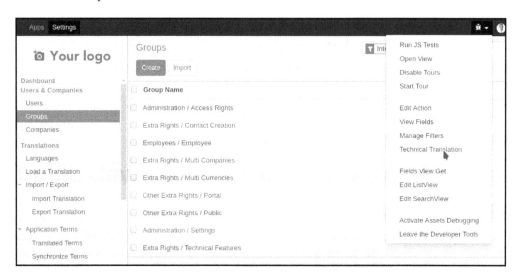

3. A list of the available translation terms for that view will be shown. Edit **Translation Value** in a line to change (or add) its translation text. If looking for a particular source string, use the listed filters to narrow down the displayed text:

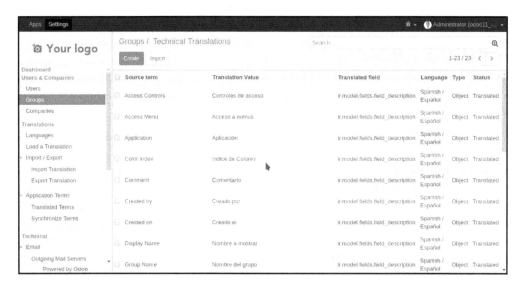

The Group name is a translatable field. Let's translate a record's value to the several languages installed:

4. Navigate again to the **User Groups** menu option, open one of the group records in the form view, and click on **Edit**:

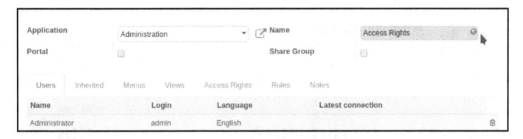

5. Note that the **Name** field has a special icon in the far right. This indicates that it is a translatable field. Clicking on the icon opens a **Translate** list with the different installed languages, allows us to set the translation for each of those languages.

How it works...

Translated terms are stored in the database table for the `ir.translation` model. The **Technical Translation** option in the **Debug** menu provides a quick access to those terms, in context with the currently selected view.

Similarly, model fields with translatable content feature an icon to access the list of the installed languages and to set the appropriate value for each language.

Alternatively, the translation terms can be accessed from the **Settings** top menu using the **Translations** | **Application Terms** | **Translated Terms** menu option. Here, we can see all the terms available for our instance, but should need to use data filters to locate the terms we might be interested in.

There's more...

Alongside the **Translated Terms** menu option, we also find the **Synchronize Terms** option. Selecting it will display a dialog window to provide the desired language, and will then launch the process to extract translatable strings from the installed addon modules and add any new ones to the **Translated Terms** table. It is equivalent to performing the **Export Translation**, followed by the **Import Translation** steps described earlier.

This can be useful after changing some models or views, to have the new strings added so that we can translate them.

It can also be used to populate the strings from the **en_US** default language. We can then make use of the translation terms to replace the original English texts with new ones, better for the end user's specific business vocabulary.

 When editing a QWeb view in a language other than the main website language, you'll notice that you can only change strings. This is because for other languages, you actually only add translations to the text content of nodes using Odoo's internationalization mechanism.

Exporting translation strings to a file

Translation strings can be exported with or without the translated texts for a selected language. This can be either to include in a module i18n data, or to later perform the translations with a text editor or perhaps with a specialized tool.

We will demonstrate how to do it using the standard mail module, so feel free to replace mail with your own module.

Getting ready

We will need to have the **Developer Mode** activated. If it's not, activate it as pointed out in *Activating the Odoo developer tools* recipe in Chapter 1, *Installing the Odoo Development Environment*.

How to do it...

To export the translation terms for the mail addon module, follow these steps:

1. In the web client user interface, from the **Settings** top menu, select the **Translations** | **Import/Export** | **Export Translation** menu option.

2. At the **Export Translations** dialog, choose the language translation to export, the file format, and the modules to export. To export a translation template file, select **New Language (Empty translation template)** from the **Language** selection list. It's recommended to use the `.po` format and to export only one `addon` module at a time—the **Discuss** (`mail` technical name) module in our example:

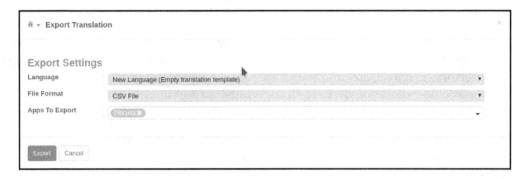

3. Once the export process is complete, a new window will be displayed, with a link to download the file and some additional advice.

4. To export a translation template file for the mail addon module from the Odoo command-line interface:

```
$ ./odoo-bin -d mydb --i18n-export=mail.po --modules=mail
$ mv mail.po ./addons/mail/i18n/mail.pot
```

5. To export the translation template file for a language, es_ES for Spanish, for example, from the Odoo command-line interface:

```
$ ./odoo-bin -d mydb --i18n-export=es_ES.po --modules=mail
  --language=es_ES
$ mv es_ES.po ./addons/mail/i18n
```

How it works...

The **Export Translation** feature does two things: it first extracts the translatable strings from the target modules, adding the new ones in the `ir.translation` model, and then creates a file with the translation terms. This can be done both from the web client and the command-line interface.

When exporting from the web client, we can choose to either export an empty translation template, that is, a file with the strings to translate along with empty translations, or export a language, resulting in a file with the strings to translate along with translation already done for the selected language.

The file formats available are CSV, PO, and TGZ. The TGZ file format exports a compressed file containing a `<name>/i18n/` directory structure with the PO or POT file.

The CSV format can be useful to perform translations using a spreadsheet, but the format to use in the addon modules is PO files. These are expected to be placed inside the `i18n` subdirectory, and if so, are automatically loaded once the corresponding language is installed. When exporting these PO files, we should export only one module at a time. The PO file is also a popular format supported by translation tools, such as Poedit.

Translations can also be exported directly from the command line, using the `--i18n-export` option. The recipe shows how to extract both the template files and the translated language files.

In Step 4 of the previous section, we exported a template file. The `--i18n-export` option expects the path and the file name to export. Mind that the file extension is required to be either CSV, PO, or TGZ. This option requires the `-d` option, specifying the database to use. The `--modules` option is also needed to indicate the addon modules to export. Note that the `--stop-after-init` option is not needed, since the export command automatically returns to the command line when finished.

This exports a template file, that in a module is expected to have the POT extension. When working on a module, after the export operation, we usually want to move the exported PO file to the module's `i18n` directory with a `<module>.pot` name.

In Step 5, the `--language` option was also used. With it, instead of an empty translation file, the translated terms for the selected language were also exported. One use case for this is to perform some translations through the web client user interface using the **Technical Translation** feature, and then exporting and including them in the module.

There's more...

Text strings in view and model definitions are automatically extracted for translation. For models, the `_description` attribute, the field names (the `string` attribute), help text, and selection field options are extracted as well as the user texts for model constraints (`_constraints` and `_sql_constraints`).

Text strings to translate inside Python or JavaScript code can't be automatically detected, so the code should identify those strings, wrapping them inside the underscore function.

In a module Python file, we should ensure that it is imported with the following:

```
from odoo import _
```

It can then be used wherever a translatable text is used with something like this:

```
_('Hello World')
```

For strings that use additional context information, we should use Python string interpolation, as shown:

```
_('Hello %s') % 'World'
```

Note that the interpolation should go outside the translation function. For example, `_("Hello %s" % 'World')` is wrong. String interpolations should also be preferred to string concatenation so that each interface text is just one translation string.

 Caution with `Selection` fields! If you pass an explicit list of values to the field definition, then the displayed strings are automatically flagged for translation. On the other hand, if you pass a method returning the list of values, then the display strings must be explicitly marked for translation.

Regarding manual translation work, any text file editor will do, but using an editor specifically supporting the PO file syntax makes the work easier by reducing the risk of formatting errors. Such editors include those listed here:

- poedit (`https://poedit.net/`)
- emacs (po-mode)
  (`https://www.gnu.org/software/gettext/manual/html_node/PO-Mode.html`)
- Lokalize (`http://i18n.kde.org/tools`)
- Gtranslator (`https://wiki.gnome.org/Apps/Gtranslator`)

Using gettext tools to ease translations

The PO file format is part of the `gettext` internationalization and localization system commonly used in Unix-like systems. This system includes tools to ease the translation work.

This recipe demonstrates how to use these tools to help translate our addon modules. We want to use it on a custom module, so my_module created in Chapter 4, *Creating Odoo Addon Modules*, is a good candidate. However, feel free to replace it with some other custom module you have at hand, replacing the recipe's my_module references as appropriate.

How to do it...

To manage translations from the command line, assuming that your Odoo installation is at ~/odoo-work/odoo, follow these steps:

1. Create a compendium of translation terms for the target language, for example, Spanish. If we name our compendium file odoo_es.po, we should write the following code:

```
$ cd ~/odoo-work/odoo  # Use the path to your Odoo installation
$ find ./ -name es_ES.po | xargs msgcat --use-first | msgattrib
   -- translated  --no-fuzzy \ -o ./odoo_es.po
```

2. Export the translation template file for the addon module from the Odoo command-line interface and place it in the module's expected location:

```
$ ./odoo-bin -d mydb --i18n-export=my_module.po --modules=my_module
$ mv my_module.po ./addons/my_module/i18n/my_module.pot
```

3. If no translation file is available yet for the target language, create the PO translation file, reusing the terms already found translated in the compendium:

```
$ msgmerge --compendium ./odoo_es.po -o
./addons/my_module/i18n/es_ES.po \
/dev/null ./addons/my_module/i18n/my_module.pot
```

4. If a translation file exists, add the translations that can be found in the compendium:

```
$ mv ./addons/my_module/i18n/es_ES.po /tmp/my_module_es_old.po
$ msgmerge --compendium ./odoo_es.po -o./addons/my_module/i18n/es_ES.po
  \ /tmp/my_module_es_old.po ./addons/my_module/i18n/my_module.pot
$ rm /tmp/my_module_es_old.po
```

5. To take a peek at the untranslated terms in a PO file, use this:

```
$ msgattrib --untranslated ./addons/my_module/i18n/es_ES.po
```

6. Use your favorite editor to complete the translation.

How it works...

Step 1 uses commands from the gettext toolbox to create a translation compendium for the chosen language, Spanish, in our case. It works by finding all the es_ES.po files in the Odoo code base, and passing them to the msgcat command. We use the --use-first flag to avoid conflicting translations (there are a few in the Odoo code base). The result is passed to the msgattrib filter. We use the --translated option to filter out the untranslated entries and the --no-fuzzy option to remove fuzzy translations. We then save the result in odoo_es.po.

Step 2 of the preceding section calls odoo.py with the --i18n-export option. You need to specify a database on the command line, even if one is specified in the configuration file and the --modules option, with a comma-separated list of modules to export the translation for.

> In the gettext world, fuzzy translations are those created automatically by the msgmerge command (or other tools) using a proximity match on the source string. We want to avoid these in the compendium.

Step 3 creates a translation file using the translated values for texts already found in the compendium. The msgmerge command is used with the --compendium option to find in the compendium files the msgid lines matching those in the translation template file generated in step 2. The result is saved in the es_ES.po file.

If you have a preexisting .po file for your addon with translations you would like to preserve, then you should rename it and replace the /dev/null argument with this file. The rename is required to avoid using the same file both for input and output.

There's more...

This recipe only skims the rich tools of the GNU gettext toolbox. Full coverage is well beyond the scope of this book. If you are interested, the GNU gettext documentation contains a wealth of precious information about PO file manipulation, and is available at `http://www.gnu.org/software/gettext/manual/gettext.html`.

Importing translation files into Odoo

The usual practice to load translations is by placing PO files inside the module's `i18n` subdirectory. Whenever the addon module is installed or upgraded, the translation files are loaded and the new translated strings are added.

However, there may be cases where we want to directly import a translation file. In this recipe, we will see how to load a translation file, either from the web client or from the command line.

Getting ready

We will need to have the **Developer Mode** activated. If it's not, activate it as pointed out in the *Activating the Odoo developer tools* recipe from `Chapter 1`, *Installing the Odoo Development Environment*. We are also expected to have a translation file to be imported, `myfile.po`, for example.

How to do it...

To import the translation terms, follow these steps:

1. In the web client user interface, from the **Settings** top menu, select the **Translations** | **Import/Export** | **Import Translation** menu option.
2. On the **Import Translations** dialog, fill out the language name and the language code, and select the file to import. Finally, click on the **Import** button to perform the action:

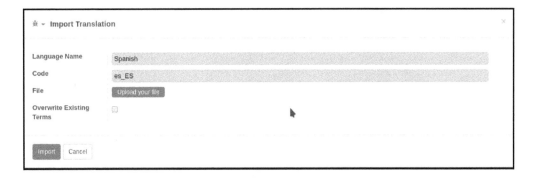

3. To import a translation file from the Odoo command-line interface, we must place it inside the server addons path and then perform the import:

```
$ mv myfile.po ./addons/
$ ./odoo.py -d mydb --i18n-import="myfile.po" --lang=es_ES
```

How it works...

Import Translation takes a PO or CSV file and loads the translation strings into the `ir.translation` table.

The web client feature asks for the language name, but this is not used in the import process. It also has an overwrite option. If selected, it forces all the translations, strings to be imported, even the ones that already exist, overwriting them in the process.

On the command line, the import can be done using the `--i18n-import` option. It must be provided with the path to the file, relative to an addons path directory; `-d` and `--language` (or `-l`) are mandatory. Overwriting can also be achieved by adding the `--i18n-overwrite` option to the command. Note that we didn't use the `--stop-after-init` option. It is not needed, since the import action stops the server when it finishes.

13
Automation, Workflows, Emails, and Printouts

In this chapter, we will cover the following recipes:

- Using Kanban stages and features
- Creating server actions
- Using Python code server actions
- Using automated actions on time conditions
- Using automated actions on event conditions
- Adding messaging and tracking features
- Email templates
- QWeb-based PDF reports
- Producing LibreOffice-based reports with Py3O

Introduction

Business applications are expected not only to store records, but also to manage business workflows. Odoo includes a workflow engine, but it is increasingly used less in later versions of the product. Instead, automation rules and Kanban boards are used whenever possible.

The automation rules are most relevant for customization than for new addon modules development, but developers should still be familiar with them. Doing so can avoid over-engineered business rules that can be implemented through functional customizations. Some of these techniques can also be used by power users or functional consultants to add some simpler process automation without the need to create custom addons.

Using Kanban stages and features

The Kanban board is a simple method to manage workflows. It is organized in columns, each corresponding to stages, and the work items progress from left to right until they are finished.

There are a few features used across several Kanban boards, providing a common pattern that can also be used in our own custom modules. Let's visit those features.

Getting ready

To follow this recipe, you will need to have the Project Management app already installed.

How to do it...

To get started with a Project Tasks Kanban board, do the following:

1. Select the **Project** top menu option and then **Create** a new Project:

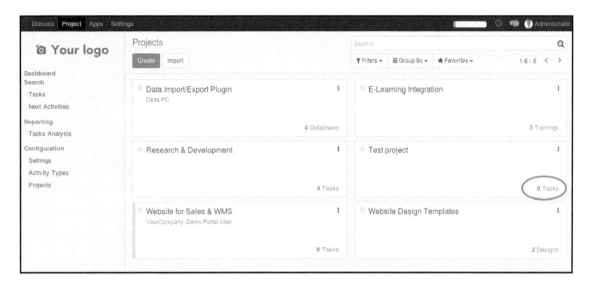

2. Give a name to the new Project, for instance, **Test project**, and click on the **Create** button. Next, press on the "**0 Tasks**" link in the bottom-right cornet of the newly created project card. This will open the Kanban view for the Project Tasks.

3. Click on the **Add New Column** vertical bar at the left, type Now in the small dialog box, and click on **Add**. Repeat to also add the **Later** and **Done** stages.

4. Hover the mouse pointer over the **Done** stage and a cog wheel icon will be shown. Click on it and pick **Edit Stage** from the option menu.

5. In the **Edit Column** window, check the **Folded in Kanban** box and save, as shown in the following screenshot:

How it works...

Kanban is one of the available view types, and it is able to organize items grouped in columns. If we use stages to group the work items, we get a **Kanban board**. The stage list can be configured to fit the user's specific needs.

Stages should have a folded attribute, meaning that the corresponding column in the Kanban view should be shown folded. Work in progress items are expected to be in an unfolded stage, and terminated items, usually **Done** and **Cancelled**, should be in **Folded** stage.

Each work item has a reference for the stage it is in. It may also have a Kanban State, represented by a traffic signal-like light, and a Priority, represented by a star. The Kanban cards can also have a color attribute, used for their background color.

While the stage represents the current status in the process for the work item, **Kanban State** provides information about its readiness to advance to the next stage. It is a **Selection** field, usually named `kanban_state`. You will normally display it in form views and Kanban views using the `kanban_state_selection` widget. This field is displayed as follows:

- A grey neutral circle, the default (the `normal` database value)
- A red *Blocked* circle (the `blocked` database value), meaning that there is some reason to retain the work item in the current stage
- A green *Ready for the next stage* circle (the `done` database value), meaning that the work item is ready to be pulled for the next stage

The **Priority** is also a **Selection** field, and is displayed with the special `priority` widget in the form and Kanban views. The selection options are expected to be either a string with a number, starting at 0, for normal value (not starred), and other values for starred options.

There's more...

Stages are added to models through a `Many2one` field referencing a stage model defining the possible stages. On form views, they can be represented with the help of the `statusbar` pipeline widget. For more details on views, widgets, and designing Kanban views, you can refer to `Chapter 10`, *Backend Views*.

The complementary Kanban state is supported by a **Selection** field and its typical definition is as follows:

```
kanban_state = fields.Selection(
    [('normal', 'Normal'),
     ('blocked', 'Blocked'),
     ('done', 'Ready for next stage')],
    'Kanban State',
    default='normal')
```

On form views, it should use the specific `kanban_state_selection` widget:

```
<field name="kanban_state" widget="kanban_state_selection" />
```

Regarding the **Priority** field, it is also a **Selection** field, and the number of options usually ranges between 2 and 4 selection items:

```
priority = fields.selection(
    [('0', 'Normal'), ('1', 'Low'), ('2', 'High'),
     ('3', 'Very High')],
    'Priority', default='0')
```

In form views, it can make use of the specific `priority` widget:

```
<field name="priority" widget="priority"/>
```

Creating server actions

Server actions underpin the Odoo automation tools. They allow us to describe the actions to perform. These actions are then available to be called by event triggers, or to be triggered automatically when certain time conditions are met.

The simplest case is to let the end user perform some action on a document by selecting it from the **More** button menu. We will create such an action for project tasks, to **Set as Priority** by starring the currently selected task and setting a deadline on it to 3 days from now.

Getting ready

We will need an Odoo instance with the Project app installed. We will also need the **Developer Mode** activated. If it's not, activate it in the Odoo Settings dashboard.

How to do it...

To create a server action and use it from the **More** menu, follow these steps:

1. On the **Settings** top menu, select the **Technical** | **Actions** | **Server Actions** menu item, and click on the **Create** button at the top of the record list:

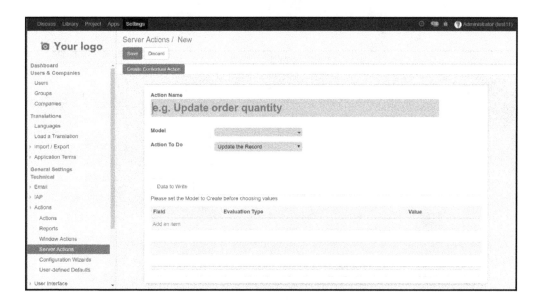

2. Fill out the server action form with these values:
    - **Action Name**: Set as Priority
    - **Base Model**: Task
    - **Action To Do**: Update the Record

3. In the server action, under the **Value Mapping** field, add the following lines:

- As the first value, we will enter the following parameters:
    - **Field**: `Deadline`
    - **Evaluation Type**: `Python expression`
    - **Value**: `datetime.date.today() + datetime.timedelta(days=3)`
- As the second value, we will enter the following parameters:
    - **Field**: `Priority`
    - **Evaluation Type**: `Value`
    - **Value**: `1`

The following screenshot shows the entered values:

4. Save the server action and click on the **Create contextual action** button at the top left to make it available in the Project task's **More** button.

5. To try it out, go to the Project top menu, select the **Search | Tasks** menu item, and open a random task. By clicking on the **More** button, we should see the **Set as Priority** option. Selecting it will star the task and change the deadline date to three days from now.

How it works...

Server actions work on a Model, so one of the first things to do is to pick the **Base Model** we want to work with. In our example, we used Project Tasks.

Next, we should select the type of action to perform. There are a few options available:

- **Execute Python Code** allows you to write arbitrary code to execute, when none of the other options is flexible enough for what we need
- **Create a new Record** allows you to create a new record on the current or on another Model
- **Update the Record** allows you to set values on the current or on another record
- **Send Email** allows choosing an email template, and will be used to send out an email when the action is triggered
- **Execute several actions** can be used to trigger a client or window action, just like when a menu item is clicked on
- **Add Followers** allows to subscribe users or channels to the record

For our example, we used **Update the Record** to set some values on the current record. We set **Priority** to 1 to star the task, and set a value on the **Deadline** field. This one is more interesting, since the value to use is evaluated from a Python expression. Our example makes use of the `datetime` Python module (visit `https://docs.python.org/2/library/datetime.html`) to compute the date 3 days from today.

Arbitrary Python expression can be used there as well as in several of the other action types available. For security reasons, the code is checked by the `safe_eval` function implemented in `odoo/openerp/tools/safe_eval.py`. This means that some Python operations may not be allowed, but this rarely proves to be a problem.

There's more...

The Python code is evaluated in a restricted context, where the following objects are available to use:

- `env`: This is a reference for the Environment object, just like `self.env` in a class method.
- `model`: This is a reference to the model class the server action acts upon. In our example, it is equivalent to `self.env['project.task]`.
- `Warning`: This is a reference to `openerp.exceptions.Warning`, allowing for validations that block unintended actions. It can be used as `raise Warning('Message!')`.

- `record` or `records`: This provides references to the current record or records, allowing you to access their field values and methods.
- `log`: This is a function to log messages in the `ir.logging` model, allowing for database side logging on actions.
- `datetime`, `dateutil`, and `time`: These provide access to the Python libraries.

Using Python code server actions

Server actions have several types available, but executing arbitrary Python code is surely the most flexible one. Used wisely, it can provide power users with the capability to implement advanced business rules from the user interface, without the need to create specific addon modules to install that code.

We will demonstrate using this type of server actions by implementing one that sends reminder notifications to the followers of a Project task.

Getting ready

We will need an Odoo instance with the Project app installed.

How to do it...

To create and try a Python code server action, follow these steps:

1. Create a new server action: on the **Settings** top menu, select the **Technical | Actions | Server Actions** menu item, and click on the **Create** button at the top of the record list.
2. Fill out the **Server Action** form with the following values:
   - **Action Name**: Send Reminder
   - **Base Model**: Task
   - **Action To Do**: Execute Python Code
3. In the **Python code** text area, remove the default text and replace it with the following:

```
if not record.date_deadline:
    raise Warning('Task has no deadline!')
```

```
deadline_dt = datetime.datetime.strptime(
    obj.date_deadline, '%Y-%m-%d')
delta = deadline_dt.date() - datetime.date.today()
days = delta.days
if days==0:
    msg =  'Task is due today.'
elif days < 0:
    msg = 'Task is %d day(s) late.' % abs(days)
else:
    msg = 'Task will be due in %d day(s).' % days
record.message_post(msg, subject='Reminder', subtype='mt_comment')
```

4. Save the **Server Action** and click on **Add in the 'More' Button** at the top-right to make it available in the Project task's **More** button.

5. Now, click on the **Project** top menu and select the **Search | Tasks** menu item. Pick a random task, set a deadline date on it, and then try the **Send Reminder** option in the **More** button.

How it works...

The *Creating server actions* recipe provides a detailed explanation on how to create a server action in general. For this particular type of action, we need to pick the **Execute Python Code** option and then write the code to run the text area.

The code can have multiple lines, as is the case in our recipe, and it runs in a context that has available references to objects such as the current record object or the session user. The references available are described in the *Creating server actions* recipe.

The used code computes the number of days from the current date until the deadline date and uses that to prepare an appropriate notification message. The last line does the actual posting of the message in the task's message wall. The subtype='mt_comment' argument is needed for email notifications to be sent to the followers, just like when we use the **New Message** button. If no subtype is given, mt_note is used as a default, posting an internal note without notification, as if we used the **Log an internal note** button.

There's more...

Python code server actions are a powerful and flexible resource, but do have some limitations compared to the custom addon modules.

Since the Python code is evaluated at runtime, in case of an error, the stack trace is not so informative and it can be harder to debug. It is also not possible to insert a break point in the code of a server action using the techniques shown in Chapter 8, *Debugging and Automated Testing*, so debugging needs to be done using logging statements. Another concern is, when trying to track down the cause from a behavior in module code, you may not find anything relevant. In that case, it's probably caused by a server action.

When carrying out a more intensive use of server actions, we can get complex interactions, so it is advised to plan properly and keep them organized.

Using automated actions on time conditions

Automated actions can be used to automatically trigger actions based on time conditions. We can use them to automatically perform some operation on records that meet certain criteria and reach time condition.

As an example, we can trigger a reminder notification for Project tasks one day before their deadline, if they have any. Let's see how this can be done.

Getting ready

To follow this recipe, we will need to have both the **Project Management** app (technical name project) and the **Automated Action Rules** addon (technical name base_automation) already installed, and have the **Developer Mode** activated. We will also need the server action created in the *Using Python code server actions* recipe.

How to do it...

To create an automated action with a timed condition on tasks, follow these steps:

1. In the **Settings** top menu, select the **Technical** | **Automation** | **Automated Actions** menu item, and click on the **Create** button.
2. Fill out the basic information on the **Automated Actions** form:
   - **Rule Name**: Deadline Near Notification
   - **Related Document Model**: Task
   - Under the **Conditions tab**, for **When to Run**, select **Based on Time Condition**
   - In **Action To Do**, select **Execute several actions**

3. To set the record criteria, click on the **Edit Domain** button in the **Apply on** section. In the pop-up dialog, set a valid domain expression in the code editor: `[('date_deadline', '!=', False), ('stage_id.fold', '=', False)]`, and click on the **Save** button. When changing to another field, information on the number of records meeting the criteria is updated, and the **Select Records** link changes to **Change Selection**. By clicking on it, we can check the records list of the records meeting the domain expression.

4. To set the time condition, on **Trigger Date** select the field to use, **Deadline**, and set the **Delay After Trigger Date** to **-1 Days**.

5. On the **Actions** tab, under **Server actions to run**, click on **Add an item** and pick **Send Reminder** from the list that should have been created previously. If not, we can still create the server action to run using the **Create** button:

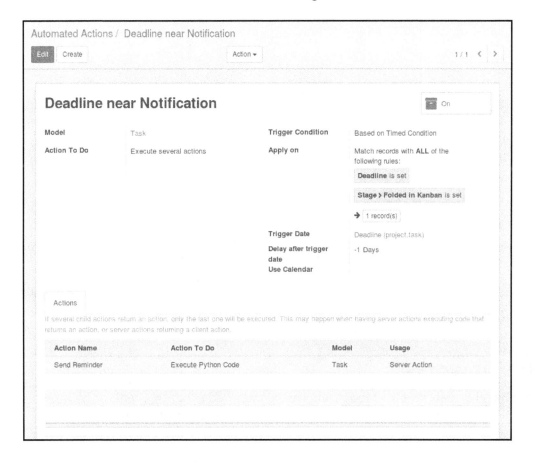

6. Click on **Save** to save the automated action.
7. Perform the following steps to try it out:
   1. Go to the **Project** top menu, **Search** | **Tasks**, and set a deadline on some task with a date in the past.
   2. Go to the **Settings** top menu, to the **Technical** | **Automation** | **Scheduled Actions** menu item, find the **Base Action Rule: Check and execute** action in the list, open its form view, and press on the **Run Manually** button in the top-left. This forces timed automated actions to be checked now. Note that this should work on a newly created demo database, but might not work like this in an existing database:

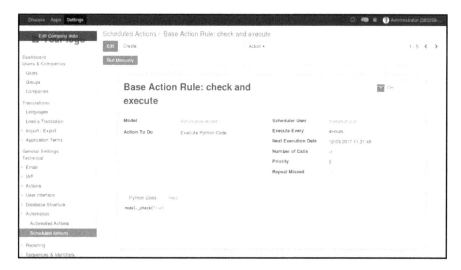

   3. Again, go to the **Project** top menu and open the same task you previously set a deadline date to. Check the message board; you should see the notification generated by the server action triggered by our automated action.

How it works...

Automated actions act on a Model, and can be triggered either by events or by time conditions. The first steps are to set the **Model** and **When to Run** values.

Both methods can use a filter to narrow down the records eligible to perform the action on. We can use a domain expression for this. You can find details on writing domain expressions in `Chapter 10`, *Backend Views*. Alternatively, you can create and save a filter on project tasks, using the user interface features, and then copy the automatically generated domain expression here, selecting it from the **Set selection based on a search filter** list.

The domain expression we used selects all the records with a non-empty **Deadline** date, in a stage where the **Fold** flag is not checked. Stages without the **Fold** flag are considered to be working in progress. This way, we avoid triggering notifications on tasks that are in the **Done**, **Canceled**, or **Closed** stages.

Then, we should define the time condition: the date field to use and when in time the action should be triggered. The time period can be in minutes, hours, days, or months, and number of periods can be positive, for time after the date, or negative, for time before the date. When using a time period in days, we can provide a **Resource Calendar** defining the working days, and the day count will use it.

These actions are checked by the **Check Action Rules** scheduled job. Note that, by default, it is run every four hours. This is appropriate for actions that work on the days or months scale, but if you need actions that work in the hour or minute timescales, you need to change the running interval to a smaller value.

Actions will be triggered for records that meet all the criteria and whose triggering date condition (field date plus the interval) is after the last action execution. This is so as to avoid repeatedly triggering the same action. Also, this is why manually running the preceding action will work in a database where the scheduled action was not yet triggered, but might not work immediately in a database where it was already run by the scheduler.

Once an automated action is triggered, the **Actions** tab tells you what should happen. This can be a list of server actions, doing things such as changing values on the record, posting notifications, and sending out emails.

There's more...

These types of automated actions are triggered once a certain time condition is reached. This is not the same as regularly repeating some action while some condition is still true. For example, an automated action will not be capable of posting a reminder every day after the deadline has exceeded.

This type of action can instead be performed by **Scheduled Actions**, stored in the `ir.cron` model. However, scheduled actions do not support server actions; they can only call an existing method of a model object. So, to implement a custom action, we need to write an addon module adding the underlying Python method.

For reference, the technical name for the **Automated Actions** Model is `base.action.rule`.

Using automated actions on event conditions

Business applications provide systems with records for business operations, but are also expected to support dynamic business rules that are specific to the organization use cases.

Carving these rules into custom addon modules can be inflexible and out of the reach of functional users. Automated actions triggered by event conditions can bridge this gap and provide a powerful tool to automate or enforce the organization procedures.

As an example, we will enforce a validation on Project tasks so that only the Project Manager can change **Tasks** to the **Done** stage.

Getting ready

To follow this recipe, you will need to have the Project Management app already installed. We also need to have the **Developer Mode** activated. If it's not, activate it in the Odoo **About** dialog.

How to do it...

To create an automated action with an event condition on tasks, follow these steps:

1. In the **Settings** top menu, select the **Technical** | **Automation** | **Automated Actions** menu item, and press on the **Create** button
2. Fill out the basic information on the **Automated Actions** form:
    - **Rule Name**: Validate Closing Tasks
    - **Related Document Model**: Task
    - **Conditions tab** | **When to Run**: On Update
    - **Action To Do**: Execute several actions

3. The `on update` rules allow you to set two record filters, before and after the update operation:
    - On the **Before Update Filter** field, click on the **Edit domain** button and set a valid domain expression—`[('stage_id.name', '!=', 'Done')]`—in the code editor and save
    - On the **Apply on** field, click on the **Edit domain** button and set the `[('stage_id.name', '=', 'Done')` domain in the code editor and save

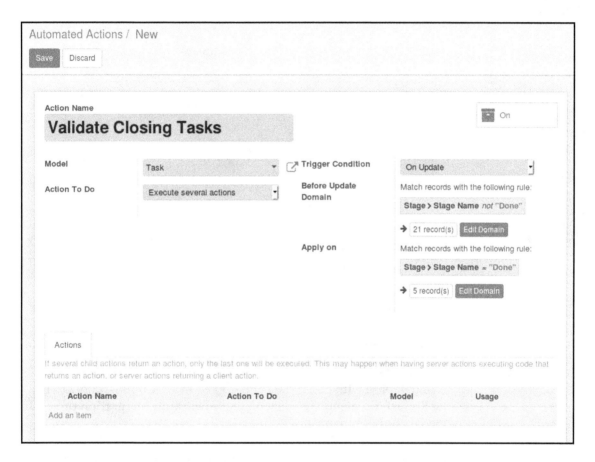

4. On the **Actions** tab, click on **Add an item**, and on the list dialog, click on the **Create** button to create a new server action

5. Fill out the server action form with the following values and then press on the **Save** button:

- **Action Name**: Validate Closing Tasks
- **Base Model**: Task
- **Action To Do**: Execute Python Code
- **Python Code**: Enter the following:

```
if user != record.project_id.user_id:
    raise Warning('Only the Project Manager can close
Tasks')
```

- The following screenshot shows the entered values:

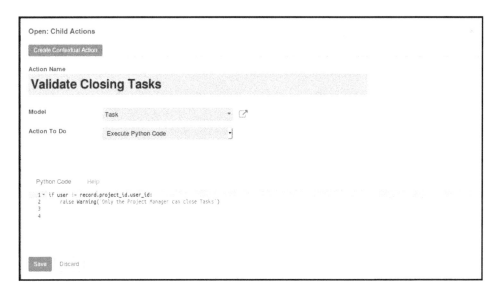

6. Click on **Save & Close** to save the automated action and try it out:

1. On a database with demo data and logged in as Administrator, go to the **Project** top menu and click on the **E-Learning Integration** project to open its task Kanban.

2. Then, try dragging one of the tasks into the **Done** stage column. Since this Project's Manager is user Demo and we are working with the user Administrator, our automated action should be triggered, and our warning message is blocking the change.

How it works...

We start by giving a name to our automated actions and setting the Model it works with. For the type of action, we choose **On Update**, but the **On Creation, On Creation & Update, On Deletion**, and **Based On Form Modification** options are also possible.

Next, we should define the filters to determine when our action should be triggered. The **On Update** actions allow us to define two filters: one to check before and the other after the changes are made to the record. This can be used to express transitions: detect when a record changes from state A to state B. In our example, we want to trigger the action when a not-done task changes to the Done stage. The **On Update** action is the only one that allows for these two filters; the other action types only allow for one filter.

> It is important to note that our example condition will only work correctly for English language users. This is so because the **Stage Name** is a translatable field that can have different values for different languages. So, filters on the translatable fields should be avoided or used with care.

Finally, we create and add one (or more) server actions with whatever we want to be done when the automated action is triggered. In this case, we chose to demonstrate how to implement custom validation, making use of a Python code server action that uses the Warning exception to block the user changes.

There's more...

In Chapter 6, *Basic Server-Side Development*, we saw how to redefine the write() methods of a model to perform actions on record update. Automated actions on record update provide another way to achieve the same, with some benefits and drawbacks.

Among the benefits, it is easy to define an action triggered by the update of a stored computed field, which is tricky to do in pure code. It is also possible to define filters on records and have different rules for different records, or for records matching different conditions that can be expressed with search domains.

However, automated actions can have disadvantages when compared to Python business logic code inside modules. As a concern, with poor planning, this flexibility can rapidly grow into complex interactions, difficult to maintain and debug. Also, the before and after write filter operations bring some overhead, so for performing sensitive actions, this can be an issue.

Adding messaging and tracking features

Odoo social features are used in many of the standard apps. They provide an easy way for the user to be updated and to collaborate around business documents. It is, therefore, important for the custom addon modules to also support them.

These features are provided by the **Discuss** app (the technical name is `mail`) and their most visible aspect is the message wall at the bottom of the form for a business document, along with the follower box on its right-hand side:

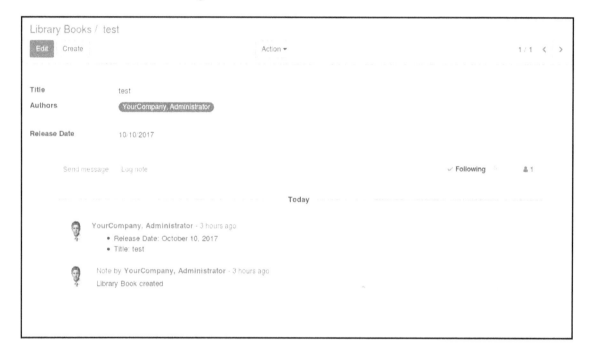

Getting ready

We will use `my_module` introduced in `Chapter 3`, *Creating Odoo Modules*, defining the `Library Book` model. You can get that code or quickly create an addon around this model:

```
from odoo import models, fields
class LibraryBook(models.Model):
    _name = 'library.book'
    name = fields.Char('Title', required=True)
```

```
date_release = fields.Date('Release Date')
author_ids = fields.Many2many('res.partner', string='Authors')
```

We will also need an XML file with the corresponding form view:

```xml
<form>
    <group>
        <field name="name"/>
        <field name="author_ids" widget="many2many_tags"/>
    </group>
    <group>
        <field name="date_release"/>
    </group>
</form>
```

How to do it...

To enable the social network and tracking features on the Library Book model, follow these steps:

1. Add the mail dependency to the addon module's __manifest__.py manifest file:

```
'depends': ['mail'],
```

2. Edit the library.book model to add the code highlighted next:

```
class LibraryBook(models.Model):
    _name = 'library.book'
    _description = 'Library Book'
    _inherit = ['mail.thread']
    name = fields.Char('Title', required=True,
                       track_visibility=True)
    date_release = fields.Date('Release Date',
                       track_visibility=True)
    author_ids = fields.Many2many('res.partner', string='Authors')
```

3. Add the following method to the library.book model:

```
def _track_subtype(self, init_values):
    if 'date_release' in init_values:
        return 'mail.mt_comment'
    return False
```

4. Add the message wall widgets into the form view, just before the `</form>` closing tag:

```
<div class="oe_chatter">
    <field name="message_follower_ids"
            widget="mail_followers"
            groups="base.group_user" />
    <field name="message_ids"
            widget="mail_thread" />
</div>
```

After installing these changes, we should see the message wall at the bottom of the `Library Book` form, and changes to the **Title** and **Release Date** fields should be logged on it.

How it works...

The Discuss addon (whose technical name is `mail`) provides the `mail.thread` model to use on other business models as a `mixin` class. Our first steps are to add the module dependency and to have the `library.book` module to inherit features from it.

Among other things, the `message_follower_ids` and `message_ids` fields are added to store the follower list and related messages. These should be added to the form view, using the `mail_followers` and `mail_thread` special widgets.

We also added the optional `_description` attribute to the model's class. It is used by some of the tracking messages, such as **Library Book created**, and will inappropriately display messages such as **Email Thread is created** if not explicitly defined. After addon installation, the display name that'll be used can also be set at **Settings | Technical | Database Structure | Models**, in the **Model Description** field.

The `mail.thread` model can keep track of changes made to a document, posting them as messages on the message wall. For this, we just need to add `track_visibility=True` (or any true value) on the fields to track. By default, these are posted as internal notes, meaning that no email messages are triggered.

 The changed values are stored in the database, in the `mail.tracking.value` model. This is accessible in the web client at **Settings | Technical | Email | Tracking Values**. This can be useful for reporting or auditing.

The message types are called **Subtypes**. The mail module comes with two subtypes: discussion messages and internal notes. The first can trigger email notifications and is visible to all the followers. The second one does not trigger notifications and can only be seen by users in the Employee security group. We can set the subtype when posting messages using their XML IDs. For these two, the corresponding XML IDs are `mail.mt_comment` and `mail.mt_note`.

The subtype for the tracking messages can be changed by the `_track_subtype()` method. It receives a dictionary with the tracked field names with changes, and their values before the changes were made. It is expected to return a string with the XML ID of the subtype to use. Subtypes provided by the `mail` addon do not need the module suffix, so we can use just `mt_comment` for discussion messages. If no specific subtype is returned, messages will use the default `mt_note` subtype.

Followers can subscribe to different subtypes, so they are able to choose when to be notified. For example, the Project addon adds subtypes such as **Task change stage** or **Task is blocked**. With `_track_subtype()`, we can detect such events and report them through messages with the proper subtype. Inside that method, `self` makes available the recordsets involved in the write operation so that distinct message subtypes can be selected based on arbitrary record values.

There's more...

Posting messages can be done using the following method:

```
obj.message_post(body="Body text", subject="Subject", subtype="mt_note")
```

The subject and subtype are optional.

Followers can be either partners or message channels. To add followers, use the following:

```
obj.message_subscribe(partner_ids=..., channel_ids=..., subtype_ids=[])
```

The `subtype_ids` argument is optional, and allows you to subscribe specific subtypes. If not provided, the defaults defined in the subtypes will be used.

Sometimes, we want to add a user as a follower. A user is also a partner, so `user.partner_id` should be used for this. However, the following specific method is also provided for this:

```
obj.message_subscribe_users(user_ids, subtype_ids=[])
```

It is reasonable to expect to be able to post messages or follow documents, even if the connected user has no write access to them. Special security logic is implemented to allow this, and these particular operations are performed with the Administrator user, through the `sudo()` ORM method.

Message subtypes can be managed in the **Settings** top menu by navigating to the **Technical** | **Email** | **Subtypes** menu item. There, we can inspect the existing subtypes and customize them. **Description** is the text displayed in the message, and the **Default** field indicates if the subtype is subscribed by default for the new followers.

Subtypes support an inheritance mechanism. It is, for example, used by projects to allow the followers to automatically subscribe events on tasks and issues, such as **Task Opened**. This is done using the fields in the **Auto Subscription** area of the subtype:

- **Parent** is the related subtype to be automatically subscribed. For the `project.project` Task Opened, this would be the `project.task` Task Opened.
- **Relation Field** is the field in the related model to use. For a `project.task` subtype, this is `project_id`, for the Project to inherit subscription from.

Odoo also supports **Activities** in a fashion similar to mail messages. Activities can be used to serve as reminders for actions related to a record that need to be performed by a user. In our library example, we can envision the creation of an activity record to repair a book that has been returned in bad condition by a user. To allow managing activities on a model, you need to inherit from `mail.activity.mixin`.

To integrate activities in the form view of the record, in the `div` of the chatter, you need to add the `activity_ids` with the `mail_activity` widget, as follows:

```
<div class="oe_chatter">
  <field name="message_follower_ids" widget="mail_followers"/>
  <field name="activity_ids" widget="mail_activity"/>
  <field name="message_ids" widget="mail_thread"/>
</div>
```

Email templates

Emails are a very convenient way of sending information to other users or third parties. Odoo has a nice way of providing templates for emails with placeholders that will get filled in with information from the record to which the email is attached when the message is posted. Such templates can be used when manually sending an email, or when a message is sent automatically for instance through a server action.

In this recipe, we will define a mail template to notify a user of the library that they forgot to bring back some documents.

Getting ready

This recipe builds on models introduced in the *Write a wizard to guide the user* recipe from Chapter 9, *Advanced Server-Side Development Techniques,* and the *Extending the business logic defined in a Model* recipe from Chapter 6, *Basic Server-Side Development.* It also uses the library.book model from Chapter 4, *Creating Odoo Addon Modules.*

Here's a rapid and simplified definition of the models we will use in this recipe:

```
from odoo import models, fields
class LibraryBook(models.Model):
    _name = 'library.book'
    name = fields.Char('Title', help='the title of the book',
required=True)

class LibraryMember(models.Model):
    _name = 'library.member'
    _inherit = 'mail.thread'
    name = fields.Char('Name', required=True)
    email = fields.Char('Email address', required=True)
    loan_ids = fields.One2many(
        'library.book.loan', 'member_id')])
class LibraryBookLoan(models.Model):
    _name = 'library.book.loan'
    book_id = fields.Many2one('library.book', 'Book',
                            required=True)
    member_id = fields.Many2one('library.member', 'Borrower',
                            required=True)
    expected_return_date = fields.Date('Due for', required=True)
    state = fields.Selection(
        [('ongoing', 'Ongoing'),
         ('done', 'Done')],
        'State',
```

```
                default='ongoing', required=True
    )
```

You will also need to have views for these models and create some demo data. The code samples provide this.

Note that the `library.member` has an email field to record the email address to which we will need to send the message. We also made the model inherit from `mail.thread` (refer to the *Adding messaging and tracking features* recipe earlier in this chapter) because it is more convenient to define the template directly from the user interface.

How to do it...

In order to send a customized mail to the library members with overdue books, you will need to do the following:

1. Find a member with a late document, and click on the **Send** message link in the chatter:

2. Use the expand arrows in the top-right corner of the textbox to get the expanded composition interface.
3. Type in the skeleton of the message as follows, and change the subject:

Recipients	Followers of the document and
	Add contacts to notify...
Subject	Late document

Dear Fabien,

It seems that you have forgotten to bring back the following documents you borrowed some time ago

- Odoo Development Cookbook

Please bring them back as other readers may be waiting on them.

--

Your friendly librarian

Attach a file   Use template

Send   Cancel   Save as new template

4. Click on the **Save as new template** button. This will create a new template and link it into the **Use template** field.

5. You can then click on the link to open and edit the new template:

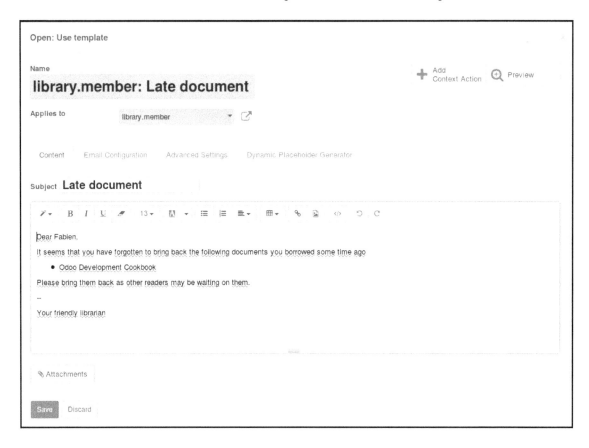

6. In that screen, replace **Fabien** with `${object.name}`.

7. Then, click on the **Code View** button (third button from the right in the preceding screenshot, displayed as **</>**).

8. In the code view screen, locate the **<ul>** opening tag, which is the one in the bullet list of the late books and insert a line break before it and another line break after it (refer to step 12 for a screen capture).

9. On the line before the opening **li** tag, insert the following text:

```
% for row in object.loan_ids:
```

10. Inside the tag, replace the text **Odoo Development Cookbook** with `${row.book_id.name}` (due on `${row.expected_return_date}`.

11. After the closing of the **li** tag, insert a line break and add the following line:

```
% endfor
```

12. This is how it should look like:

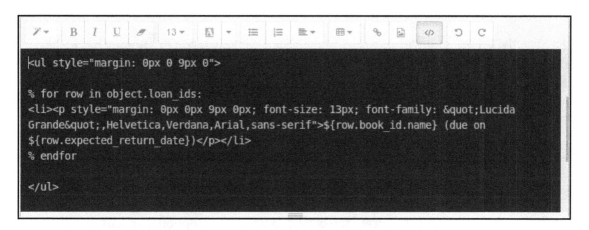

13. In the email configuration page, set the **To (Emails)** field to `${object.email}`.
14. Click on the **Save** button. You will get back to the email composition window, and the text will have been updated to use the expected return date of the document.
15. You can click on **Send** to send the email.
16. Next time you want to remind a member about late documents, you can select the mail template in the **Use template** field of the mail composition window.

How it works...

In steps 1 to 3, we create a normal manual email.

Step 4 creates a new email template from the text we typed. If you need to always send the same message, without any placeholder values you can stop there. However, you will often want to customize the message a bit.

In steps 5 and 6, we insert a placeholder to get the name of the member inside the mail rather then hard-coding it. Placeholders use the `${object.field_name}` syntax.

Historically, mail templates were formatted using Mako templates (http://www.makotemplates.org/). It turns out that this was posing a security risk by allowing to execute arbitrary user-supplied Python code when formatting the emails, so now the templates still use a trimmed down version of the Mako templating language, processed in a Jinja2 sandboxed environment.

Between the braces, you will generally use a dotted name to navigate from `object`, which is the record from which the email template is generated to whatever field you need to display. There are a few other variables and functions that can be used inside the braces:

- `object`: The record from which the mail is being generated
- `user`: The user generating the email
- `ctx`: The current context dictionary
- `format_date(date, format)`: A function to format a date according to the given format or to the default format is the second argument is omitted
- `format_tz(timestamp, timezone, format)`: A function to format a timestamp (in UTC) using the provided timezeone (optional, defaults to the current user's timezone) and an optional format
- `format_amount(amount, currency)`: Format an amount expressed in a currency using the expected way for that currency

Actually, inside the braces, you can have any valid Python expression. A common trick to deal with non mandatory fields and avoid having False inside the email is to use, for instance, `${object.fieldname or ''}`.

This `${name}` notation is nice, but it does not allow us to use control structures such as loops and tests. However, to use this, we need to exit the WYSIWYG editor and get to the raw HTML editor (steps 7 and 8); otherwise the control structures we are going to insert will not be processed by the templating engine. Steps 8 to 12 insert a `for` loop in the template to generate bullet list elements (`<li>` in HTML) inside an unnumbered list (`<ul>` in HTML).

There are different control structures available:

- Variable definitions are done with `% set varname = expression`. It allows us to define a new variable. The expression must be valid Python and can use other previously defined variables as well as the globally available variables you can use in `${varname}` placeholders. A variable defined that way can be used in a placeholder expression.

- Tests use `% if condition:`, `% else:` (optional), and `% endif` to test for a condition. The condition can use any valid Python expression with the variables and functions available. It is a multiline structure that will look like this in the template code:

```
% if condition:
block printed if condition is True
% else:
block printed if condition is False
% endif
```

- Loops use `% for varname in iterable:` and `% endfor`. The iterable is generally a recordset or a list defined in another variable. The block inside the loop will typically use `${varname}` to display the variable or `${varname.fieldname}` to display the value of a field of a record from the recordset. This construct is very useful to create bullet list items or table rows.

When you have the developer tools activated, you can access the mail templates in the **Settings > Technical > Email > Templates** menu. You can create a new template from scratch there and link it to a document type in the **Applies to** field. Of course, you can also create a `mail.template` record directly in the data of your addon. If you need to do so and to include HTML tags in the body of your message, it is often useful to use a **CDATA section** in the XML file. This allows you to omit escaping the < and & characters in the value of the `body_html` field:

```
<record id='late_document' model='mail.template>
  <field name="name">library.member: Late Document</field>
  <field name="email_from">${'%s &lt;%s&gt;' % (user.name,
  user.email)|safe}</field>
  <field name="subject">Late documents</field>
  <field name="email_to">${object.email}</field>
  <field name="model_id" ref="my_module.model_library_member"/>
  <field name="body_html"><![CDATA[
<p>Dear ${object.name},</p>
<p>It seems that you have forgotten to bring back the following
documents:</p>
```

```
<ul>
% for row in object.loan_ids:
<li>${row.name}</li>
% endfor
</ul>
<p>Best regards,</p>
<p style="color:#888888;">
% if user.signature:
    ${user.signature | safe}
% endif
</p>
]]>
  </field>
</record>
```

The | safe used in the signature is a Jinja filter that prevents escaping of HTML from the signature field. More information on Jinja filter is available at http://jinja.pocoo.org/docs/2.10/templates/#filters.

There's more...

Mail templates are a very versatile tool in Odoo and can be used in many places:

- As we saw in the recipe, you can use them to fill in an email that you are creating manually.
- Some applications inside Odoo configure Kanban stages so that when a record lands in a new stage, an email can be sent using a template. This is the case for the Project app and the Recruitment app, for instance.
- In the email template edit form, if you click on the **Add context action** button in the top-right corner, you will add an action linked to this template that will be available when you select multiple records in a list view, and will generate an outgoing email for each of them.
- You can also can be used inside server actions if you set **Action to do** to **Send email**. The server action can then be linked to an automated actions send the mail for instance based on a time condition or when a record is created or modified. Refer to the *Using automated actions on event conditions* recipe earlier in this chapter.

See also

For more information about the Mako templating language, check out http://www.makotemplates.org/.

QWeb-based PDF reports

When communicating with the outside world, it is often necessary to produce a PDF document from a record in the database. Odoo uses the same templating language as the one used for form views, QWeb.

In this recipe, we will create a QWeb report to print the book currently borrowed by a member of our library example. This recipe will reuse the models presented in the *Email templates* recipe from this chapter.

Getting ready

In case you haven't done it till now, install wkhtmltopdf as described in Chapter 1, *Installing the Odoo Development Environment*, otherwise you won't get shiny PDFs as a result of your efforts.

Also, double-check that the configuration parameter—web.base.url (or alternatively, report.url)—is a URL accessible from your Odoo instance, otherwise report generation takes ages and the result looks funny.

How to do it...

1. Define a view for your report in reports/book_loan_templates.xml:

```xml
<?xml version="1.0" encoding="utf-8"?>
<odoo>
<template id="my_module.book_loans_template">
  <t t-call="web.html_container">
  <t t-foreach="docs" t-as="doc">
  <t t-call="web.internal_layout">
    <div class="page">
      <div class="oe_structure">
        <h1>Book Loans for <t t-esc="doc.name"/></h1>
        <table class="table table-condensed">
```

```
          <thead>
            <tr><th>Title</th><th>Expected return date</th></tr>
          </thead>
          <tbody>
            <tr t-foreach="doc.loan_ids" t-as="loan" >
              <td><t t-esc="loan.book_id.name" /></td>
              <td><t t-esc="loan.expected_return_date" /></td>
            </tr>
          </tbody>
        </table>
      </div>
    </div>
  </t>
  </t>
  </t>
 </template>
</odoo>
```

2. Use this view in a report tag in `reports/book_loan_report.xml`:

```
<?xml version="1.0" encoding="utf-8"?>
<odoo>
  <report id="report_book_loans"
          name="my_module.book_loans_template"
          model="library.member"
          string="Book Loans"
          report_type="qweb-pdf" />
</odoo>
```

3. Add both files in the manifest of the addon:

```
{
    'name': 'Chapter 13 code for the qweb report recipe',
    'depends': ['mail'],
    'data': [
        'views/library_book.xml',
        'views/library_member.xml',
        'reports/book_loan_report.xml',
        'reports/book_loan_report_template.xml',
    ],
    'demo': ['demo/demo.xml'],
}
```

Now, when opening a library member form view or when selecting members in the list view, you should be offered to print the book loans.

How it works...

In step 1, we are defining the structure of the report using the **QWeb** templating language. Instead of using the `record` syntax as we did earlier, we use the `template` element here. This is entirely for convenience; QWeb reports are just views as all the others. The reason to use this element is that the `arch` field of QWeb views has to follow quite strict rules, and the `template` element takes care to generate an `arch` content that fulfils these rules.

Don't worry about the syntax within the `template` element now. This topic will be addressed extensively in the *QWeb* recipe in `Chapter 16`, *CMS Website Development*.

In step 2, we declare the report in another XML file. The `report` element is another shortcut for an action of the `ir.actions.report.xml` type. The crucial part here is that you set the `name` field to *the complete XML ID* (that is, `modulename.record_id`) of the template you defined, otherwise the report generation will fail. The `model` attribute determines on which type of record the report operates, and the `string` attribute is the name shown to the user in the print menu.

By setting `report_type` to `qweb-pdf`, we request that the HTML generated by our view is run through `wkhtmltopdf` in order to deliver a PDF to the user. In some cases, you may want to use `qweb-html` to just render the HTML within the browser.

There's more...

There are some marker classes in a report's HTML that are crucial for the layout. Ensure that you wrap all your content in an element with the class `page` set. If you forget that, you'll see nothing at all. To add a header or footer to your record, use the class `header` or `footer`.

Also, remember that this is HTML, so make use of CSS attributes such as `page-break-before`, `page-break-after`, and `page-break-inside`.

You'll have noted that all of our template body is wrapped in two elements with the `t-call` attribute set. We'll examine the mechanics of this attribute later, but it is crucial that you do the same in your reports. These elements take care that the HTML generated links to all the necessary CSS files and contains some other data needed for the report generation. While `web.html_container` doesn't really have an alternative, the second `t-call` can also be `web.external_layout`. The difference is that the external layout already comes with a header and footer displaying the company logo, the company's name, and some other information you expect from a company's external communication, while the internal layout just gives you a header with pagination, the print date, and the company's name. For the sake of consistency, always use one of the two.

Note that `web.internal_layout`, `web.external_layout`, `web.external_layout_header`, and `web.external_layout_footer` (the last two are called by the external layout) are just views by themselves, and you already know how to change them by inheritance. To inherit with the template element, use the `inherit_id` attribute.

In the previous versions of Odoo, these templates were defined in the `report` module, not `web`. When porting a module to Odoo 11, don't forget to change the identifiers in you calls to `t-call`.

Producing LibreOffice-based reports with Py3O

Odoo's native way of producing PDF documents uses QWeb templates and `wkhtmltopdf` (refer to the *QWeb-based PDF reports* recipe). The drawback of this approach is that editing the layout of a report is tricky and requires some technical knowledge. Similarly, styling a report to match a graphic charter is tedious. Fortunately, the Odoo Community Association hosts a project called **report_py3o**, which allows using LibreOffice to define a report template. Then, the styling can be done easily by end users.

At the time of writing this, **report_py3o** has not yet been migrated to Odoo 11. The recipe was tested using Odoo 10. It is expected that it will work with Odoo 11.0 with only minor changes, if at all. You can check whether the `report_py3o` module was ported on `https://github.com/OCA/reporting-engine/tree/11.0`.

In this recipe, we will print a document with the books borrowed by a library member. We will use the same models as in the *Email templates* recipe earlier in this chapter.

Getting ready

This module requires us to invest some time in the setup.

Getting the report_py3o module in Odoo

Using `report_py3o` requires some additional Python libraries; install them in your virtualenv with this:

```
$ pip3 install py3o.template
$ pip3 install py3o.formats
```

 Caution: The mentioned commands use **pip3** as this will be used for Odoo 11. However, if you are testing with Odoo 10, you need to use **Python 2.7** and **pip**.

Then, you will need to download **report_py3o** from the OCA reporting-engine `https://github.com/OCA/reporting-engine/` project and make it available in your addons path and install it in your instance.

Refer to the *Installing addon modules from GitHub* recipe from `Chapter 2`, *Managing Odoo Server Instances*, for more information on this.

Installing and running a py3o.fusion server

To produce the reports, report_py3o does not run LibreOffice from Odoo, which is a major difference from qweb reports, for which Odoo will call `wkhtmltopdf` directly. Rather, report_py3o relies on an external service called **py3o.fusion**. This service provides a REST API and will receive rendering requests via HTTP. It runs a headless LibreOffice, which will do the rendering and return the styled reports. This service can be shared among different Odoo instances if needed.

 Headless means that there is no graphical user interface that makes for a lighter installation on the server.

In order to save time in the setup of `py3o.fusion`, which has a large chain of dependencies, we will use a dockerized version so that you will also need to have **Docker** installed on your system. The instructions to install Docker Community Edition for Debian GNU/Linux are on `https://docs.docker.com/engine/installation/linux/docker-ce/debian/` (and the instructions for installing Docker for other platforms are available by clicking on the platform in the side bar of that page).

You will also need `docker-compose`, which is packaged for Debian stretch:

```
# apt-get install docker-compose
```

 If you had rather run `py3o.fusion` without Docker, it is of course possible. Refer to the README file that comes with report_py3o for instructions.

Create a directory called `py3o_fusion`, and in that directory, create a `docker-compose.yml` file with the following content:

```
py3ofusion:
    image: xcgd/py3o.fusion
    ports:
        - "8765:8765"
    links:
        - "py3orenderserver"

py3orenderserver:
    image: xcgd/py3oserver-docker
    links:
        - "oooserver"
    volumes_from:
        - "oooserver"

oooserver:
    image: xcgd/libreoffice
```

In the directory, run the `docker-compose up -d` command to download the docker images and start the `py3o.fusion` server.

How to do it...

In order to print the book loan report with `report_py3o`, you need to do the following:

1. In `my_module/data`, add a file called `py3o_server.xml` with the following content:

```xml
<?xml version="1.0" encoding="utf-8"?>
<odoo>
  <record id="local_py3o_server" model="py3o.server">
    <field name="url">http://localhost:8765/form</field>
  </record>
</odoo>
```

2. In `my_module/reports`, add a file called `book_loan_report.xml` with the following content:

```xml
<?xml version="1.0" encoding="utf-8"?>
<odoo>
  <record id="report_book_loans_py3o" model="ir.actions.report.xml">
    <field name="name">Book Loans</field>
    <field name="model">library.member</field>
    <field name="report_name">library.member.loans</field>
    <field name="report_type">py3o</field>
    <field name="py3o_filetype">pdf</field>
    <field name="py3o_server_id" ref="local_py3o_server"/>
    <field name="module">my_module</field>
    <field
    name="py3o_template_fallback">reports/book_loans.odt</field>
  </record>

</odoo>
```

3. Add both files to the manifest of the addon, and declare a dependency on `report_py3o`:

```python
{
    'name': 'Chapter 14 code the py3o recipe',
    'depends': ['mail', 'report_py3o'],
    'data': [
        'data/py3o_server.xml',
        'reports/book_loan_report.xml'
        # ...
    ],
}
```

4. Create an empty LibreOffice ODT document and save it in
   `reports/book_loans.odt`

5. Place the cursor at the beginning of the document, and choose **Insert >
   Hyperlink...** in the menu

6. In the dialog, set the following as shown in the screen capture below:
   - **Target**: **py3o://for="member in objects"**
   - **Text**: **for="member in objects"**

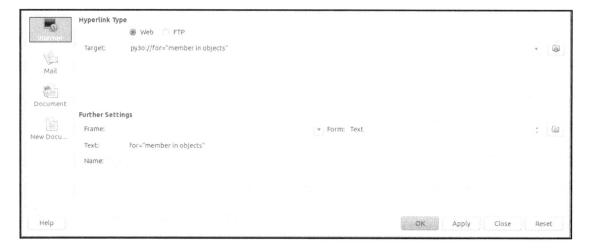

7. After the hyperlink, set the format as **Title**, and type **Book loans for**

8. With the cursor after "for", choose **Insert > Field > More Fields... (Ctrl+F2)** in the
   menu

9. In the dialog, choose the **Variables** tab:
   - Set the **Type** to **User Field**
   - Set **Name** to **py3o.member.name**
   - Set **Value** to **Member Name**
   - Click on the **Insert** button:

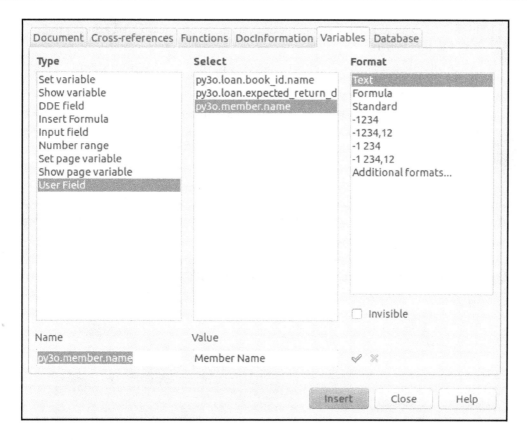

10. Insert a table with two columns and four rows

11. In the first row, type **Book title** and **Expected return date**

12. In the second row, insert a hyperlink as you did in step 6. The **Target** is **py3o://for="loan in member.loan_ids"** and the **Text** is **for="loan in member.loan_ids"**

13. In the third row, insert these to the user fields as you did in step 9:
    - In the first column, the **Name** is **py3o.loan.book_id.name** and the **Value** is **Book Title**
    - In the second column, the **Name** is **py3o.loan.expected_return_date** and the **Value** is **Expected Return Date**

14. In the last row, insert a hyperlink as you did in step 12. The **Target** is **py3o:///for** and the text is **/for**

15. After the table, insert a hyperlink as you did in step 14 with the same **Target** and **Text**

In steps 14 and 15, pay attention to the number of slashes: there are three consecutive slashes before **for**.

Here's what your document should look like:

for="member in objects"¶

Book Loan report for Member Name¶

Book Title¶	Expected return date¶
for="loan in objects.loan_ids"¶	¶
Loaned book title¶	Loaned book return date¶
/for¶	¶

/for¶

To test your report, install your module. Display a library member and select **Print > Book Loans**.

How it works...

Step 1 declares a `py3o.fusion` server that the rendering will use to produce the PDF document. This is mainly for convenience as we can also do so from the user interface.

Step 2 declares the report itself. We need to use the record element because the additional fields for py3o reports are not handled by the report shortcut we used in the *QWeb based PDF reports* recipe earlier in this chapter.

The rest of the recipe deals with creating the report template in LibreOffice writer. Such a template is a normal ODT document with some special conventions to handle placeholders and structure control.

Placeholders

Placeholders are created by inserting **Fields** of type **User Value** (take a look at steps 8 and 9). To allow distinguishing these fields from other user values, the convention is to give them a name starting with `py3o.`, followed by a dotted path to get the required value. The type of the **User Value** is used to determine how the value is displayed. The **Name** is how the **Field** is displayed in the template.

The namespace in which the path can find variable names includes `objects`, which contain the recordset being printed, `user`, which is a reference to the user performing the action, plus any local variable declared by control structures.

Control structures

Control structures include loops and tests, and they are normally inserted using hyperlinks with the `py3o://` protocol.

In the current version of the `py3o.` template, two control structures exist: `py3o://for="varname in iterable"` and `py3o://if="condition"`. Both need to be closed with `py3o:///for` and `py3o:///if`, respectively. Note that there is no else in a condition; you need to make a second `py3o://` if blocked with the opposite condition.

TIP

Caution: There are two forward slashes in the opening hyperlink URL and three in the closing hyperlink URL.

With the constraint of using a hyperlink in mind, the result is very similar in spirit to the templating of emails explained in the *Email Templates* recipe earlier in the chapter.

There's more...

The `report_py3o` is evolving. It was recently contributed by its authors to the Odoo Community Association, and this contribution means an increased exposure, so it is expected that new contributions and improvements will keep coming in. We advise you to track the online documentation of `py3o.template` at `http://py3otemplate.readthedocs.io/en/latest/`, which will give you the latest news about what is available for your templates. Ensure that you also check the `README` file of report_py3o for important updates.

14
Web Server Development

In this chapter, we'll cover the following topics:

- Making a path accessible from the network
- Restricting access to web accessible paths
- Consuming parameters passed to your handlers
- Modifying an existing handler
- Using the RPC API

Introduction

We'll introduce the basics of the web server part of Odoo in this chapter. Note that this covers the fundamental pieces. For high-level functionality, you should refer to Chapter 15, *Web Client Development*.

All of Odoo's web request handling is driven by the Python library `werkzeug` (`http://werkzeug.pocoo.org`). While the complexity of `werkzeug` is mostly hidden by Odoo's convenient wrappers, it is an interesting read to see how things work under the hood.

Making a path accessible from the network

In this recipe, we'll see how to make a URL of the `http://yourserver/path1/path2` form accessible to users. This can either be a web page or a path returning arbitrary data to be consumed by other programs. In the latter case, you would usually use the JSON format to consume parameters and to offer your data.

Getting ready

We'll make use of the `library.book` model of Chapter 5, *Application Models*, so in case you haven't done so yet, grab its code to be able to follow the examples.

We want to allow any user to query the full list of books. Furthermore, we want to provide the same information to programs via a JSON request.

How to do it...

We'll need to add controllers, which go into a folder called `controllers` by convention:

1. Add a `controllers/main.py` file with the HTML version of our page:

```
from odoo import http
from odoo.http import request

class Main(http.Controller):
    @http.route('/my_module/books', type='http', auth='none')
    def books(self):
        records = request.env['library.book'].sudo().search([])
        result = '<html><body><table><tr><td>'
        result += '</td></tr><tr><td>'.join(records.mapped('name'))
        result += '</td></tr></table></body></html>'
        return result
```

2. Add a function to serve the same information in the JSON format:

```
@http.route('/my_module/books/json', type='json', auth='none')
def books_json(self):
    records = request.env['library.book'].sudo().search([])
    return records.read(['name'])
```

3. Add the `controllers/__init__.py` file:

```
from . import main
```

4. Add controllers to your `__init__.py` addon:

```
from . import controllers
```

After restarting your server, you can visit /my_module/books in your browser and get presented with a flat list of book names. To test the JSON-RPC part, you'll have to craft a JSON request. A simple way to do that would be using the following command line to receive the output on the command line:

```
curl -i -X POST -H "Content-Type: application/json" -d "{}"
localhost:8069/my_module/books/json
```

If you get **404** errors at this point, you probably have more than one database available on your instance. In this case, it's impossible for Odoo to determine which database is meant to serve the request.

Use the --db-filter='^yourdatabasename$' parameter to force using the exact database you installed the module in. Now, the path should be accessible.

How it works...

The two crucial parts here are that our controller is derived from odoo.http.Controller and that the methods we use to serve content are decorated with odoo.http.route. Inheriting from odoo.http.Controller registers the controller with Odoo's routing system in a similar way as models are registered, by inheriting from odoo.models.Model; also, Controller has a metaclass that takes care of this.

In general, paths handled by your addon should start with your addon's name to avoid name clashes. Of course, if you extend some addon's functionality, you'll use this addon's name.

odoo.http.route

The route decorator allows us to tell Odoo that a method is to be web accessible in the first place, and the first parameter determines on which path it is accessible. Instead of a string, you can also pass a list of strings in case you use the same function to serve multiple paths.

The type argument defaults to http and determines what type of request is to be served. While strictly speaking JSON is HTTP, declaring the second function as type='json' makes life a lot easier, because Odoo then handles type conversions for us.

Don't worry about the `auth` parameter for now, it will be addressed in the *Restricting access to web accessible paths* recipe in this chapter.

Return values

Odoo's treatment of the functions' return values is determined by the `type` argument of the `route` decorator. For `type='http'`, we usually want to deliver some HTML, so the first function simply returns a string containing it. An alternative is to use `request.make_response()`, which gives you control over the headers to send in the response. So, to indicate when our page was last updated, we might change the last line in `books()` to the following:

```
return request.make_response(
  result, [
    ('Last-modified', email.utils.formatdate(
      (
        fields.Datetime.from_string(
        request.env['library.book'].sudo()
        .search([], order='write_date desc', limit=1)
        .write_date) -
        datetime.datetime(1970, 1, 1)
      ).total_seconds(),
      usegmt=True)),
  ])
```

This code sends a `Last-modified` header along with the HTML we generated, telling the browser when the list was modified for the last time. We extract this information from the `write_date` field of the `library.book` model.

In order for the preceding snippet to work, you'll have to add some imports on the top of the file:

```
import email
import datetime
from odoo import fields
```

You can also create a `Response` object of `werkzeug` manually and return that, but there's little gain for the effort.

Generating HTML manually is nice for demonstration purposes, but you should never do this in production code. Always use templates, as demonstrated in the *Creating or modifying templates – QWeb* recipe in `Chapter 16`, *CMS Website Development*, and return them by calling `request.render()`.

This will give you localization for free and make your code better by separating business logic from the presentation layer. Also, templates provide you with functions to escape data before outputting HTML. The preceding code is vulnerable to cross-site-scripting attacks if a user manages to slip a `script` tag into the book name, for example.

For a JSON request, simply return the data structure you want to hand over to the client; Odoo takes care of serialization. For this to work, you should restrict yourself to data types that are JSON serializable, which are roughly dictionaries, lists, strings, floats, and integers.

odoo.http.request

The `request` object is a static object referring to the currently handled request, which contains everything you need to take useful action. Most important is the `request.env` property, which contains an `Environment` object that is just the same as in `self.env` for models. This environment is bound to the current user, which is none in the preceding example because we used `auth='none'`. Lack of a user is also why we have to `sudo()` all our calls to model methods in the example code.

If you're used to web development, you'll expect session handling, which is perfectly correct. Use `request.session` for an `OpenERPSession` object (which is quite a thin wrapper around the `Session` object of `werkzeug`), and `request.session.sid` to access the session ID. To store session values, just treat `request.session` as a dictionary:

```
request.session['hello'] = 'world'
request.session.get('hello')
```

Note that storing data in the session is no different from using global variables. Use it only if you must, that is usually the case for multirequest actions such as a checkout in the `website_sale` module. Also, in this case, handle all functionality concerning sessions in your controllers, never in your models.

There's more...

The `route` decorator can have some extra parameters to customize its behavior further. By default, all HTTP methods are allowed, and Odoo intermingles the parameters passed. Using the `methods` parameter, you can pass a list of methods to accept, which would usually be one of either `['GET']` or `['POST']`.

To allow cross-origin requests (browsers block AJAX and some other types of requests to domains other than where the script was loaded from for security and privacy reasons), set the `cors` parameter to `*` to allow requests from all origins, or some URI to restrict requests to ones originating from this URI. If this parameter is unset, which is the default, the `Access-Control-Allow-Origin` header is not set, leaving you with the browser's standard behavior. In our example, we might want to set it on `/my_module/books/json` in order to allow scripts pulled from other websites to access the list of books.

By default, Odoo protects certain types of requests from an attack known as cross-site request forgery by passing a token along on every request. If you want to turn that off, set the `csrf` parameter to `False`, but note that this is a bad idea in general.

See also

If you host multiple Odoo databases on the same instance and each database has different web accessible paths on possibly multiple domain names per database, the standard regular expressions in the `--db-filter` parameter might not be enough to force the right database for every domain. In that case, use the `dbfilter_from_header` community module from `https://github.com/OCA/server-tools` in order to configure database filters on the proxy level. This module was not migrated to version 11 at the time of writing, but at the time of publication, it probably will be.

To see how using templates makes modularity possible, check out the *Modifying an existing handler* recipe later in the chapter.

Restricting access to web accessible paths

We'll explore the three authentication mechanisms Odoo provides for routes in this recipe. We'll define routes with different authentication mechanisms in order to show their differences.

Getting ready

As we extend code from the previous recipe, we'll also depend on the `library.book` model of `Chapter 5`, *Application Models*, so you should get its code in order to proceed.

How to do it...

Define handlers in `controllers/main.py`:

1. Add a path that shows all books:

```
@http.route('/my_module/all-books', type='http', auth='none')
def all_books(self):
    records = request.env['library.book'].sudo().search([])
    result = '<html><body><table><tr><td>'
    result += '</td></tr><tr><td>'.join(records.mapped('name'))
    result += '</td></tr></table></body></html>'
    return result
```

2. Add a path that shows all books and indicates which was written by the current user, if any:

```
@http.route('/my_module/all-books/mark-mine', type='http',
auth='public')
def all_books_mark_mine(self):
    records = request.env['library.book'].sudo().search([])
    result = '<html><body><table>'
    for record in records:
        result += '<tr>'
        if record.author_ids & request.env.user.partner_id:
            result += '<th>'
        else:
            result += '<td>'
        result += record.name
        if record.author_ids & request.env.user.partner_id:
            result += '</th>'
        else:
            result += '</td>'
        result += '</tr>'
    result += '</table></body></html>'
    return result
```

3. Add a path that shows the current user's books:

```
@http.route('/my_module/all-books/mine', type='http', auth='user')
def all_books_mine(self):
    records = request.env['library.book'].search([
        ('author_ids', 'in', request.env.user.partner_id.ids),
    ])
    result = '<html><body><table><tr><td>'
    result += '</td></tr><tr><td>'.join(records.mapped('name'))
    result += '</td></tr></table></body></html>'
    return result
```

With this code, the /my_module/all-books and /my_module/all-books/mark_mine paths look the same for unauthenticated users, while a logged in user sees their books in a bold font on the latter path. The /my_module/all-books/mine path is not accessible at all for unauthenticated users. If you try to access it without being authenticated, you'll be redirected to the login screen in order to do so.

How it works...

The difference between authentication methods is basically what you can expect from the content of request.env.user.

For auth='none', the user record is always empty, even if an authenticated user is accessing the path. Use this if you want to serve content that has no dependencies on users, or if you want to provide database agnostic functionality in a server wide module. The auth='public' value sets the user record to a special user with XML ID base.public_user for unauthenticated users, and to the user's record for authenticated ones. This is the right choice if you want to offer functionality to both unauthenticated and authenticated users, while the authenticated ones get some extras, as demonstrated in the preceding code.

Use auth='user' to ensure that only authenticated users have access to what you've got to offer. With this method, you can be sure that request.env.user points to some existing user.

There's more...

The magic for authentication methods happens in the `ir.http` model from the base addon. For whatever value you pass to the `auth` parameter in your route, Odoo searches for a function called `_auth_method_<yourvalue>` on this model, so you can easily customize this by inheriting this model and declaring a method that takes care of your authentication method of choice.

As an example, we provide an authentication method called `base_group_user`, which enforces a currently logged in user who is a member of the group with XML ID `base.group_user`:

```
from odoo import exceptions, http, models
from odoo.http import request

class IrHttp(models.Model):
  _inherit = 'ir.http'

  def _auth_method_base_group_user(self):
    self._auth_method_user()
    if not request.env.user.has_group('base.group_user'):
      raise exceptions.AccessDenied()
```

Now you can say `auth='base_group_user'` in your decorator and be sure that users running this route's handler are members of this group. With a little trickery, you can extend this to `auth='groups(xmlid1, ...) '`; its implementation is left as an exercise to the reader, but is included in the example code.

Consuming parameters passed to your handlers

It's nice to be able to show content, but it's better to show content as a result of some user input. This recipe will demonstrate the different ways to receive this input and react to it. As in the previous recipes, we'll make use of the `library.book` model.

How to do it...

First, we'll add a route that expects a traditional parameter with a book's ID to show some details about it. Then, we'll do the same, but we'll incorporate our parameter into the path itself:

1. Add a path that expects a book's ID as a parameter:

```
@http.route('/my_module/book_details', type='http', auth='none')
def book_details(self, book_id):
    record = request.env['library.book'].sudo().browse(int(book_id))
    return u'<html><body><h1>%s</h1>Authors: %s' % (
        record.name,
        u', '.join(record.author_ids.mapped('name')) or 'none',
    )
```

2. Add a path where we can pass the book's ID in the path:

```
@http.route("/my_module/book_details/<model('library.book'):book>",
            type='http', auth='none')
def book_details_in_path(self, book):
    return self.book_details(book.id)
```

If you point your browser to `/my_module/book_details?book_id=1`, you should see a detail page of the book with ID `1`. If this doesn't exist, you'll receive an error page.

The second handler allows you to go to `/my_module/book_details/1` and view the same page.

How it works...

By default, Odoo (actually `werkzeug`) intermingles the GET and POST parameters and passes them as keyword argument to your handler. So, by simply declaring your function as expecting a parameter called `book_id`, you introduce this parameter as either GET (the parameter in the URL) or POST (usually passed by forms with your handler as action). Given that we didn't add a default value for this parameter, the runtime will raise an error if you try to access this path without setting the parameter.

The second example makes use of the fact that in a `werkzeug` environment, most paths are virtual anyway. So, we can simply define our path as containing some input. In this case, we say we expect the ID of a `library.book` as the last component of the path. The name after the colon is the name of a keyword argument. Our function will be called, with this parameter passed as keyword argument. Here, Odoo takes care of looking up this ID and delivering a browse record, which, of course, only works if the user accessing this path has appropriate permissions. Given that `book` is a browse record, we can simply recycle the first example's function by passing `book.id` as parameter `book_id` to give out the same content.

There's more...

Defining parameters within the path is a functionality delivered by `werkzeug`, which is called **converters**. The `model` converter is added by Odoo, which also defines the converter `models` that accept a comma-separated list of IDs and pass a recordset containing those IDs to your handler.

The beauty of converters is that the runtime coerces parameters to the expected type, while you're on your own with normal keyword parameters. These are delivered as strings, and you have to take care of the necessary type conversions yourself, as seen in the first example.

Built-in `werkzeug` converters include `int`, `float`, and `string`, but also more intricate ones such as `path`, `any`, or `uuid`. You can look up their semantics at `http://werkzeug.pocoo.org/docs/0.11/routing/#builtin-converters`.

See also

Odoo's custom converters are defined in `ir_http.py` in the base module and registered in the `_get_converters` class method of `ir.http`. As an exercise, you can create your own converter that allows you to visit the `/my_module/book_details/Odoo+cookbook` page to receive the details of this book (if you added it to your library earlier). This converter's implementation is included in the example code for this recipe.

Modifying an existing handler

When you install the website module, the `/website/info` path displays some information about your Odoo instance. In this recipe, we override this in order to change this information page's layout, and also to change what is displayed.

Getting ready

Install the `website` module and inspect the `/website/info` path. Now, craft a new module that depends on `website` and uses the following code.

How to do it...

We'll have to adapt the existing template and override the existing handler:

1. Override the qweb template in a file called `views/templates.xml`:

```xml
<?xml version="1.0" encoding="UTF-8"?>
<odoo>
  <template id="show_website_info"
            inherit_id="website.show_website_info">
    <xpath expr="//dl[@t-foreach='apps']" position="replace">
      <table class="table">
        <tr t-foreach="apps" t-as="app">
          <th>
            <a t-att-href="app.website">
            <t t-esc="app.name" /></a>
          </th>
          <td><t t-esc="app.summary" /></td>
        </tr>
      </table>
    </xpath>
  </template>
</odoo>
```

2. Override the handler in a file called `controllers/main.py`:

```python
from odoo import http
from odoo.addons.website.controllers.main import Website

class Website(Website):
    @http.route()
```

```
def website_info(self):
    result = super(Website, self).website_info()
    result.qcontext['apps'] = result.qcontext['apps'].filtered(
        lambda x: x.name != 'website'
    )
    return result
```

Now, when visiting the info page, we'll only see a filtered list of installed applications, and in a table as opposed to the original definition list.

How it works...

In the first step, we override an existing QWeb template. In order to find out which that is, you'll have to consult the code of the original handler. Usually, it will end with something similar to the following line, which tells you that you need to override template.name:

```
return request.render('template.name', values)
```

In our case, the handler uses a template called website.info, but this one is immediately extended by another template called website.show_website_info, so it's more convenient to override this one. Here, we replace the definition list showing installed apps with a table. For details about how QWeb inheritance works, consult Chapter 16, *CMS Website Development*.

In order to override the handler method, we must identify the class that defines the handler, which is odoo.addons.website.controllers.main.Website in this case. We import the class to be able to inherit from it. Now, we override the method and change the data passed to the response. Note that what the overridden handler returns is a Response object and not a string of HTML, as the previous recipes did for the sake of brevity. This object contains a reference to the template to be used and the values accessible to the template, but is only evaluated at the very end of the request.

In general, there are three ways to change an existing handler:

- If it uses a QWeb template, the simplest way to change it is to override the template. This is the right choice for layout changes and small logic changes.
- QWeb templates get a context passed, which is available in the response as the member qcontext. This is usually a dictionary where you can add or remove values to suit your needs. In the preceding example, we filter the list of apps to only contain apps that have a website set.
- If the handler receives parameters, you can also preprocess those in order to have the overridden handler behave the way you want.

There's more...

As seen in the preceding section, inheritance with controllers works slightly differently than model inheritance; you actually need a reference to the base class and to use Python inheritance on it.

Don't forget to decorate your new handler with the `@http.route` decorator; Odoo uses it as a marker for which methods are exposed to the network layer. If you omit the decorator, you actually make the handler's path inaccessible.

The `@http.route` decorator itself behaves similar to field declarations: every value you don't set will be derived from the decorator of the function you're overriding, so we don't have to repeat values we don't want to change.

After receiving a `response` object from the function you override, you can do a lot more than just change the QWeb context:

- You can add or remove HTTP headers by manipulating `response.headers`
- If you want to render an entirely different template, you can overwrite `response.template`
- To detect whether a response is based on QWeb in the first place, query `response.is_qweb`
- The resulting HTML code is available by calling `response.render()`

See also

Details of QWeb templates will be explained in `Chapter 16`, *CMS Website development*.

Using the RPC API

One of Odoo's strengths is its interoperability, which is helped by the fact that basically any functionality is available via JSON-RPC 2.0 and XMLRPC. In this recipe, we'll explore how to use both of them from client code. This interface also enables you to integrate Odoo with any other application. Making functionality available via any of the two protocols on the server side is explained in the *There's more...* section of this recipe.

We'll query a list of installed modules from the Odoo instance so that we can show a list like the one displayed in the previous recipe in our own application or website.

How to do it...

The following code is not meant to run within Odoo, but as simple scripts:

1. First, we query the list of installed modules via XMLRPC:

```
#!/usr/bin/env python3
from xmlrpc.client import ServerProxy

db = 'odoo11'
user = 'admin'
password = 'admin'
uid = ServerProxy('http://localhost:8069/xmlrpc/2/common')\
    .authenticate(db, user, password, {})
odoo = ServerProxy('http://localhost:8069/xmlrpc/2/object')
installed_modules = odoo.execute_kw(
    db, uid, password, 'ir.module.module', 'search_read',
    [[('state', '=', 'installed')], ['name']],
    {'context': {'lang': 'fr_FR'}},
)
for module in installed_modules:
    print(module['name'])
```

2. Then, we do the same with JSONRPC:

```
import json
from urllib.request import Request, urlopen

db = 'odoo11'
user = 'admin'
password = 'admin'

request = Request(
    'http://localhost:8069/web/session/authenticate',
    json.dumps({
        'jsonrpc': '2.0',
        'params': {
            'db': db,
            'login': user,
            'password': password,
        },
    }).encode('utf8'),
    {'Content-type': 'application/json'})
result = urlopen(request).read()
result = json.loads(result.decode('utf-8'))
session_id = result['result']['session_id']
request = Request(
```

```
            'http://localhost:8069/web/dataset/call_kw',
            json.dumps({
              'jsonrpc': '2.0',
              'params': {
                'model': 'ir.module.module',
                'method': 'search_read',
                'args': [
                  [('state', '=', 'installed')],
                  ['name'],
                ],
                'kwargs': {'context': {'lang': 'fr_FR'}},
              },
            }).encode('utf8'),
            {
                'X-Openerp-Session-Id': session_id,
                'Content-type': 'application/json',
            })
    result = urlopen(request).read()
    result = json.loads(result.decode('utf-8'))
    for module in result['result']:
      print(module['name'])
```

Both code snippets will print a list of installed modules, and because they pass a context that sets the language to French, the list will be in French if there are translations available.

How it works...

Both snippets call the `search_read` function, which is very convenient because you can specify a search domain on the model you call, pass a list of fields you want to be returned, and receive the result in one request. In older versions of Odoo, you had to call `search` first to receive a list of IDs and then call `read` to actually read the data.

`search_read` returns a list of dictionaries, with the keys being the names of the fields requested and the values the record's data. The ID field will always be transmitted, no matter whether you requested it or not.

Now, we need to look at the specifics of the two protocols.

XMLRPC

The XMLRPC API expects a user ID and a password for every call, which is why we need to fetch this ID via the `authenticate` method on the `/xmlrpc/2/common` path. If you already know the user's ID, you can skip this step.

As soon as you know the user's ID, you can call any model's method by calling `execute_kw` on the `/xmlrpc/2/object` path. This method expects the database you want to execute the function on, the user's ID and password for authentication, then the model you want to call your function on, and then the function's name. The next two mandatory parameters are a list of positional arguments to your function, and a dictionary of keyword arguments.

JSONRPC

Don't be distracted by the size of the code example; that's because Python doesn't have built-in support for JSONRPC. As soon as you've wrapped the `urllib` calls in some helper functions, the example will be as concise as the XMLRPC one.

As JSONRPC is stateful, the first thing we have to do is to request a session at `/web/session/authenticate`. This function takes the database, the user's name, and their password.

The crucial part here is that we record the session ID Odoo created, which we pass in the header `X-Openerp-Session-Id` to `/web/dataset/call_kw`. Then, the function behaves the same as `execute_kw` from; we need to pass a model name and a function to call on it, then positional and keyword arguments.

There's more...

Both protocols allow you to call basically any function of your models. In case you don't want a function to be available via either interface, prepend its name with an underscore; Odoo won't expose those functions as RPC calls. This is also a security measure—never expose methods you don't want or need to be called via one of the RPC protocols.

Furthermore, you need to take care that your parameters as well as the return values are serializable for the protocol. To be sure, restrict yourself to scalar values, dictionaries, and lists.

As you can do roughly the same with both protocols, it's up to you which one to use. This decision should be mainly driven by what your platform supports best. In a web context, you're generally better off with JSON, because Odoo allows JSON handlers to pass a CORS header conveniently (refer to the *Making a path accessible from the network* recipe of this chapter for details). This is rather difficult with XMLRPC.

See also

The most interesting business methods to call on models are explained in Chapter 6, *Basic Server-Side Development*.

15
Web Client Development

In this chapter, we will cover the following recipes:

- Creating custom widgets
- Using client-side QWeb templates
- Making RPC calls to the server
- Writing tests for client-side code
- Debugging your client-side code

Introduction

Odoo's web client, or backend, is the place where employees spend most of their time. In `Chapter 10`, *Backend Views*, you saw how to use the existing possibilities the backend offers. Here, we'll take a look at how to extend and customize those possibilities. All the following code will depend on the web module. Note that at the time of writing, there exist two versions of the web module for Odoo 11.0: the community version and the enterprise version, which are quite different from each other, even though they share the same name. We'll only talk about the community version here.

Creating custom widgets

As you saw in `Chapter 10`, *Backend Views*, there's a plethora of widgets that display your data in a certain way. To demonstrate how to create your own widget, we'll write one that lets the user choose a `many2one` reference from a predefined selection of values in the form of a list of buttons. The result looks somewhat similar to the `many2many_checkboxes` widget, but with buttons instead of checkboxes.

Getting ready

You'll need to create an empty addon that depends on the web module; we call it **r1_widgets** here.

How to do it...

We'll add a JavaScript file that contains our widget's logic, and a CSS file to do some styling. Then, we also choose one field on the partner form to use our new widget. Follow the given steps:

1. Add a `static/src/js/r1_widgets.js` file. For the syntax used here, refer to the *Extending CSS and JavaScript for the website* recipe from `Chapter 16`, *CMS Website Development*:

```
odoo.define('r1_widgets', function(require)
{
    var registry = require('web.field_registry'),
        AbstractField = require('web.AbstractField');
```

2. Create your widget by subclassing `AbstractField`:

```
var FieldMany2OneButtons = AbstractField.extend({
```

3. Set the CSS class for the widget's root div element:

```
className: 'oe_form_field_many2one_buttons',
```

4. Override `init` to do some initialization:

```
init: function()
    {
        this._super.apply(this, arguments);
        this.user_list = {
            1: {
                name: 'Administrator',
            },
            4: {
                name: 'Demo user',
            },
        };
    },
```

5. Capture some JavaScript events:

```
events: {
    'click .btn': '_button_clicked',
},
```

6. Override `_render` to set up DOM elements:

```
_render: function()
{
    var self = this;
    this.$el.empty();
    _.each(this.user_list, function(description, id)
    {
        self.$el.append(
            jQuery('<button>').attr({
                'data-id': id,
                'class': 'btn btn-default btn-sm',
            })
            .text(description.name)
            .toggleClass(
                'btn-primary',
                self.value ? self.value.res_id == id : false
            )
        );
    });
    this.$el.find('button').
        prop('disabled', this.mode == 'readonly');
},
```

7. Define the handlers we referred to earlier:

```
_button_clicked: function(e)
{
  this._setValue(parseInt(jQuery(e.target).attr('data-id')));
},
```

8. Don't forget to register your widget:

```
registry.add('many2one_buttons', FieldMany2OneButtons);
```

9. Make it available for other addons:

```
return {
    FieldMany2OneButtons: FieldMany2OneButtons,
}
```

10. Add some CSS in `static/src/css/r1_widgets.css`:

```
.oe_form_field_many2one_buttons button
{
    margin: 0em .2em .2em 0em;
}
```

11. Register both files in the backend assets in `views/templates.xml`:

```xml
<?xml version="1.0" encoding="UTF-8"?>
<odoo>
    <template id="assets_backend" inherit_id="web.assets_backend">
        <xpath expr="." position="inside">
            <link
                href="/r1_widgets/static/src/css/r1_widgets.css"
                rel="stylesheet" type="text/css"
            />
            <script
                src="/r1_widgets/static/src/js/r1_widgets.js"
                type="text/javascript"
            />
        </xpath>
    </template>
</odoo>
```

12. Finally, make the partner form use our widget for choosing the sales person:

```xml
<?xml version="1.0" encoding="UTF-8"?>
<odoo>
    <record id="view_partner_form" model="ir.ui.view">
        <field name="model">res.partner</field>
        <field name="inherit_id" ref="base.view_partner_form" />
        <field name="arch" type="xml">
            <field name="user_id" position="attributes">
                <attribute name="widget">many2one_buttons</attribute>
            </field>
        </field>
    </record>
</odoo>
```

When you open a partner form after installing the module, you'll see two buttons on the sales person field that allow you to select a user. The currently selected user's button is highlighted.

How it works...

The first choice when developing a widget is to choose the correct base class. The fundamental base class for widgets is `Widget` (defined by `web.Widget`), but we didn't choose it because it's too basic. It only takes care of handling events and rendering, but we want more functionality for free. Still, this is an interesting class to study if you want to dig into Odoo's JavaScript internals.

We chose `AbstractField` (defined by `web.AbstractField`) because it brings all the functionality we need for our widget to behave as a field. It does this by inheriting from `Widget`, which includes things such as communicating with the parent form and saving the current field's value. You should study both classes, but the most important functions are overridden in the code example to make this widget do anything in the first place.

The `init` function should be used to do synchronous initialization tasks. Then, for asynchronous initialization, either use `willStart` (runs before rendering) or `start` (runs after rendering). Both these functions are supposed to return a deferred object, which can simply be obtained from super.

We use init to set up a list of users (this is only to keep it simple for now; generally, hard-coded data is a horrible idea, of course). We'll fix this in the *Making RPC calls to the server* recipe and to bind an event. Another possibility for binding events is using the mapping `events`, where you map an event name, possibly followed by a jQuery selector, to a function name. We use this to have click events for the buttons we create later set up automatically. For events that the Odoo framework provides, use the mapping `custom_events`.

The actual UI is created in `_render`, where we simply create one button per user, and mark the appropriate button with the `btn_primary` class. The `_button_clicked` event handler is then necessary to implement our widget's behavior, that is, select the user a button displays, but don't allow selections in read-only mode.

After we've defined our new widget, it's crucial to register it with the form widget registry, which lives in `web.field_registry`. Note that all view types look at this registry, so if you want to create another way of displaying a field in a list view, you also add your widget here and set the `widget` attribute on the field in the view definition.

This was heavily changed from the previous version of Odoo. There, we had one registry per view type with quite different paradigms; you'll have to deal with this when migrating pre-11.0 code. In case you need different code for different views, register your specialized widget with the view type prepended, as in `list.many2many_buttons` if we had a specialized widget for this.

Finally, we export our widget class so that other addons can extend it or inherit from it.

The rest of the code is some quite unspectacular styling for our buttons, registering our JavaScript and CSS files with the system, and using our widget on the partner form.

There's more...

The `web.mixins` namespace defines a couple of very helpful `mixin` classes you should not miss out on when developing form widgets. You used them earlier already as `AbstractField` inherits from `Widget`, which in turn inherits from them: `EventDispatcherMixin` offers a simple interface for attaching event handlers and triggering them. `ServicesMixin` provides functions for RPC calls and actions.

 When doing your overrides, always study the base class to see what the function is supposed to return. A very common cause of bugs is forgetting to return super's Deferred object, which causes trouble with asynchronous operations.

Widgets are responsible for validation. Use the `isValid` function to implement your customization of this aspect.

See also

In case you want to use something very similar to this in real life, take a look at the `radio` widget provided by the web addon; it supports selection and many2one fields.

A very good source for more widgets is the community repository at `https://github.com/OCA/web`, where developers share their general purpose widgets (and other addons related to the web client).

Using client-side QWeb templates

Just as it's a bad pattern to programmatically create HTML code in controllers, you should create only the minimum amount of DOM elements in your client-side JavaScript code. Fortunately, there's a templating engine available for the client side too and, even more fortunately, it's just the same as for server-side code.

We'll use Qweb to make the module from the *Creating custom widgets* recipe more modular by moving the DOM element creation to QWeb.

Getting ready

This recipe is just a modified version of the *Creating custom widgets* recipe code, so grab a copy of it and use it to create the r2_clientside_qweb module.

How to do it...

We add the QWeb definition in the manifest and change the JavaScript code to use it:

1. Add a member called template:

```
var FieldMany2OneButtons = AbstractField.extend({
    template: 'FieldMany2OneButtons',
```

2. Change the _render function to simply render the element (inherited from Widget):

```
_render: function()
    {
        this.renderElement();
    },
```

3. Add the template file in static/src/xml/r2_clientside_qweb.xml:

```
<templates>
  <t t-name="FieldMany2OneButtons">
    <div class="oe_form_field_many2one_buttons">
      <t t-foreach="widget.user_list" t-as="user_id">
        <button
          t-att-disabled=
              "widget.mode == 'readonly' ? 'disabled' : False"
          t-att-data-id="user_id"
```

```
                t-attf-class="btn btn-default btn-sm
                {{(widget.value and widget.value.res_id == user_id) and
                                                'btn-primary' or ''}}">
                    <t t-esc="widget.user_list[user_id].name" />
                </button>
            </t>
        </div>
    </t>
</templates>
```

4. Register the QWeb file in your manifest:

```
"qweb": [
    'static/src/xml/r2_clientside_qweb.xml',
],
```

Now, other addons have a much easier time changing the HTML code our widget uses, because they can simply override it with the usual QWeb patterns.

How it works...

As there is already a comprehensive discussion of the basics of QWeb in the *Creating or modifying templates – QWeb* recipe from `Chapter 16`, *CMS Website Development*, we'll focus on what is different here. First of all, you need to realize that we're dealing with the JavaScript QWeb implementation here as opposed to the Python implementation on the server side. This means that you don't have access to browse records or the environment; you only have access to the current widget via variable widget and some helper objects such as date-time with a subset of Python as described in the *Passing parameters to forms and actions – Context* recipe from `Chapter 10`, *Backend Views*.

This means that you should have all the intelligence in the widget's JavaScript code and have your template only access properties, or possibly functions, on the widget. Fortunately, the original version of our widget does this already, so the only thing we have to do is to iterate through the object we prepared in init and create buttons accordingly. Given that we can access all properties available on the widget, we can simply ask it whether it should behave as read-only by checking the mode property, which returns **readonly** if the field should be rendered in read-only mode, and **edit** if the user should be able to edit the field.

As client-side QWeb has nothing to do with QWeb views, there's a different mechanism to make those templates known to the web client; add them via the key qweb to your addon's manifest in a list of file names relative to the addon's root.

There's more...

The reason for making the effort to use QWeb here was extensibility, and this is the second big difference between client-side and server-side Qweb. On the client side, you can't use Xpath expressions; you need to use jQuery selectors and operations. If we, for example, want to change our widget in yet another module, we'd use the following code to have each of our buttons show a user icon before the user's name:

```
<t t-extend="FieldMany2OneButtons">
    <t t-jquery="button" t-operation="prepend">
        <i class="fa fa-user" />
    </t>
</t>
```

If we also gave a t-name attribute here, we'd have made a copy of the original template and left that one untouched. Other possible values for the t-operation attribute are append, before, after, inner, and replace, which cause the content of the t element to be either appended to the content of the matched element, put before or after the matched element, replace the content of the matched element (inner), or replace the complete element (replace). There's also t-operation='attributes', which allows you to set an attribute on the matched element, following the same rules as server-side QWeb.

Another tacit difference is that names in client-side QWeb are not namespaced by the module name, so you have to choose names for your templates that are probably unique over all addons you install, which is why developers tend to choose rather long names.

See also

The client-side QWeb engine has less convenient error messages and handling than other parts of Odoo. A small error often means that simply nothing happens and it's hard for beginners to continue from there. Fortunately, there are some debug statements for client-side QWeb templates described later in the chapter, in the *Debugging your client-side code* recipe.

Making RPC calls to the server

Sooner or later, your widget will need to look up some data from the server. This recipe shows you how to do that. We'll replace the hard-coded list of users in the `many2one_buttons` widget with a list queried from the server, depending on the field's domain.

Getting ready

This recipe is just a modified version of the previous recipe, *Using client-side QWeb templates* code, so grab a copy of it and use it to create the `r3_rpc_calls` addon.

How to do it...

We just have to adapt some JavaScript code at the right place:

Delete the `init` function and replace it with an implementation of `willStart`:

```
willStart: function()
{
    var deferred = new jQuery.Deferred(),
    self = this;
     self.user_list = {};
      this._rpc({
          model: this.field.relation,
          method: 'search_read',
          fields: ['display_name'],
          domain: this.field.domain,
      })
      .then(function(records)
      {
          _.each(records, function(record)
          {
              self.user_list[record.id] = record;
              self.user_list[record.id].name =
                record.display_name;
          });
          deferred.resolve();
      });
      return jQuery.when(
          this._super.apply(this, arguments),
          deferred
      );
```

```
        },
```

Now, you should see all users of your system and not just the two hard-coded ones, as you did before. Also, the widget can be used for any `many2one` field now, because it just queries what is available and doesn't need any knowledge about this beforehand. If you set a domain on the field, the buttons will be restricted to records matching this domain. In this specific case, you might want to restrict the selection to users of the **Sale | User** group.

How it works...

The `willStart` function is called before rendering, and, more importantly, returns a deferred object that must be resolved before rendering starts. So, in a case like ours, where we need to run an asynchronous action before rending can occur, this is the right function to do it.

When dealing with data access, we rely on the `_rpc` function provided by the `ServicesMixin` class explained earlier. This function allows you to call any public function on some model such as `search` or `read`, or in this case, `search_read`. You could also have required `web.rpc` and have called the `query` function on it; this is what `_rpc` does under the hood.

In any case, we'll have to collect the results asynchronously in our success handler. This will set up the internal data structure `user_list` the same way we did earlier in the hard-coded version, which is great, because this way, we don't have to change anything else.

Note that we request the `display_name` field here instead of `name`, because we can be sure that every model has a `display_name` field, whereas that's not guaranteed with the `name` field. Then, we just assign the `name` property the same value as `display_name`; again, this is in order to not have to change the existing code more than necessary. Do this too instead of a lot of overrides if you just need to divert display to another field or something similar. For details about the `display_name` field, refer to the *Defining the Model representation and order* recipe in `Chapter 5`, *Application Models*.

The end of the handler contains the crucial part, resolving the deferred object we created earlier. This, in combination with returning the deferred object wrapped along with super's result in a new deferred object created by the `jQuery.when` call, causes rendering to only happen after the values are fetched and whatever asynchronous action super was busy with finished too. This way, you can be sure in the template code that `widget.user_list` is accessible and contains the values we need.

There's more...

The `AbstractField` class comes with a couple of interesting properties, one of which we just used. The `field` property contains roughly the output of the model's `fields_get` function for the field the widget is displaying. Apart from the relation key that gives you the co-model for x2x fields or the domain, you can also use it to query the field's string, size, or whatever other property you can set on the field during model definition.

Another helpful property is `nodeOptions`, which contains data passed via the `options` attribute in the form definition. This is already JSON parsed, so you can access it like any object.

See also

Odoo's RPC heavily relies on jQuery's deferred objects, so it can't be repeated often enough that you should dive into jQuery's documentation about this at `https://api.jquery.com/jQuery.Deferred`.

Writing tests for client-side code

The more code you have on the client side, the more it becomes a liability. For server-side code, there's the well-entrenched unit tests, and for JavaScript, we have QUnit (`https://qunitjs.com`), which Odoo uses.

Getting ready

We'll add our tests to the addon developed in the previous recipes, so grab the code from the *Making RPC calls to the server* recipe and put it in a new module called `r4_tests`.

How to do it...

We have to add our test file and make it known to the test mechanism in the appropriate template:

1. Add the `static/test/r4_tests.js` file:

```
odoo.define('r4.tests', function (require) {
```

2. Require what we need:

```
var test_utils = require('web.test_utils'),
    FormView = require('web.FormView');
```

3. Provide some test data:

```
QUnit.module(
    'r4',
    {
        beforeEach: function()
        {
            this.data = {
                'res.partner': {
                    fields: {
                        user_id: {
                            string: 'User id',
                            type: 'many2one',
                            relation: 'res.users',
                        },
                    },
                    records: [
                        {
                            id: 1,
                            user_id: 1,
                        },
                    ],
                },
                'res.users': {
                    fields: {
                        display_name: {
                            string: 'Display name',
                            type: 'char',
                        },
                    },
                    records: [
                        {
                            id: 1,
                            display_name: 'Administrator',
                        },
                        {
                            id: 4,
                            display_name: 'Demo user',
                        },
                    ],
                },
            };
```

```
        },
```

4. Run the actual test:

```
function()
    {
        QUnit.test('Test many2one_buttons widget', function(assert) {
            assert.expect(2);
            var view = test_utils.createView({
                View: FormView,
                model: 'res.partner',
                data: this.data,
                arch: '<form><field name="user_id"
                widget="many2one_buttons" /></form>',
            });
            assert.strictEqual(2, view.$('.btn').length);
            view.on('field_changed', view, function(e)
            {
                assert.strictEqual(1, e.data.changes.user_id.id);
            });
            view.$('.btn[data-id=1]').click();
        });
    }
```

5. Make the test file known to the test mechanism in `views/templates.xml`:

```
<template id="qunit_suite" inherit_id="web.qunit_suite">
    <xpath expr="//t[@t-set='head']" position="inside">
        <script src="/r4_tests/static/test/r4_tests.js"
                type="text/javascript" />
    </xpath>
</template>
```

When you navigate to `/web/tests` now, the web client will run all tests available. You should find our test in this list, too, hopefully with a positive result. Given that a lot of tests will run there, it can be simpler to also pass the module you want to test. In our case, select **r4** in the upper-right drop-down box.

 Note that what you need to select as the module in the test page is not necessarily the name of your addon, but whatever section name you defined in your QUnit.module call earlier.

How it works...

You define your JavaScript tests in a very similar manner to how you would make normal JavaScript code known to Odoo. You call a function that gets your code as a parameter. In the case of tests, this function is called `QUnit.module` and expects a logical name for the tests to be run, an optional object with some hook functions, and a function that sets up the tests themselves.

Every test is a function added by calling `QUnit.test`, passing a name and a function provided with an assert object. Within this last function, the actual testing happens. We use the `createView` helper here, which does nearly all the work for us. It creates a view with the definition we passed and renders it with the data we set up in the `beforeEach` function of the hook object.

Note that the framework needs to be told how many assertions you expect; it's because of the asynchronous nature of most Javascript code.

For doing those checks, the assert object has a few functions such as `equal`, `deepEqual`, `notEqual`, and `notDeepEqual`, which all deal with equality, but the `deep*` variants recurse into compound types such as arrays and objects. Then there's `ok` and `notOk`, which can be used to assert true or false value and `throws`, to assert that a function throws a certain exception or error message.

There's more...

The example code contains two peculiarities that make this test more complicated than others; it needs to request data from the server, and as a consequence of that, run asynchronously; both pose challenges to the test framework.

For fetching data, Odoo offers an object called MockServer, which we can fill with data that will be returned when code requests data from the server. So, what we do here is assign a mapping per model that our test code is expected to query so as to have the function return what we consider the expected result. Then, the test is whether the client-side code reacts to this data appropriately. If your test code makes calls to model functions, you can pass a `mockRPC` function to `createView`, which will have to react to those calls. However, as we only read data, it suffices to add the data with the `data` parameter. If your own code involves more interactions with the server, you'll probably need a smarter handler that actually looks at its parameters and returns different results for different requests.

See also

Unfortunately, at the time of writing, many of the more complex JavaScript community modules are not yet migrated to Odoo 11.0, so there are not many examples of client-side tests in the wild. Consult the web module's tests for some examples, which are available at `https://github.com/OCA/OCB/tree/11.0/addons/web/static/tests`.

Debugging your client-side code

For debugging server-side code, this book contains a whole chapter, that is, `Chapter 8`, *Debugging and Automated Testing*. For the client-side part, you'll get a kick start in this recipe.

Getting ready

This recipe doesn't really rely on specific code, but if you want to be able to reproduce exactly what's going on, grab the previous recipe's code.

How to do it...

What makes debugging client-side script difficult is that the web client heavily relies on jQuery's asynchronous events. Given that breakpoints halt execution, the chance is high that a bug caused by timing issues will not occur when debugging. We'll discuss some strategies for this later:

1. Turn on debug mode with assets. For details, consult the *Activating the Odoo developer tools* recipe from `Chapter 1`, *Installing the Odoo Development Environment*.

2. In the JavaScript function you're interested in, call the debugger:

   ```
   debugger;
   ```

3. If you have timing problems, log to the console in some JavaScript function:

   ```
   console.log("I'm in function X currently");
   ```

4. If you want to debug during template rendering, call the debugger from QWeb:

   ```
   <t t-debug="" />
   ```

5. You can also have QWeb log to the console by saying the following:

```
<t t-log="myvalue" />
```

All of this relies on your browser offering appropriate functionality for debugging. While all the major browsers do that, we'll only look at Chromium here for demonstration purposes. To be able to use the debug tools, open them by clicking on the top-right menu button and selecting **More tools** | **Developer tools**:

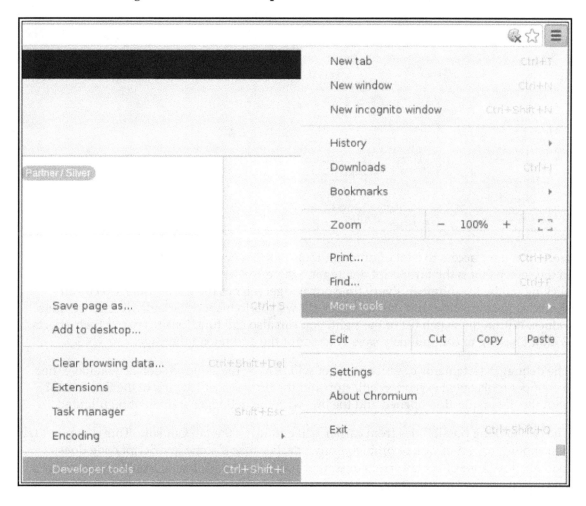

How it works...

When the debugger is opened, you should see something similar to the following screenshot:

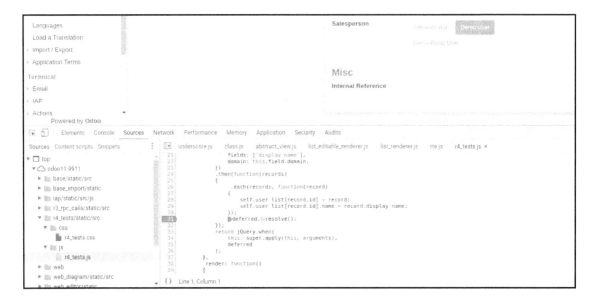

Here, you have access to a lot of different tools in the separate tabs. The currently active tab in the screenshot is the JavaScript debugger, where we set a break point in line 31 by clicking on the line number. Every time our widget fetches the list of users, execution should stop at this line, and the debugger allows you to inspect variables or change their values. Within the watch list to the right, you can also call functions to try out their effects without having to continuously save your script file and reload the page.

The debugger statements described earlier will behave the same as soon as you have the developer tools open: execution will stop and the browser will switch to the **Sources** tab, with the file in question opened and the line with the debugger statement highlighted.

The two logging possibilities from earlier will end up in the tab **Console**. This is the first tab you should inspect in case of problems anyway, because if some JavaScript code doesn't load at all because of syntax errors or similar fundamental problems, you'll see an error message there explaining what's going on.

There's more...

Use the **Elements** tab to inspect the DOM representation of the page the browser currently displays. This will prove helpful to make yourself familiar with the HTML code the existing widgets produce, and will also allow you to play with classes and CSS attributes in general. This is a great resource for testing layout changes.

The **Network** tab gives you an overview of which requests the current page made and how long it took. This is helpful to debug slow page loads, as you'll usually see the culprit in one glance here, represented by a long bar. Then, you can check on the server side why this call takes as long as it does. Also, this view helps you determine whether it makes sense to parallelize calls; this will look like several long bars, one after another. If you select a request, you can inspect the payload passed to the server and the result returned, which helps you figure out the reason for unexpected behavior on the client side. You'll also see the status codes of requests made, for example, 404, in case a resource can't be found, for example, because you misspelled a filename.

For other browsers, you'll have to look up similar functionality in the documentation. Firefox, for example, has the very powerful firebug addon, which lets you perform most of the mentioned actions.

As stated earlier, debugging becomes complicated as soon as asynchronous operations are involved. Break points are of limited use here, because they interrupt code execution and the call stack won't contain the place where an event handler was attached, but mostly internal jQuery functions and the browser's implementation of the event system. The **Profiling** tab helps you here by showing call graphs, including timings. This can hint at event handlers being called in the wrong order. Another strategy is to spread out `console.log` statements throughout your handlers in order to plot a sort of call graph in the JavaScript console. Before diving into this, take a critical look at all your custom code in order to check whether you forgot to return super's result in case it is a deferred object. This is a very common cause of timing problems.

16
CMS Website Development

In this chapter, we will cover the following recipes:

- Extending CSS and JavaScript for the website
- Creating or modifying templates – QWeb
- Offering snippets to the user

Introduction

Odoo comes with a fully-featured CMS system implemented by the **website** addon. Some low-level functionality is provided by the **web** addon, so if you need to look up code, keep both modules in mind.

Extending CSS and JavaScript for the website

In this recipe, we'll see how to add custom style sheets and JavaScript to the website.

Getting ready

Create an empty module named `r1_css_js` and install it in your test database. Ensure that this module depends on the `website` module, as we use some of its functionality.

How to do it...

Override the main website template to inject your code:

1. Add a file called `views/templates.xml` and add an empty view override:

```
<odoo>
    <template id="assets_frontend"
                inherit_id="website.assets_frontend">
        <xpath expr="." position="inside">
            <!-- points 2 & 3 go here /-->
        </xpath>
    </template>
</odoo>
```

2. Add a reference to your CSS file:

```
<link href="/r1_css_js/static/src/css/r1_css_js.css"
        rel="stylesheet" type="text/css"/>
```

3. Add a reference to your JavaScript file:

```
<script src="/r1_css_js/static/src/js/r1_css_js.js"
        type="text/javascript" />
```

4. Add some CSS code to `static/src/css/r1_css_js.css`:

```
body
{
    background: yellow;
}
```

5. Add some JavaScript code to `static/src/js/r1_css_js.js`:

```
odoo.define('r1_css_js', function(require)
{
    var core = require('web.core');
    alert(core._t('Hello world'));
    return {
        // if you created functionality to export, add it here
    }
});
```

After updating your module, you should see that Odoo websites have a yellow background and a somewhat annoying **Hello world** popup on each page load.

How it works...

At the base of Odoo's CMS lies an XML templating engine called QWeb, which is discussed in detail in the following recipe. For now, it's enough to know that we can use it to inject nodes into existing documents. In the example, we change the `website.assets_frontend` view to link to our CSS and JavaScript files. This view will be pulled to construct all the HTML for the website, so you can be sure that your code is available on all pages.

As we can be sure that the `website.assets_frontend` view is pulled within a HTML **head** node, we can simply add the files we need and possibly adjust or add other nodes in the **head** element, too.

For CSS files, order matters. So, if you need to override a style defined in another addon, you'll have to take care that your file is loaded after the original file you want to modify. This can be done by either adjusting your view's **priority** field or directly inheriting from the addon's view that injects the reference to the CSS. For details, refer to the *Changing the existing views – View inheritance* recipe in `Chapter 10`, *Backend Views*.

To avoid ordering issues with JavaScript, Odoo uses a mechanism very similar to RequireJS (`http://requirejs.org`). In your JavaScript file, you call `odoo.define()`, which receives the namespace you want to define as the first argument, and a function that contains the actual implementation as the second argument.

The name to be defined should be your addon's name. In case you export a lot of logically different parts of functionality, define them in different functions, with your addon's name prepended and separated by dots to avoid naming conflicts in the future. This is what the `web` module does, which defines, among others, `web.core` and `web.data`. The definition function receives only one parameter, `require`, which is a function you can use to obtain references to JavaScript namespaces defined in other modules or in the core. Use this for all interactions with Odoo and never rely on the global `odoo` object.

Your own function can then return an object pointing to the references you want to make available for other addons, or nothing if there are no such references. Be lavish with exporting your own objects; few things are more frustrating than having to jump through hoops in order to use some existing functionality just because its developer didn't bother to export it properly. The object you return here is what other code gets when it calls `require('yourmodule')`.

As per convention, your files should be called as your module with the appropriate extension added and live in `static/src/css` or `static/src/js`, respectively. Only if your files become large enough to be a maintenance issue should you split them up into smaller chunks.

 The `require` mechanism discussed here was introduced for Odoo 9.0. In older versions, addons dealing with JavaScript need to define a function with the same name as the addon in the `openerp` namespace. This function receives a reference to the currently-loaded instance as a parameter, from which API functions are to be accessed. So, in order to upgrade the existing code, change this to a `odoo.define` clause and import the necessary objects via `require`.

There's more...

Instead of passing plain CSS to Odoo, you can also make use of **less** (`http://lesscss.org`), which is a higher-level notation for CSS that helps you write more efficient CSS code. Certainly for big code bases, it will improve maintainability a lot. Given Odoo uses this internally anyway, you can rely on it being available. So, to use less instead of plain CSS, just point to the less file in your `link` element and use `type="text/less"`; this will make Odoo run `lessc` on your file in order to generate CSS on the fly without you having to do anything for it.

Creating or modifying templates – QWeb

We'll add website capabilities to the library addon developed in Chapter 5, *Application models*, and following. What we're interested in is allowing users to browse through the library and, if they are logged in with the appropriate permissions, enable them to edit book content right from the website interface.

Getting ready

As we make use of the `library.book` model, get the code in Chapter 5, *Application Models*, for `my_module`. For convenience, this recipe's code contains a copy of it. We'll create a module called `r2_templates`.

How to do it...

We'll need to define a couple of controllers and views:

1. Add a template that displays a list of books in
   `views/library_book_templates.xml`:

```xml
<odoo>
  <template id="books">
    <t t-call="website.layout">
      <section>
          This is an editable text before the list of books.
      </section>
      <t t-foreach="books" t-as="book">
          <article itemscope="itemscope"
                  itemtype="http://schema.org/Book"
                  t-attf-class="row book-#{book_parity}">
              <h2 t-field="book.name" class="col-md-12" />
              <t t-if="book.date_release">
                  <div class="col-md-2"
                      t-att-dateCreated="book.date_release"
                      t-field="book.date_release" />
              </t>
              <ul class="col-md-10">
                  <li t-foreach="book.author_ids"
                      t-as="author" itemprop="author">
                      <t t-esc="author.name" />
                  </li>
              </ul>
          </article>
      </t>
      <section contenteditable="False">
          This is a non-editable text after the list of books.
      </section>
    </t>
  </template>
</odoo>
```

2. Add a controller that serves the list of books in `controllers/main.py`:

```python
@http.route('/books', type='http', auth="user", website=True)
def route(self):
    return request.render(
        'r2_templates.books',
        {
            'books': request.env['library.book'].search([]),
        })
```

With this code in place, users can query the existing books and see their details. Given appropriate permissions, users will also be offered to change book details and a couple of other texts.

How it works...

First, we create a template called `books` that is used to generate the HTML necessary to display a list of books. All the code is wrapped in a t element with the `t-call` attribute set, which makes Odoo render the `website.layout` template and insert our content at the place the called template has designated for it. This way, we get a full Odoo web page with the menu, footer, and so on, without having to repeat any code. If you leave out this call, you'll have to generate this or similar code yourself.

Loops

For working on record sets, you need a construct to loop through lists. Take a look at the inside of the `t-call` element, where the actual content generation happens. The template expects to be rendered with a context that has a variable called `books` set and iterates through it in the `t-foreach` element. Iteration can happen in a t element, in which case its contents are repeated for every member of the iterable that was passed in the `t-foreach` attribute. You can also place the `t-foreach` and `t-as` attributes in some arbitrary element; then, this element and its contents will be repeated for every item in the iterable. The `t-as` attribute is mandatory and will be used as the name of the iterator variable to use for accessing the iterated data. While the most common use for this construction is to iterate over record sets, you can use it on any Python object that is iterable.

Attributes

We use as many of the semantic HTML5 elements as possible, which is why the actual data is wrapped in an `article` tag. For machine readability, some `item*` properties are attached. You can read more about this in this recipe's *See also* section.

Now, focus on the `t-attf-class` attribute here. This will be evaluated by QWeb to be the `class` attribute with the contents evaluated as a format string. That is, the string `row book-` is passed as it is, and the contents of the `#{...}` snippet are evaluated as Python code. This is different from `t-att-dateCreated` (note the missing 'f', the first is an attribute format string, the latter an evaluation) used below, where the whole content is evaluated as Python code. Both forms just pass the part of their name after the second dash as the name of the attribute to be constructed.

It is pretty much up to you when to choose a `t-attf-*` construction and when to use `t-att-*`, the rule of thumb is to use a format string if the result contains a lot of string literals anyway and an evaluation otherwise.

Fields

The `h2` and `div` tags use the `t-field` attribute. This attribute needs to be passed a field within a record set with length one, and transparently allows the user to change the content displayed when the website's edit mode is activated. Of course, this is subject to a permission check and is only allowed if the current user has write permissions on the displayed record. With an optional `t-options` attribute, you can give a dictionary of options to be passed to the field renderer, including the widget to be used. Currently, there's no vast amount of widgets for the backend, so the choices are a bit limited here.

Conditionals

Note that the division showing the publication date is wrapped by a `t` element with the `t-if` attribute set. This attribute is evaluated as Python code and the element only rendered if the result is truthy. In the example, we only show the `div` class if there is actually a publication date set.

Inline editing

Changes made by a user will either be propagated to the connected database record if the change happened within a `t-field` node, or to the view in question if it is some other node marked as editable. Content nodes such as `section` elements don't need to be marked as editable; they are editable by default. To turn an editable element read-only, use the `contenteditable=False` attribute.

Note that editing a view via the website editor sets the **noupdate** flag on this view. This means that subsequent code changes will never make it into your customer's database. In order to also get the ease of use of inline editing and the possibility of updating your HTML code in subsequent releases, create one view that contains the semantic HTML elements and a second one that injects editable elements. Then, only the latter view will be **noupdate**, and you can still change the former.

For the CSS classes used here, consult bootstrap's documentation, as linked in this recipe's *See also* section.

The controller in step 2 just renders the template; refer to the *Modify an existing handler* recipe in `Chapter 14`, *Web Server Development*, for details.

There's more...

Given the way `t-call` elements are evaluated, you can use `t-set` elements to pass information to the template you call. This can be very useful if you have some generalized templates such as `website.layout` or `web.external_layout`, which display data you want to see almost always. Adapt them not to print certain elements if some variable is set and set it via a `t-set` element on the page or report where you want to suppress the element in question. This helps avoid a lot of code duplication.

Within `t-foreach` loops, you've got access to a couple of variables whose names are derived from the accompanying `t-as` attribute. As it is `book` in the preceding example, we have access to the `book_parity` variable that contains the value `even` for even indices while iterating and `odd` for odd ones. In this example, we use this to be able to have alternating background colors in our list. Other interesting variables in this case would be `book_index`, which returns the current (zero-based) index in the iteration, `book_first` and `book_last`, which are `True` if this is the first or last iteration respectively, and `book_value`, which would contain the item's value if the `book` variable we iterate over were a dictionary; in this case, `book` would iterate through the dictionary's keys.

The **template** element is a shorthand for a `record` element that sets some properties on the record for you. While there's never a reason not to use the convenience of the template element, you should know what happens under the hood: the element creates a record of the `ir.ui.view` model with the `qweb` type. Then, depending on the `template` element's **name** and `inherit_id` attributes, the `inherit_id` field on the view record will be set. In case the template has the `primary` attribute set to `True`, the view record's `mode` field will be set to `primary`. Finally, an `arch` field is crafted with the correct root element (`t` for non-inheriting views, `data` for inheriting views) and a `t-name` attribute is set for primary views.

Keep in mind that QWeb is a perfectly generic templating engine, so whenever you need to generate content in an Odoo context, use a Qweb view that you render by calling `env['ir.ui.view'].render('xmlid', parameters)`. Especially for generating XML documents, this is convenient, but you can generate every other kind of text too.

See also

For a more in-depth discussion of controllers, refer to the *Make a path accessible from the network* and *Restrict access to web accessible paths* recipes in `Chapter 14`, *Web Server Development*.

For details on view inheritance, take a look at the *Changing the existing views – View inheritance* recipe in `Chapter 10`, *Backend Views*.

The code generated here makes use of microdata (`https://html.spec.whatwg.org/multipage/microdata.html`) using definitions from `http://schema.org` - it is advised that you do the same for your publicly accessible websites in order to simplify reading your pages for machines. This also makes your content more accessible for search engines.

Odoo as a whole makes extensive use of bootstrap (`http://getbootstrap.com`), which you should use to get adaptive designs without much effort.

Offering snippets to the user

The website designer offers building blocks in website edit mode, which can be dragged on the page. This recipe discusses how to offer your own blocks, called snippets, internally.

Getting ready

As we make use of the `library.book` model, get the codes from Chapter 5, *Application Models*, for `my_module`. For convenience, this recipe's code contains a copy of it.

How to do it...

A snippet is actually just a QWeb view that gets injected in the **Insert blocks** bar, which is defined by a QWeb view itself:

1. Add a file called `views/snippets.xml`:

```xml
<?xml version="1.0" encoding="UTF-8"?>
<odoo>
    <template id="book_snippet" inherit_id="website.snippets">
        <!-- points 2, 3 go here /-->
    </template>
</odoo>
```

2. Add a view for your snippet:

```xml
<xpath
expr="//div[@id='snippet_feature']/div[hasclass('o_panel_body')]"
position="inside">
    <div>
        <div class="oe_snippet_thumbnail">
            <div style="background: white; box-shadow:none"
                class="oe_snippet_thumbnail_img">
                <i class="fa fa-book fa-5x text-muted" />
            </div>
            <span class="oe_snippet_thumbnail_title">
                                Latest books
            </span>
        </div>
        <div class="oe_snippet_body book_snippet">
            <section class="container">
                <h2>Latest books</h2>
                <table class="table">
```

```
                    <tr>
                        <th>Name</th>
                        <th>Release date</th>
                    </tr>
                </table>
            </section>
        </div>
    </div>
</xpath>
```

3. Add options:

```
<xpath expr="//div[@id='snippet_options']" position="inside">
    <div data-selector=".book_snippet">
        <li class="dropdown-submenu">
            <a href="#">Show books</a>
            <ul class="dropdown-menu">
                <li data-select-class="book_snippet-show3">
                    <a>3</a>
                </li>
                <li data-select-class="book_snippet-show5">
                    <a>5</a>
                </li>
                <li data-select-class="book_snippet-show10">
                    <a>10</a>
                </li>
                <li data-select-class="book_snippet-show15">
                    <a>15</a>
                </li>
            </ul>
        </li>
    </div>
    <div data-selector=".book_snippet table">
        <li class="dropdown-submenu">
            <a href="#">Table style</a>
            <ul class="dropdown-menu">
                <li data-toggle-class="table-striped">
                    <a>Striped</a></li>
                <li data-toggle-class="table-bordered">
                    <a>Bordered</a></li>
                <li data-toggle-class="table-condensed">
                    <a>Condensed</a>
                </li>
            </ul>
        </li>
    </div>
</xpath>
```

4. Add JavaScript code to populate our snippet:

```javascript
odoo.define('r3_snippets', function(require)
{
    "use strict";
    var rpc = require('web.rpc'),
        Animation = require('website.content.snippets.animation');

    Animation.registry.book_snippet = Animation.Class.extend({
        selector: '.book_snippet',
        start: function()
        {
            var self = this,
                number = 3;
            _.each(this.$el.attr('class').split(/\s+/), function(cls)
            {
                if(cls.indexOf('book_snippet-show') == 0)
                {
                    number = parseInt(cls.substring(
                                        'book_snippet-show'.length));
                }
            });
            this.$el.find('td').parents('tr').remove();
            rpc.query({
                model: 'library.book',
                method: 'search_read',
                domain: [],
                fields: ['name', 'date_release'],
                sortBy: ['date_release desc'],
                limit: number,
            })
            .then(function(data)
            {
                var $table = self.$el.find('table');
                _.each(data, function(book)
                {
                    $table.append(
                        jQuery('<tr />')
                        .append(
                            jQuery('<td />').text(book.name),
                            jQuery('<td />').text(book.date_release)
                        )
                    );
                })
            });
        },
    });
```

```
    });
```

After updating your module, you're offered a snippet called **Latest books,** which shows a configurable amount of books in a list, ordered by their publication date.

How it works...

You inject your snippet directly into the snippet bar's view. What is crucial is that you attach the right classes and insert your code at the right place.

A snippet needs to have one root element (in our case, the outermost `div`) that contains an element with the `oe_snippet_thumbnail` class and another with the `oe_snippet_body` class. The first is used to display the snippet in the bar, and the second contains the actual definition of the snippet. For the thumbnail, it makes sense to use a `fontawesome` icon and add some classes for the layout. For the snippet body, you can add whatever HTML you need for your goals. In general, it's a good idea to use **section** elements and the bootstrap classes, because for them, Odoo's editor offers edit and resize controls out of the box.

The position to insert the snippet determines in which section of the bar it shows up. Our choice was `//div[@id='snippet_feature']/div[@class='o_panel_body']`, which places it in the features section. With the `snippet_structure`, `snippet_content` and `snippet_effect` IDs, you can place your snippet in the respective other sections.

The `div` we injected in `//div[@id='snippet_options']` offers the user choices in the customize menu. Note the attribute `data-selector` that contains a JQuery selector determining for which element the option is to be shown. In the example, the first option list is shown when the whole container is selected, while the second one, about the table style, is shown when the table is selected.

The `data-drop-near` and `data-drop-in` attributes determine where the snippet can be placed when dragging it out of the snippet bar. Those are also JQuery selectors and, in the example, we allow putting the snippet basically anywhere that content can go.

For the options themselves, the `data-select-class` and `data-toggle-class` attributes allow the user to set either one (select) or multiple (toggle) classes on the element selected by the `data-selector` attribute. Our first set of options sets classes later used by the JavaScript code. The second set of options sets classes directly in the table, which will change its layout accordingly.

The JavaScript code uses the snippet animation framework to execute some code every time the snippet is loaded. We use it to query the current list of books to be presented to the user. The key property here is the `selector` defined, which instructs the framework to run our class when there's an element matching this selector.

There's more...

After completing this recipe, you know enough to create Odoo themes. An addon is considered a theme if it contains only data files, CSS, and JavaScript code. Use QWeb views and snippets to adapt the website's HTML code as necessary and CSS for styling. For the addon to be recognized as such in the app store, the addon's manifest must set the **application** key to `True` and use a subcategory of theme, as found on `https://www.odoo.com/apps/themes`.

If you need more control than setting classes, you can add an option class by inheriting from `web_editor.snippets.options.Class` and passing the classes name in the `data-js` property of an option. That's quite analogous to the animation the example code uses.

Other Books You May Enjoy

If you enjoyed this book, you may be interested in these other books by Packt:

Odoo 10 Implementation Cookbook
Mantavya Gajjar

ISBN: 978-1-78712-342-7

- Learn the modern way of doing sales and managing sales contracts
- Create and configure your products and manage your sales quotations
- Set up an online shop and start selling online with Odoo eCommerce
- Manage multi-currency transactions and create a deferred revenue plan and link it with products
- Administer vendors and products and request quotations, confirm orders, and get them delivered
- Manage quality control in the warehouse and manual and real-time inventory stock valuations.
- Manage projects and project forecasting via grid and Gantt views
- Implement Human Resource apps and manage the employee appraisal process
- Manage Workcenters and the product lifecycle
- Track worker activity with tablets and launch new changes in production

Working with Odoo 10
Greg Moss

ISBN: 978-1-78646-268-8

- Configure a functioning customer relationship management system
- Set up a purchasing and receiving system
- Implement manufacturing operations and processes using real-world examples
- Discover the capabilities of Odoo's financial accounting and reporting features
- Integrate powerful human resource applications
- Utilize Odoo's project management application to organize tasks
- Customize Odoo without writing a line a code

Leave a review - let other readers know what you think

Please share your thoughts on this book with others by leaving a review on the site that you bought it from. If you purchased the book from Amazon, please leave us an honest review on this book's Amazon page. This is vital so that other potential readers can see and use your unbiased opinion to make purchasing decisions, we can understand what our customers think about our products, and our authors can see your feedback on the title that they have worked with Packt to create. It will only take a few minutes of your time, but is valuable to other potential customers, our authors, and Packt. Thank you!

Index

www.ingramcontent.com/pod-product-compliance
Lightning Source LLC
Chambersburg PA
CBHW060644060326
40690CB00020B/4507